*In the Office of Constable*

# MANCHESTER CITY POLICE.

## Conditions of Service for the Appointment of Constable.

### Declaration of Service.

I, *Robert Mark* 262

declare that I will well and truly serve our Sovereign Lord King George VI. in the Office of Constable for the City of Manchester, without favour or affection, malice or ill will, and that I will, to the best of my power, cause the peace to be kept and preserved, and prevent all offences against the persons and properties of His Majesty's subjects, and that while I continue to hold the said office I will, to the best of my skill and knowledge, discharge all the duties thereof faithfully according to law. *Robert Mark.*

Declared before me this ___2nd___ day of ___September___ 1957.

*JW Grime*

Justice of the Peace for the City of Manchester.

I, *Robert Mark*

in consideration of the Watch Committee of the City of Manchester appointing me to be a Constable in the Manchester City Police, do hereby acknowledge that I am to be so appointed on the following conditions, that is to say :—

    1. That I will deposit with the Chief Constable my certificate of birth, certificate of marriage (if married), and testimonials as to character, which shall be retained on behalf of the Watch Committee, the testimonials to be liable to forfeiture in case of my dismissal.

    2. That I will devote my whole time to the service, and at all times serve and reside where required, and will not, without the sanction of the Chief Constable,

        (a) hold any other office or employment, or carry on any business for hire or gain, or

        (b) reside at any premises where my wife, or any member of my family, keeps a shop or carries on any like business, or

        (c) hold, or my wife or any member of my family living with me hold, any licence granted in pursuance of the Liquor Licensing laws or laws regulating places of public entertainment in the City of Manchester, or have any pecuniary interest in such licence, or

        (d) allow my wife to keep a shop or carry on a like business in the City of Manchester, or

        (e) occupy premises in the capacity of caretaker, or reside outside the boundaries of the City of Manchester ;

provided that in the case of refusal of consent, there shall be an appeal to the Watch Committee, whose decision shall be final, and for the purpose of this regulation the expression "member of my family" shall include parent, son or daughter, brother or sister.

# SIR ROBERT MARK

# *In the Office of Constable*

FONTANA/COLLINS

First published by William Collins Sons & Co. Ltd
1978
First issued in Fontana Paperbacks 1979

Copyright © Robert Mark 1978

Made and Printed in Great Britain
by William Collins Sons & Co. Ltd, Glasgow

CONDITIONS OF SALE
This book is sold subject to the condition
that it shall not, by way of trade or otherwise,
be lent, re-sold, hired out or otherwise circulated
without the publisher's prior consent in any form of
binding or cover other than that in which it is
published and without a similar condition
including this condition being imposed
on the subsequent purchaser

My wife, like most policemen's wives, has indirectly given much to a service to which we are both devoted. She has asked me to dedicate this book to the men and women of the British police.

I do so with gratitude and humility, remembering in particular those who lost their lives or suffered grievous injury in the service of their country.

# Contents

# Illustrations

The Mark children and some friends.

A Manchester street scene with a police box at the time the author joined the police.
*(Manchester Public Libraries)*

The IRA bomb explosion at the House of Commons, June 1974
*(Press Association)*

Spaghetti House siege, September 1975
*(Press Association)*

The release of Sheila Matthews: a surrendering gunman helps his hostage to safety, covered by an armed police officer.
*(Press Association)*

A Special Patrol Group covering the Matthews's flat in Balcombe Street.
*(Press Association)*

Robert Mark with his wife and daughter outside Buckingham Palace, 15 February 1977.
*(Press Association)*

Robert Mark's farewell speech at Central Hall, Westminster, 4 November 1976.
*(Press Association)*

# Acknowledgements

I would like to thank my wife and son, Christopher, whose frank and helpful comments have made it easier to maintain a sense of perspective. Also, James Anderton, Chief Constable of Greater Manchester, and Jean Stead of the *Guardian* for researching the accuracy of some of my recollections.

# CHAPTER I

# Beginnings

For twenty years I have been a chief officer in a service which, though continually fascinating to the public, has never had a diarist and, even worse, has been misrepresented continually by those who write or make films about crime and wrongdoing. I like to think also that some of my activities during the past twenty years have had a significant and permanent effect on policing Great Britain, and that the conditioning of attitudes leading to the initiation of those changes may be of some interest. Why, for example, was I willing to admit wrongdoing in a service which enjoyed a longstanding and traditional reputation for spotless integrity? Why did I choose to criticize a system of justice which had for many years been generally accepted as the envy of other less fortunate countries? I was not consciously inspired by any mission to do either, but the gradual effect of life in the police service compelled me to do both, though well aware of the hostility likely to be aroused amongst police and public alike. This sense of compulsion, however, was long in coming, and reflected the cumulative experience and reaction to many years of police service. It may be of interest therefore, particularly to the student of social history to explain how it all came about, all the more curious in that much of my police career was haphazard and significantly affected by chance.

I was born on 13 March 1917 in a Manchester suburb with the unlikely but ancient name of Chorlton-cum-Hardy. Family tradition and later unkind speculation encouraged the belief that my birthday was a Friday. In fact, it was a Tuesday. I was the youngest of five children born of Yorkshire parents, who had emigrated from Leeds to Manchester in their late thirties.

Family legend has it that my father left home when very young and was apprenticed in the rag trade, by which I mean the manufacture of clothing as distinct from Steptoe and Son. He must have worked extremely hard because by his late thirties he was appointed a departmental manager in the Manchester firm of J. & N. Philips Ltd. Such a move, for one of his limited education, suggests considerable initiative and determination to succeed. After a few years, he established his own business in Jersey Street, Ancoats, as a mantle manufacturer, employing a hundred or so people, with a subsidiary retail business under the name Harvey Thomson Ltd. Thus he continued until his death in 1962 in his 83rd year. My mother is still alive, a sturdy but failing 98.

My father had three great passions: his family, Yorkshire cricket and Leeds United, though I am not sure of the precedence of the first two. He really was one of those legendary characters who regarded the Roses match as a cause for celebration or mourning and who could not resist the verbal cut and thrust on the Members' Side at Old Trafford. So much so, that even at quite a tender age, I stopped going with him. The great names of Holmes, Sutcliffe, Rhodes, Leyland and Verity ranked in my home only slightly below, if indeed at all below, those of the twelve apostles. Leeds United were at that time in much the same position as Manchester United. They graced the Second Division, and poorly at that. Only after my father's death did their fortunes turn and I suspect that he, rather than Don Revie or Jack Charlton is largely responsible for it. Or at least I would think that, were it not for the inexplicable fall from grace of Yorkshire cricket.

Like many northern parents of that time and background my father's real ambition was for his children to have a good education. I doubt whether he had any clear idea of what a good education was, but he wanted his children to have a better start in life than he had had. Until I was ten we lived in a small but well-built semi-detached house in Clarendon Road West, backing on to a large field, part of a small private estate. Conditions were cramped, but not unhappy. My mother was a superb cook and tireless worker and as we grew we were all expected to help. The family philosophy could be summed up by the old northern adage 'Them as don't work don't eat', a philosophy with which, excluding the young, the sick, and the aged, to this day I entirely agree. All five children went to what were called in those days elementary schools, mine being Manley Park, which was, I seem to recall, built of some kind of corrugated iron. The teaching at any rate was good, as was the discipline. My elder brothers and I, in turn, got free places at both Manchester Grammar School and William Hulme's Grammar School. The eldest chose Hulme and, of course, we both followed suit. That was the end of my academic distinction. From 1928 onwards the graph took a steadily downward line until 1935, when, after having narrowly got Higher School Certificate at the first attempt, I failed at the second, thus writing a new chapter in school history. I should have mentioned, by the way, that when I went to Hulme my family moved to a late-Victorian house at the junction of Upper Chorlton Road with Seymour Grove, just where Charlie Peace shot Constable Nicholas Cock late in the last century. It was called Tintern Lodge and consisted of five storeys without central heating but it made it possible for a large family such as ours to live in reasonable comfort.

The trouble was I enjoyed Hulme too much. I regarded work as a nuisance to be avoided if possible. I played the clarinet, my brothers playing the oboe and bassoon. James, the bassoonist, who was taught by Archie Camden, became so good I still think he should have followed a musical career but Cambridge, the army and the civil service put an end to all that. All the instruments belonged to the school. I was never more than competent, just about managing the fairly simple Haydn and Mozart symphonies, with the odd squeak here and there. I did, however, achieve the unusual distinction of singing Pamina in the school production of Mozart's

15

*Magic Flute* but I think it better to draw a veil over that. There is much to be thankful for in that the production escaped the notice of Neville Cardus and that Bernard Levin was not then around.

One marked difference from present-day school life is worth mentioning. We had no money. My weekly pocket money amounted to fourpence until my last year at school. The tram fare to school, about one and a half miles away, was 2½d. We walked both ways, twice a day, and thought nothing of it. That is not to say that as a family we were poor. We were well fed and reasonably clothed but times were hard in the late twenties and early thirties and I do not think my parents had an easy time financially.

I discovered early the joy of books. Whilst sharing measles with my brother James he told me for several nights the story of King Solomon's Mines. I couldn't wait to join the local public library, which in those days was excellent, and I progressed from Rider Haggard to Edgar Wallace and eventually almost anything readable. I must be one of the most consistent users of the public library service for the last forty-six years and have had immeasurable pleasure from it. It even provided me with a wife, but more of that later.

My eldest brother did well in his Higher School Certificate exam and went into that admirable firm, the Scottish Widows, but the first day of family rejoicing came when my elder brother got an Open to Trinity, Cambridge. I wasn't sure what it meant at the time but was suitably impressed and not a little delighted at my father's obvious pride and satisfaction, which used to clear the bar at the Northleigh Club just across the road in double quick time even though he was always generous at standing his round.

My brother's return home during University vacations was an occasion for rejoicing, for about twenty-four hours. Thereafter, his occasional disappearances in the small hours of the morning in response to a 'phone call from his contemporary at Cambridge, John Midgley, now the Washington correspondent of *The Economist*, used to wear parental patience pretty thin. However, James made up for all that by getting a First and then going on to read medieval German at Münster and Munich, eventually achieving a doctorate in Philosophy.

Though my time at school was wasted academically in every other way it was fulfilling. I finished as captain of rugby, vice-captain of cricket and lacrosse and Head Prefect. Even now I look back on the school with a gratitude I find hard to describe. It was not a scholarship factory, though it did well enough. It was a civilized place where maturity and freedom of expression were allowed to flower. It had its less pleasurable moments. I am probably the only medium fast bowler to be hit right over the Old Trafford pavilion into the car park and to finish the match with 0 for 98. But its tutelage went far beyond academic subjects and I shall always remember it, its Headmaster, Trevor Dennis, and its persuasion to maturity with intense gratitude.

There is one person, apart from the Headmaster, whom I should mention in particular. The school secretary, J. A. Barber, began work there at the princely wage of £1 per week at the turn of the century and served the school efficiently and faithfully for over fifty years. He ran the business affairs of the school with an iron hand, commanded the cadet corps, breathed life and energy into lacrosse at the school and outside it and was always immaculately turned out. His language could, on rare occasions, be as colourful as his probity was unquestioned. His plain, down-to-earth honesty is happily demonstrated by an incident in the days of the eleven plus exam when competition to get into Hulme was intense. Legend has it that a father, dragging his unwilling offspring to the exam, said, ' 'ere, Mr Barber, 'ow would ten quid affect the boy's chances?' and got the unhesitating reply, 'It'd just about bugger 'em.' Known for forty years as Ac, after the hill Achi Baba in the Dardanelles, he was a respected and devoted servant of the school, whose brusque manner discouraged any demonstration of the affection in which he was widely held.

Leaving school was not quite so traumatic as I had feared.

I had, of course, realized that I would have to get a job. The family business was not all that prosperous and by then my eldest brother was contemplating leaving the Scottish Widows to join it. I was too young and inexperienced at that time to appreciate the rigours of the labour market and how little a higher education at grammar school counted in the world of commerce. I applied for, and obtained, a job at the Manchester office of James Templeton and Co. of Glasgow, the largest firm of carpet manufacturers in Great Britain, and I began work there as a clerk/salesman/trainee in mid-1935 at a weekly wage of seventeen shillings and sixpence. The Templeton warehouse was in Piccadilly overlooking the very heart of Manchester. The hierarchy consisted of a manager, two travelling salesmen, four or five clerk/salesmen/trainees, one or two warehousemen and, of course, the usual typing staff. For the salesmen the prospect was of a reasonably, but not generously, paid job at the age of thirty after ten years' exploitation at disgracefully low wages even for those days. All the trainees were from grammar schools and some were highly intelligent. But the state of the labour market, our youth and inexperience, the general harmony amongst the staff, who were a remarkably pleasant and loyal group, tended to blind us to reality. Of my seventeen shillings and sixpence I gave ten shillings to my mother, the rest going on tram fares, cigarettes and lunches. Balm cakes or sandwiches with tea in an upstairs room cost about sevenpence a day. Cigarettes were sixpence for ten.

I not only survived this period, I quite enjoyed it. I was playing rugby at weekends for a newly established Old Boys club, taking part in amateur dramatics and my wants were simple. Romance had not at that stage reared its ugly head. To have a girl-friend, much less to bring a girl home, was to run the risk of derision or worse, or to provoke parental invocation of the old Yorkshire warning to those courting, 'Remember, lad. A twopenny pie costs fourpence!' I had nevertheless met by then my future wife who was a librarian in Manchester Central Library and earned three times my wage. Slowly the realization dawned that this was not really the life for me. But what to do? Jobs were valuable in 1937 and unemployment, unlike today, meant what it said. It was really one of H. G. Wells's short stories that put into my head the idea of joining the police. It contained the sentence 'In the country of the blind the one-eyed man is King.' My reasoning ran thus. You have thrown away any chance of an academic career, or a job in public service needing academic qualifications, but you are well built, fit, good at games and not entirely stupid. Why not take on a job without popular appeal in which those qualifications will give you a positive advantage? With that in mind I applied to join the Manchester police. Both Templetons and my father were horrified. The manager was so moved he went so far as to offer me two shillings and sixpence rise. My father protested that it was only one step better than going to prison. Ironically, but happily, he lived long enough to tell me, when I was Chief Constable of Leicester, that I might, after all, have turned out to be his best investment.

Hardly any, even of the older generation are likely to remember public attitudes to the police in the last century. At first they were hated by public and Press alike. In only a few years they achieved grudging acceptance because of the rapidly increasing safety of the London streets. For decades thereafter they were regarded with patronizing if slightly contemptuous approval, a ready target for the satirist commenting on their more obvious failings.

> Every member of the Force
> Has a watch and chain of course.
> If you want to know the time
> Ask a policeman.

This verse from the old music hall song did not have today's paternal aura. It relates to the 'acquisition' of watches by policemen finding drunken 'nobs' or 'toffs' on their beat. A lesser-known song of the same period is rather more explicit.

That all our men a watch can boast
Is quite a matter of course, sirs!
If they don't get one in a month at most
We turn 'em out of the Force, sirs!
And often, too, in their first week,
They finds a chap 'in liquor',
And it only wants a little cheek
To be master of a 'ticker'.

The no less widespread association of police and liquor, which led to many arbitrary dismissals in the early days of the force, attracted similar comments in the music halls.

If you want to get a drink, ask a p'liceman!
He will manage it, I think, will a policeman!
If the pubs are shut or not
He'll produce the flowing pot
He can open all the lot, can a p'liceman!

I was to find the latter, but happily not the former, tradition still in existence. Many pubs and breweries in my early days in the police used to leave bottles of beer outside at night for the patrolling policeman.

That these practices should in the thirties be regarded with benevolent humour is an apt comment on the change in the relationship between the police and the public. Indeed, in my limited experience few people today are aware of the real significance of 'If you want to know the time ...' But, of course, though this may have influenced my father's reaction, I was happily unaware of it.

Against the reality of my lot at Templetons, however, and my growing sense of resentment at what I regarded as exploitation, I persisted and after a few weeks was accepted. It is an indication of the labour market at that time that I then went on a waiting list and was not called for appointment until three weeks later. On 21 July 1937 I reported to the police headquarters in South Street and began a thirteen weeks' training course at Manchester's main fire station.

Looking back, this was the end of Disneyland for me and the discovery of a world of harsh reality.

# CHAPTER 2

# The Police I Joined

The Manchester force at that time was about 1450 strong and was commanded by a former Scottish coalminer who was also head of the fire brigade. The force also ran the ambulance service and the mortuaries. There was a one-room training school at the South Street headquarters but this was reserved for an intake of recruits to neighbouring forces. There were about 126 police forces in England and Wales at that time, some dozen of them in Lancashire and many of these were too small to run their own training schools. Those of us destined for police duty in Manchester were therefore relegated to a dismal schoolroom at the main fire station. There were about thirty of us. Our two instructors, Detective Sergeant Robert Malcolm Morrison Sloss and Sergeant James William Bland were good and conscientious. Both were, however, drawn from ordinary duty. Sloss was an experienced and efficient detective, tall, well built, good looking and impressive in every way. Bland was from the court staff, an old timer who might have been a publican in disguise. The method of teaching was to spend most of each day dictating laws, orders and regulations to be painstakingly copied in longhand and learned each evening. At the end of the week there was, of course, an exam. My class were a mixed bag, mostly lower working class, former servicemen with a sprinkling of the better educated. One, Jack Dennis, a former guardsman and hard as nails, was to serve in the Long Range Desert Group and to be severely wounded. Another, Raymond Ball, was to die in the RAF in the early days of the war. Yet another was to lose his life by accident early in the war catching a rifle thrown to him with a live round up the spout. The Mancunians amongst us were not allowed to live at home and had to move to approved lodgings in which the chip pan was usually a prominent feature. The pay was sixty-two shillings weekly, with six shillings rent allowance and one shilling boot allowance, sixty-nine shillings in all. Good digs cost thirty shillings. Most of us invested in bicycles not only to save fares but because public transport was not always available on shift duties, called 'Reliefs'. There were three basic reliefs, 6 a.m.–2 p.m., 2 p.m.–10 p.m., and 10 p.m.–6 a.m., called mornings, afternoons and nights with occasionally 8 a.m.–4 p.m. and 4 p.m.–12 midnight, called days and evenings. Regular day duties, such as traffic posts, were generally reserved for men with twenty or more years' service.

We were lucky in our instructors. They did their best to break us in gently and in their own way to forewarn us about the kind of life we were to lead, wholly different from the police of today. The Manchester force was dominated by a philosophy not unlike that of Victoria's army. There was no suggestion of leadership by example. Seniors battened on and bullied juniors and the force as a whole did the same to that part of the public not able effectively to look after itself. There was a kind of comradeship born of sharing the same conditions and there were plenty of basically kind and decent men. But the system was harsh, unimaginative, unintelligent and ruthless. The final stage in our training was in itself an indication of going by the book. We were all supposed to have reached a minimal standard of proficiency in shorthand before we finished our training and we received weekly instruction from the chief constable's private secretary, a Scot known to us as Saxpence. When the time for the final test came, most of us couldn't do a stroke. We needn't have worried. Model answers were distributed before dictation began and all we did was to write our names on them. Saxpence undoubtedly got the most uniformly satisfactory results of any instructor I have known in forty years. We all duly received a certificate of proficiency in shorthand signed by Saxpence himself on a form bearing a facsimile of the chief constable's signature. It was never my most treasured possession.

The training course was followed by three consecutive months on night duty, the principle being that you were not fit to be seen in uniform until 'your number was dry'. I actually did four, not for any malicious or other reason, just to fill a gap in the duty roster. I was posted to C Division, covering eastern Manchester from the slums of Ancoats in the city centre to Levenshulme on the border with Stockport and Clayton further north. My divisional number was 202. For the next two years I had no name.

C Division was a Box Division. It consisted of an antiquated headquarters in Mill Street, Bradford, a suburb of Manchester boasting its own colliery, one or two small section stations and about thirty wooden boxes each equipped with a small electric fire, a red light which could be switched on from divisional headquarters to attract attention, and a telephone. The division consisted of six sections each of six beats and was worked throughout the three reliefs by eighteen sergeants and one hundred and eight constables with a further three sergeants and eighteen constables to relieve those taking weekly rest days. There was also a patrolling inspector for each relief, a number of fixed traffic posts and special patrols. There was, of course, a CID complement under a detective inspector and a 'vice detail'', or 'plain clothes branch' of one sergeant and six constables. At the top sat the All Highest, the superintendent, and that was just about all he did in my day.

The Box Division sprang from a belief that it would avoid capital expenditure on buildings and save time in travel from police stations to beats. No consideration at all was given to physical comfort, the value of contact with fellow officers or the need to promote a sense of corporate identity. You paraded for duty by 'ringing in' on the box telephone fifteen minutes before your relief and 'retired' from duty in the same way. Half an hour was allowed for refreshments and each box contained a list of nearby places where hot water could be obtained to brew tea in the box jug. It was a weird life. The only policemen you saw were those on adjoining beats, the section sergeant twice nightly and the patrol inspector. Pay was drawn from divisional headquarters each Friday, less compulsory voluntary subscriptions for retiring officers. Each beat had four fixed points and forty-five minutes were allowed between each. The method of working varied each day, the starting point and direction, clockwise or anti-clockwise, being changed to make our movements less predictable. Many of the inspectors and sergeants looked on their juniors in much the same way as the force looked upon the public, fair game if you could get away with it. To hide behind a building to catch a constable two or three minutes late on his point was routine, the result being a discipline form and a two shillings and sixpence fine. Habitual lateness, say three or four times in a few months meant the sack. The lower orders fought back as best they could. Torches were used to warn the man on the next beat of the approach of a sergeant or inspector. Generally speaking, each rank stuck together, whilst maintaining distance above and below.

I soon stopped worrying about the futility of shaking hands with doorknobs all night. Like most of my colleagues I rapidly acquired a knowledge of unlocked outside lavatories in which I could smoke a peaceful pipe out of the wind. Most beat books had an unofficial list of peepshows and calling places and the night watchman with his coke fire was a friend indeed.

The small hours in the slums of Manchester were eerie in those days. The tacklers, or knockers up, carrying long sticks with wire fans at the end to rap bedroom windows, who claimed to have parted more couples than divorce courts. The street cleaners, in the distance like grey ghosts in the half light of dawn. Even working on the section based on Mill Street had its snags. We ate in a giant kitchen and were lucky to have a large tripe works next door. One of the less attractive antics of the reserve constable, usually an old war horse, was to bamboozle a young probationer into the mortuary to help with tidying up after a post-mortem in order to put him off his tripe. It usually worked. It certainly did with me. I thought one incident funny at the time. I don't think so now. The night relief decided to take the mickey out of a rather cocky and pompous young probationer and the station inspector agreed to help. When the youngster came in to report for refreshments at 1.15 a.m. he was handed the mortuary keys and told to count the bodies, of which there were about six. The reserve man, not of noticeably delicate or sensitive disposition, had removed all the lights but one, removed his false teeth, taken off his shoes and socks, rolled his trousers up to the knees, tied a label to his big toe, covered himself with a paper shroud and lain on a slab in the darkest corner of the mortuary. A mortuary is not a pleasant place at the best of times but that one, in the small hours, was certainly not a place to be. The rest of the relief were, of course, concealed behind cars in the yard outside. In the middle of an increasingly nervous count the reserve man let out an unearthly moan and started to rise from his slab. The probationer emerged from the mortuary at a speed that would have left Jesse Owens standing. Unfortunately he tore out of the station towards Philips Park and when everyone had stopped laughing we realized we had a problem. It took over an hour to find him and though he had recovered his nerve was emotionally shattered. Most important, his self-respect had gone. No one likes showing fear in front of his fellows. Although we all did our best in a rough way to make amends he did not stay, not surprisingly.

It was on my first tour of day duty that I saw my first dead body. Even to this day I can remember the sense of shock. He was a young man, about twenty, who had been crushed by a heavy lorry whilst riding a bicycle in Hyde Road. A wheel had gone over part of his head and the result was both unpleasant and indescribably pathetic. Sudden deaths, as we called them, were usually handled by section sergeants but there being none available I got the job. For a young man of twenty-one from a sheltered background it was a grim experience. Unfortunately, I made so good a job of it that the inspector in charge of my relief decided to give me all the uncomplicated sudden deaths for the next few weeks. If was not meant unkindly. He simply thought it would be good experience and in a way he was right. But it certainly wasn't a way to earn a living. One was a poor old woman in a virtually furniture-less hovel in Bradford. She had starved to death. There was one stale crust, a little sour milk, no fire and bare floorboards. As I helped to strip the poor, pathetic body in the mortuary for the post-mortem I thought my heart would break but was terrified of showing weakness before the reserve constable. Another taught me a valuable lesson about the vagaries of police humour. The body was that of an old vagrant. It had lain undiscovered for days on a flock mattress in the upstairs room of a house in Ardwick. It was badly decomposed, verminous and stank. The police ambulance driver was an old hand and no delicate flower. He smartly produced a flexible canvas stretcher and said, 'Right, 202. You take the bottom end.' As we descended the narrow stairs I was covered in the most indescribable filth, much to his amusement. I could cheerfully have shot him. I suppose I handled about a dozen deaths in about ten weeks and was thankful to be relieved of the job when the station inspector changed. But at least it taught me early about the finality and pathos of death and in a way prepared me for some of the harsh realities to follow, both in the police and the army.

I am ashamed to this day of my first arrest. He was a little Irishman, like a bantam cock, and he had had far too much to drink on New Year's Eve. He was surrounded by a grinning crowd in Devonshire Street and was offering to fight the lot. I'm afraid 'Move along there' in the best George Dixon style didn't help very much. He was dancing round me with his fists up like the featherweight champion of Europe. I was in a quandary. I did not want to lock up a drunk on New Year's Eve. On the other hand I couldn't back off in front of a jeering crowd. Accordingly I grabbed him and to my surprise found he was a real handful. At that time, wistfully, I only weighed ten stone. Having dragged him about fifty yards he suddenly stopped struggling and said, 'Sure, officer, let's call it off and be friends. I live there,' pointing to a lodging house. But I remembered the awful warnings in training school about the dire fate of any policeman losing a prisoner so I resumed the struggle and landed exhausted with him at Upton Street station. The next morning he was fined ten shillings, was profusely apologetic and we had coffee together for which he insisted on paying. It wasn't exactly a headline-making first case.

I had been known for some time by some of my colleagues as the 'grammar school lad' and after a year felt that I was living down the distrust and suspicion reserved for anyone who seemed reasonably well educated. I had even gained the qualified approval of two of the most feared sergeants of C Division, Bert Cliff and Jos Smith. The latter, a six-foot-four former guardsman, used to greet all new recruits with the enquiry 'Was you in the Guards, chum?' and if you wasn't your prospects seemed poor indeed. I spent only eighteen months actually on the beat. They contained one or two memorable moments, but nothing spectacular or historic. Holding on to a lunatic trying to throw himself off a balcony of the flats in Kirkmanshulme Lane behind Belle Vue until help came; patrolling in pairs in Ancoats on Friday and Saturday nights, chasing and losing an Irishman whose jacket was charred from a premature explosion in Higher Temple Street. That kind of thing. I caught no burglars or criminals of any significance. There was, however, one incident not without a wry humour in retrospect. I had been posted for point duty at the corner of London Road with Fairfield Street, a very busy crossing. I had not done much point duty and was still naïvely thrilled at the godlike power which caused all traffic to stop at the raising of a hand. It was a splendid feeling inducing a sense of confidence all too dangerous for the unwary or the inexperienced. I had noticed that whilst all the Manchester Corporation trams went straight on to and from Piccadilly, the smaller Stockport trams turned left before reaching the officer on point duty, which meant that he had only to avoid vans and cars whilst trams were actually passing him. On this particular occasion

I nonchalantly waved on cars from Manchester and one from Stockport at the same time. Too late I realized the Stockport car was coming straight on and that I was going to be sandwiched between them. The look of horror on the Stockport driver's face was enough for me. I stood not upon the order of my going and even though I could not see whether there was any traffic coming up on his nearside I held my greatcoat skirt in my hand and jumped for dear life landing on my backside with a resounding thump in the gutter. It was morning rush hour and the street was crowded with pedestrians who laughed and cheered with understandable lack of restraint. It is not often one sees the majesty of the law in full, if brief, flight. I did the only thing possible. Having recovered my helmet, I doffed it with a graceful bow to my public and then fled into nearby Whitworth Street station. Despite the odd brawl and punch-up I think that was certainly the nearest I came to death in the line of duty.

I did however pick up a few points on policing, one of which illustrates well the ingenuity and practicality of the police in those days. On the border of Openshaw and Clayton with Droylsden there was a canal lock, a favourite place for suicides. Providing that the beat officer found the body and no members of the public were present, two shillings would induce the lock keeper to open the gates to allow the body to be pushed through into the county. I did this once and suffered the indignity of finding the body back on my side of the lock the following morning. I suppose the eventual police amalgamations put an end to that, as well as reducing the tax free perks of the lock keeper.

The first break came when divisional orders advertised a vacancy in the plainclothes branch. Successful candidates usually had not less than five years' service but I thought 'nothing ventured' and applied. To my astonishment and that of everyone else I was selected. It was another lesson in reality. The primary tasks of the one sergeant and six constables were to deal with soliciting, brothels, living on immoral earnings and street betting. Not like the home life of our own dear Queen, in fact. I did this for six months and it was valuable experience. There were scores of bookies on C Division and it would have been impossible with our slim resources to enforce the rather fatuous law at that time. On the other hand we could make life hell for any one of them. So by common agreement they took it in turn to put up stooges, runners with false betting slips and money, usually from the ranks of the unemployed. They were 'arrested' by appointment, the bookie was waiting at the station to bail them and, if previously unconvicted, they were fined ten pounds. The courts were perfectly well aware of this farce. It was not unusual for the magistrates to see off ten such cases in less minutes, though there were occasional flashes of humour, as when one 'runner' stumped out of the dock on a wooden leg and another admitted a previous conviction, thus doubling the fine.

Notwithstanding the impression to be gained from some newspapers, prostitution is not in itself unlawful. Procuring women for immoral purposes, or soliciting so as to annoy people are. Not even the most ingenious and puritanical legislation is likely to put an end to prostitution which has always been with us and always will be. Indeed, in these days of easy abortion and contraception the real threat to the prostitute is the increase in sexual freedom and its growing acceptance. In the thirties, however, police were expected to prevent prostitutes from annoying people on the street and to ensure that those who did were made to pay for it in much the same way as bookies' runners. In other words, a routine number of arrests was expected from those areas where soliciting was traditional. If these were not forthcoming, both senior officers and the Press were quick to assume petty corruption of the plainclothes men by the girls or their ponces. There was, therefore, an implicit pressure to get results. Penalties were small, complaints were few. Most of our efforts were thus devoted to achieving a defensive record of fairly pointless work.

Public lavatories also figured in our work. My simple mind was quite astonished to find the things that men get up to there, and no pun is intended. We were not so unlucky as the central, or A Division, where this was something of a problem and two officers were permanently assigned to the task. They were known traditionally as Plink and Plonk. It always amused me, by the way, long after I left Manchester when a new and very able chief constable was fiercely criticized by the civil libertarians when his annual report revealed a sudden upsurge in the activities of Plink and Plonk. I don't suppose he knew anything about it until he saw the figures. I should think the two veterans just happened to have found a more prolific hunting ground for their activities or used a brace and bit to provide a few peepholes. I remember years later being chided gently by a Home Secretary for this kind of thing in central London, until I reminded him courteously that men having recourse to public urinals were sometimes not a little put out to find that three hands were necessary for the purpose.

Each weekend the sergeant and six constables used to patrol Brunswick Street and Ardwick Green in strength because prostitutes and drunks frequently started fights there and good time was had by all. One such incident, had it occurred in today's enlightened conditions, would certainly have ended my career. Most of us carried, wholly improperly, short rubber truncheons made in a nearby Dunlop factory. One Friday night an enormous navvy pushed the head of a constable through a shop window and started quite a battle in which uniformed and plainclothes men cheerfully joined. It grew to quite serious proportions, stopping the traffic in Ardwick Green. At the most critical moment we had this great so-and-so almost in the van, face upwards with one of us pulling him in by the hair and the rest of us trying to help. The crowd was jeering and becoming unpleasantly restive. The man had enormous boots on and his feet were splayed outwards to stop us from getting the last bit of him into the van. I was standing on the van step astride his legs and decided on desperate measures. I stretched out the left side of my mackintosh for cover, drew my rubber with my right hand and gave him a hefty whack on the shin. Even in his drunken state that registered. He let out a yell, closed his legs and he was in with three of us sitting on various portions of him. The next morning at court, looking sheepish and surprisingly clean, he pleaded guilty, apologized to the court, thanked the officers in the case and was fined the customary ten shillings. As he left the dock my heart stood still. His right leg below the knee was encased in plaster of Paris. He had been taken to the Royal Infirmary during the night and treated for a suspected fracture of the small bone in the lower leg, the tibia or fibula, I can never remember which. Far from there being any hard feelings he greeted me cheerfully and we went off for a drink together. Nowadays, of course, it would have meant a complaint, an enquiry, papers to the Director of Public Prosecutions and a prosecution or discipline case. Not that I didn't deserve it, but times were different, thank goodness.

In between our excursions to Rusholme Road, Ardwick Green and Brunswick Street we occasionally called at the Ardwick Wrestling Stadium. It was hilarious, especially behind the scenes, where the broad northern dialect of Hassan the Assassin or The Terrible Turk would have don. credit to Mike Yarwood. Fortune was not always on our side. On one occasion a colleague and I arrested a young man copulating on the pavement in broad daylight in Brunswick Street with a most revolting prostitute. Admitted, this was unusual, but the truth was too much for the magistrate to accept, especially after looking at the woman, and the case was dismissed. A bucket of cold water might have done more good. On another we arrested a man and two women showing unusual sexual dexterity in public. The arrest was near the boundary with A Division in which most C Division officers were unknown. The van unfortunately took us with the prisoners to Whitworth Street station which was on that division. I led the way into the charge room, my colleague bringing up the rear. The charge was accepted and the station officer pressed the bell for the gaoler. The door behind me leading to the cells opened, two hands seized me firmly by the scruff of the neck and the seat of the pants and a second later a cell door clanged behind me. There were apologies all round, hysterical laughter from the prisoners, one of whom assured me that she wouldn't have missed it for all the world! Looking back on it all, though, it was a pretty sordid business. I didn't see it objectively at the time. It was just a job to be done, sometimes with a touch of excitement, occasionally quite funny but I suppose all we were doing was not really far removed from the job of the garbage man.

As the end of my probation approached, there were more important things happening elsewhere. Chamberlain had returned from Munich before I began plainclothes duty and in Manchester, if not elsewhere, there was a general feeling that war was inevitable. I was just at the point of wondering vaguely whether to look for another job when I was suddenly whisked away to Force Headquarters at South Street and appointed a detective constable in Special Branch. It sounds more glamorous than it was. In those days there were only three Special Branch men in Manchester, an inspector, sergeant and constable. We had, as today, no special powers or immunity. Our task was to gather information about any organization seeking the achievement of political objectives by unlawful means, minorities of the right and the left being of equal interest. In addition, of course, organizations of alien origin or with alien loyalties were of no less interest. Initially it was not a very happy set-up. The inspector and sergeant detested each other and since neither had been consulted about my appointment each took me for a henchman of the other. In fact, I had never heard of either. However, once the inspector had decided he was mistaken, we became firm friends and he taught me a lot. His name was Edward Pierpoint and he was to play quite a part in my CID career. He was painstaking, slow, methodical and scrupulously honest but he was excessively frightened of his seniors and had, unnecessarily, quite an inferiority complex which caused him to put off making decisions to an extent which got him into continual trouble. He was nevertheless very capable and I learnt a lot from him, including the perils of procrastination!

Until war broke out there was very little visible end product to Special Branch work and this taught me early a very useful lesson. Police reports and enquiries which are not tested in court or by similar impartial process should never be allowed to impair freedom or employment without suitable safeguards for those to whom they relate. The early years of the war brought this home to me forcibly and in a manner never to be forgotten. The incident, in fact, had a profound effect on my whole police career. It occurred soon after the Italian entry into the war in 1940. There was a panic reaction by the government. Police forces were ordered to arrest for internment under the Defence Regulations a large number of Italian citizens, some of whom had lived here for many years. One such order related to one Ernani Landucci, a waiter at a Manchester hotel for about thirty years with a British born daughter. Pierpoint and I arrived at the Landucci home about midnight, having worked for three days and two nights without sleep. Far from looking like an enemy agent even to our tired eyes, Landucci looked like a simple, decent but very frightened Italian waiter. We showed him the Order and explained the position. He burst into tears and called his wife and daughter. He admitted readily that he was a member of the Fascio di Manchester but said this meant nothing. He owned a tiny piece of land in southern Italy and was required on account of it to pay two shillings and sixpence annually to the Italian Consul General. That was the sum of his subversive activities. We believed him and said that although we had no choice but to execute the Order we would report immediately our view that he was harmless and should be released. He opened a bottle of white wine and as all five of us raised our glasses he gave us the toast 'Bugger da fasc'. We duly reported our views on the following day, but within three days he was dead. It was his misfortune to be put with hundreds of other so-called enemy aliens on the liner *Arandora Star*, which was torpedoed and sunk on the high seas by a U-boat. The sense of injustice, of shock, of tragedy has remained with me to this day. The irresponsibility, the futility still arouses the strongest feelings in me. I suppose more than anything else that experience taught me that there was neglect, carelessness and worse in the police system. It was a lesson I never forgot.

My arrival in Special Branch, or CID Headquarters, as we called it, began my association with a legendary Manchester policeman who was largely to determine my future. He was called Moses Idwal Valentine, the son of a Welsh Methodist minister and the brother of Lewis Valentine, the Welsh academic who gave himself up after setting fire to an RAF bombing range in North Wales before the war. Valentine was a big man, about six-foot-two, with a bald head, long nose and a permanent hacking cough. He was a chief superintendent, third man in the Manchester force, honest to the point of hair-shirtedness and a detective of great skill and determination. Unfortunately, his honesty made him some powerful enemies. In the late thirties a well-known Manchester sporting figure of thoroughly undesirable habits and background severely injured a man in a pub brawl. His friends and backers, seeing the end of his career and a prison sentence, are said to have paid £100 to the victim by way of compensation, a lot of money in those days, and £200 to a lay magistrate of equally dubious background, to go on the bench out of turn to dismiss the case or impose a nominal penalty. Valentine got wind of this and went to see the then Director of Public Prosecutions, Sir Theobald Mathew, who sent a senior representative to insist on committal for trial. Not only did the offender go to prison but the magistrate and the victim are said to have refused to disgorge their ill-gotten gains. All very Damon Runyon, but unfortunately the magistrate was an influential figure in the local Labour Party and Valentine was to pay dearly for his naïve belief in equality before the law when, in 1942, the Home Office insisted on the appointment of a second assistant chief constable who was obviously intended to be the heir apparent. Valentine, then an Acting Inspector of Constabulary and incontestably the best candidate, was blocked by sufficient members of the Watch Committee to deny him the job. The other members, however, would not agree on a nominee and after much argument and adverse publicity the committee agreed to appoint a candidate unknown to any of them but acceptable to the Home Office. The successful candidate duly succeeded the retiring chief constable and Valentine thereupon moved back from the Regional Commissioner's office to become the only assistant chief constable.

All this did not affect me at the time. My Special Branch work was quite interesting and socially convenient and life at force headquarters was a great deal more civilized than in C Division. Moreover my future wife worked just across the road at the Central Library, on which I still look with a great deal of sentimental regard. We were, however, not by any means idle. The fall of France had led to the panic internment of Austrian, German and Italian aliens of whom there were thousands. I suppose this was understandable for a nation staring defeat in the face and for which the term fifth column had suddenly acquired a new meaning. But it was a painful, sad process. I remember escorting batches of tearful and frightened refugees to a camp at Prees Heath, Shropshire which consisted of nothing more than a few huts surrounded by barbed wire. Rather less depressing was the taking of Manchester's Mosleyites to Walton gaol, though most of them made no secret of their belief in a German victory.

One unimportant, but odd, incident occurred before this part of my service ended. After the fall of France I was sent for by the head of CID who had with him the Regional Security Liaison Officer, the security service in those days operating on a regional basis. I was told to pack a bag for a week or so and be ready to go to a Manchester hotel. There I was to live, my cover being that I worked for my family business and was temporarily without a home. I was to do no more than await the arrival of a man at the hotel and thereafter to do nothing except to note his arrivals and departures and particulars of anyone who called on him. I was told that surveillance of visitors would be provided but that all I had to do was to notify the need for them to start work. I did as I was told but on the appointed day the order to move never came. The following day the Regional Security Liaison Officer said that I must wait another day whilst he did some checking. On the third day I was told to stand down. All this meant little to me, except, of course, that I guessed that the man was a German agent who had been denounced by our own collaborators. I thought no more about it until about six years later, in 1947, when, having just returned from the army I ran into a Manchester solicitor who had been in the Regional Security Liaison Office at the relevant time. He greeted me with unusual animation and said, 'Did you read the account of the inquest in this morning's *Manchester Guardian*?' I looked blank and he said, 'You know. The body found in Trow Ghyll pothole.' I still looked mystified and he said, 'I happened to look in "the office" in London yesterday and they think this was the chap you were supposed to look out for. He certainly left but never arrived.' According to the paper there was a metal container containing sodium cyanide beside the body but the unfortunate man had not made any use of it. He had died from starvation and exposure. How he came to be so far north of his objective and to die in a pothole I suppose no one will ever know. If he got into the pothole by accident it must have been a chance in a million. If, on the other hand, someone put him down it, it was certainly never reported. Of course, some pretty unpleasant things happened to some of our airmen landing in Germany, especially at the height of our sustained bombing of it. Still, it seemed an odd story with a very unsatisfactory ending.

Soon after this aborted mission I was seconded to the Regional Police Office at Arkwright House in Deansgate. It was headed by Valentine, who had selected me and there were about eight or nine of us working round the clock. The Regional Commissioner, Sir Hartley (now Lord) Shawcross was assisted also by an Inspector of Constabulary, a dear old man, Major-General Sir Llewellyn Atcherley, the father of the RAF's famous flying twins. The work was purely administrative and rather dull. We arranged support for forces hard pressed by air raids and made plans against the possible consequences of invasion. It was during this period that I married. My wife, Kathleen Mary Leahy, was the only daughter of the works manager of Kemsley Newspapers at Withy Grove. We had known each other for some years. Indeed, my foray into the police could be said to be our first exercise in joint forward planning. We were able to rent a small, semi-detached house in Daventry Road, where we spent our honeymoon to the accompaniment of a battery of heavy anti-aircraft guns at the end of the road in Hough End Fields. My first child, Christopher, was born whilst I was serving in the Regional Police Office and I still regard pushing a newly-bought empty pram from Deansgate to Chorlton-cum-Hardy as one of my more memorable achievements.

By the middle of 1942 the war on the eastern front was well under way, air raids had fallen to an insignificant level and the government decided that the time had come to release a proportion of the police for military duties. The choices were restricted to flying duties with the RAF, the commandos, the field artillery, the armoured corps or the infantry. I chose the armoured corps on the principle that anything was likely to be better than walking and was duly posted to a Primary Training Centre in the Isle of Wight to begin general military training. My reaction, on the whole, was one of relief. We were no longer an embattled country. My eldest brother was learning to fly in the RAF. My elder brother was already a GSO 2 in the western desert. My brother-in-law, a territorial major in the Royal Army Service Corps, was a prisoner of the Japs in Changi Jail. Whilst no hero, I thought it was high time I joined in and at that time, having a horror of flying, was glad of the chance to serve in the army, which had held my affection ever since my Cadet Corps days. Needless to say, my romantic illusions about military service were soon to be rudely shattered.

# CHAPTER 3

# Soldiering

I began my service as a soldier in August 1942 at a Primary
Training Centre, consisting of Nissen huts right outside HM
Prison Parkhurst, the inmates of that establishment being
generally better accommodated than we were. We crossed
to the island on a ferry which happened to be carrying
walking wounded from the unsuccessful Dieppe raid. It was
not an auspicious beginning. The Centre housed three pla-
toons, almost all of whom were policemen. At that time the
fortunes of war were running against us, Tobruk had fallen
and the enemy stood at the gates of Cairo and the Middle
East. The Russians had not yet recovered from the German
onslaught the previous winter. We were not to know that
the battle of Alam Halfa was soon to give us new heart and
that American equipment was pouring into the war zones.
All we knew was that an order had gone forth that training
was to be intensified so as to simulate the reality of warfare
and that a proportion of casualties was acceptable.

Primary training consisted mostly of weapon training and
simple fieldcraft, which for a Mancunian was something of
a revelation. In Manchester birds and plant life required a
real talent for survival. There were also countless inocula-
tions. It was important to protect us from every germ until
the moment of truth. The only really irritating feature of
this six weeks was the aggravation from the prisoners at
Parkhurst who kept inviting us to come in and join them.
They certainly looked fitter, healthier and more capable of
striking terror into the enemy than we did.

On 1 October we entrained for Catterick where we were
assigned to barrack rooms designed for twelve. We had
thirty in each, there being six wash basins which we shared

with an adjoining barrack room. Speed was essential for both shaving, washing and lavatories. There were no beds. We slept on what were called biscuits, or felt pads, on the floor.

I had only one frightening experience at Catterick. I was detailed to box as a middleweight in a Saturday night contest in the regimental gym. I was no boxer but there was no question of backing out. My opponent had been released from Dartmoor on volunteering for military service. I had visions of a premature demise far from the battlefield but my apprehensions were in the event entirely unfounded. Prison had not improved his fitness. As I fled smartly around the ring avoiding his flailing fists I became aware that his wind was failing and that he was in danger of collapsing from exhaustion. I therefore stood my ground in the second round and he ran on to my outstretched fist with sufficient energy to justify his lying down for the count. His military career was short-lived. A pound of butter was planted in his kit by the regimental police and he was arrested. We never saw him again.

I had applied for a commission during a routine interview and in due course was summoned before a War Office Selection Board. Its routine was entirely predictable and I got the surprisingly high rating of B. I took the trouble, whilst undergoing this test, to make a careful note of its procedures and the assault course, which was supposed to be a surprise, and circulated it to all my friends on my return. I was not to know whether my ploy was successful because almost immediately I was posted to 100 (Sandhurst) OCTU, RAC and left for the Pre-OCTU at Blackdown for the preliminary three months' course. My arrival at Blackdown by bus from Ashdown station was enough to congeal the blood of the bravest. There on the parade square was a squad drilling with a precision that could only have been achieved by threats of death or worse, the major domo being an emaciated six-foot monster in either the Scots or Irish Guards with a falsetto scream that made the hair stand on end.

Our troop of about thirty consisted of all sorts. One or two old regulars of thirty or so, a former RAF squadron leader who had refused to take his men into action on a night flight because he thought his controller was mad. Although military discipline had to be upheld, clearly the powers that be thought he was right or he would have been cashiered. Most of us, however, were youngsters, like my friend Monty Holt, from Wilmslow, who at nineteen years of age was killed at Arnhem. Unlike the motley crew at Catterick they were a splendid bunch. The barrack room was immaculate and actually had metal beds and japanned stoves which were never lit. They were polished daily with pumice stone and boot polish. After all, the outcome of the war depended on it. Blackdown was the nearest thing to hell in my five years in the army. If the object was to make us glad to go to war, I can only say that it was achieved. I was fit, immaculately clean and turned into a near robot. However, even this came to an end. Came the great day when the survivors were packed with their kit into a three-tonner en route for Sandhurst. On arrival we were formed up on the perimeter of a ceremonial passing out parade at which the adjutant traditionally rode up the college steps after the passing out troop. We were then marched on to the square to take the place vacated by those who had passed out and marched past the reviewing officer. When the rest of the parade was dismissed we were marched to the old building where we met for the first time the legendary Regimental Sergeant Major Brand. His first words, in a stentorian bellow, have lived in my memory. 'Now then, gentlemen, remember this. Whilst you're 'ere, I'm sir to you, sir, and you're sir to me, sir. Do you understand, all of you?' To which we replied with a concerted roar of 'Sir!', anything more than that in response to a rhetorical question constituting sufficient cause for a charge of 'gossiping'. I grew to admire and respect the footguards' instructors at Sandhurst. Their bark was worse than their bite, they led by example and their parade square patter was worthy of a book on its own. To see Brand drilling several hundred cadets before

41

dismissing them to 'them nasty smelly things on the Tank Park' was a sight never to be forgotten. 'What's your name, sir?' 'You've lost it, sir.' 'Take his name, sarn't major. Wearing an idle tie.' A bugler whose lip split whilst blowing the single note half-hour call provoked the falsetto scream, 'Sarn't major.' 'Sir.' 'Take his name for idle blowing of the 'orn.' Perhaps the most memorable of all was Brand, when drilling the women ATS who drove vehicles and did administrative work, letting out one continuous exhortation to the marching column. 'Keep your 'ead and eyes to the front or you'll be turned into pillars of salt like Lot's wife!' All this, of course, was part of an old tradition. True, it carried extra drills, but whenever there was anything really tough to be done we noticed that our instructors were always with us, even though this was not strictly required of them. It wasn't like the mindless bullying at Blackdown. There was an underlying sense of humour and mutual loyalty. Training was hard. To run three miles or more in full kit. To spend a week on a Welsh mountain without cover for seven days and nights. To do a lake crossing in canvas boats under fire from live ammunition, in our case the instructor gunner actually hitting and sinking the boat at the water's edge, all this took some doing. And our Grenadier sergeant instructor did the whole thing with us even though he didn't have to. 'Can't let you down gentlemen. Some of you 'aven't been away from your mothers for long. You might get 'urt.' They were a marvellous lot and for the first time I began to realize what soldiering was all about.

We spent seven weeks on general infantry training before moving on to the more sophisticated instruction necessary to command three tanks. The troop in its last week always did a combined exercise with the infantry on Thursley Common. All this was interspersed by ruthless physical training, one incident of which deserves recounting. We had done a three or four miles' run and walk, involving a little way crawling underground and some swarming across ropes between trees. The final stage was to swim the 'back' lake. This was not the ornamental lake in front of the college but an evil-looking narrow stretch of dirty and deep water behind the college. We were wearing steel helmets, boots, denims but were not carrying rifles. We did this in tank crews of five and as the old man of my crew I brought up the rear. To my horror, on leaving the raft in the middle of this horrible pool I got acute cramp in both hands for the first time in my life. I daren't cry out, because lack of moral fibre was the shortest route to RTU (returned to unit). I decided to complete the swim by backstroke but as soon as I turned over my helmet filled with water and began to pull my head back. I bobbed up and down for a moment or two until I realized that I really was in trouble. At that point I lost my moral fibre but I was twelve inches under water and it therefore did me neither good nor harm. I remember at the end feeling a moment or two of intense fear, pushing my helmet forward over my head and seeing it swirl away into a murky cloud and suddenly all fear left me. I can only remember thinking '. . . it!' and then passing out. As luck would have it a member of my troop who was off duty happened to be sunbathing at the side of the lake. His name was Stanley Dwyer, and he was a fellow Mancunian employed by Thomas Hedley, the Trafford Park soap people. He also happened to be a superb and powerful swimmer. Sensing something wrong he did a long underwater dive, seized me by the cross straps of my equipment and hoisted me to the surface, where he held on to the raft until help came. When I woke up I was being pumped clean of the filth and slime I had swallowed. As soon as I looked alive I was told to 'get fell in'. The following morning the squadron sergeant major addressed me in no uncertain manner. 'Squadron Leader's orders 0900 hours. The charge, by neglect, carelessly losing a steel helmet, the property of His Majesty, whilst on active service.' I just replied 'Sir'. I was learning. The squadron leader was an elegant Grenadier major called Gregory Hood, who had won an MC in Norway. As we stood in front on him the sergeant major said, 'Sir! The officer cadet pleads "Not Guilty". 'e produces this eight figure map reference. It denotes precisely where the steel

'elmet is. It is beyond 'is physical means to recover it.'
Whereupon Gregory Hood without lifting his head from the
papers he was reading said, 'Not guilty. Ordered to pay nine
shillings and sixpence, the cost of one steel helmet.' Thus
was military protocol satisfied and the books balanced. In
fact I never got a replacement until I was commissioned
and bought one from the regimental quartermaster. I only
tell this story because it has a postscript. In 1976 I was
lecturing at the Staff College as Commissioner of Police of
the Metropolis. At the end of the session the curtains behind
me suddenly drew apart and there stood the Commandant,
Sir Hugh Beach. He said, 'Commissioner. We have heard
of your tribulations and think it is about time that Sandhurst
made amends.' He then walked forward bearing a cushion
on which rested a steel helmet, which is now one of my
treasured possessions, though honesty compels me to confess
that it was not the one I lost.

Another interesting experience at Sandhurst was the test
for claustrophobia, essential for tank crews. We were taken
to Monkey Hill and were tipped head first down a drainpipe
which descended at an angle of about forty-five degrees to
an underground chamber too small to allow standing. Three
drainpipes led off from the chamber, so small as only to
allow crawling. Two finished with damp, solid earth. The
other gave access to a larger chamber. Of course, all this
was in Stygian blackness and, although we did not know it,
there was an escape hatch for use by the training staff in
case anyone lost his nerve. Some did. But I had heard all
about this and had a book of matches in my denims. They
do wonders for anyone suffering from claustrophobia in the
dark and I came through that test with flying colours.

I was sorry to leave Sandhurst. It taught me a lot. I was
superbly fit. More important I had begun to suspect that
somewhere in the army there might, after all, be someone
with a grain of sense.

One final memory. In my last three weeks we got a new
squadron leader. He was from the 9th Lancers and had been
very badly wounded in the western desert, winning an MC

in the process. I only heard one lecture from him before I was commissioned. Thirty-two years later I was to recognize him as one of the judges at the Metropolitan Police Horse Show at Imber Court, the son of a former assistant commissioner, Sir Percy Laurie, David Laurie, the last colonel of that distinguished regiment. Few people know that when he came to Sandhurst the army had written him off. He had been wounded very severely in the left arm and was thought unfit to fight again. Undeterred he went to his own doctor and asked him if he could find a surgeon to patch him up sufficiently to resume active service. It seemed impossible. But it was achieved and David Laurie, though suffering considerable disability, was able to rejoin his regiment in Italy for the drive northwards by the Eighth Army and I for one, am quite sure his men were not at all surprised. That is what Sandhurst at its best is all about.

I was posted to 108 Tank Brigade which was assigned to the 38th Welsh Division as Lines of Communication troops. Goodness knows I am no hero and never had the slightest desire to die on the battlefield – or anywhere else – but to go home and tell one's family of three years training to be a railway porter at the greatest moment in history. For God's sake! I was fortunate. My brother James, having served for some time in the western desert, had been posted to the War Office and I asked him if he could help. He arranged an interview for me with a Major J. A. T. Morgan of Phantom (GHQ Liaison Regiment) of which I had never heard. I was both relieved and curious when he agreed to take me on.

I had better explain the purpose of the regiment. One of the most important features of warfare is communication. It is important for the high command to know where the enemy is with absolute certainty. This cannot be achieved by signals having to pass from platoon or troop to battalion, brigade, division, corps and army. Apart from time, something always gets lost on the way. Phantom was designed to overcome this. The officers were, with few exceptions, from fighting units. The other ranks, again with a few exceptions were from the Royal Corps of Signals. We maintained a wireless net entirely separate from all other military formations and had our own code book for wireless transmission. The idea was to deploy patrols, each consisting of one officer and five other ranks, to every division, with listening stations at corps and army and with the headquarters at army group. In addition, one squadron was dropped by parachute behind the enemy and transmitted from special sets to a receiving station in Britain which retransmitted the messages to army group overseas. I was one of a small group whose training was inadequate to enable us to take part in the Overlord operation on D-Day. We were called FLRs or first line reinforcements. We therefore trained hard at Richmond as the great day approached. Richmond Park, at that time, was closed to the public because it had in it a device to attract enemy bombers. It was also just at the limit of the range of the V1, the pilotless bomb used by the Germans just after D-Day. They came over in considerable numbers, serving no useful military purpose, but spreading death and destruction indiscriminately. We had a splendid vantage point in the park and counted over eighty in one day. One dropped just behind the 'Lass of Richmond Hill' late one night when I was duty officer. The only casualty was a trooper who on diving for the floor had his leg penetrated by a sliver of glass from a shattered window.

At long last came D-Day and the dawn of the liberation of Europe. I was at Selsey Bill, where we had our rear link and to our immense satisfaction Phantom worked perfectly. Monty had without any delay an accurate picture, or sitrep, as we called it, of the British and Canadian front whilst the Americans, who were having a very difficult time, had nothing. Thereafter a squadron, designated L Squadron, was assigned to the Americans on a wholetime basis. It could not, of course, deploy to a level lower than corps, except for specific operations, because of shortage of numbers, but as each corps or army entered the war zone it was assigned its Phantom patrol. In this way, not only was the high command sure of the disposition of its forward troops; corps and divisional commanders were similarly well informed. Situation reports were transmitted from army group twice daily so that every army commander was kept fully in the picture about the situation on his flanks. It was perhaps one of the most imaginative and successful planning operations of the war.

I did not join all this excitement until the end of July, when the Normandy bridgehead, manned by thousands of Allied Troops, was on the point of exploding. I disembarked at the Mulberry, the floating harbour created especially for the invasion, and joined Phantom rear headquarters in an orchard where the wasps were very much more threatening than the enemy. After only a few weeks came the break-through at Avranches, Patton's drive east and the butchery of the Falaise gap. Michael Astor, with an armoured brigade at the tip of the gap, had the terrifying experience of being heavily bombed on two consecutive days, once by the Americans and once by the RAF. He lost three men and two vehicles and was lucky to emerge alive.

The advance through France to Belgium, through Amiens, Mantes-Gassicourt and eventually to Brussels will never be forgotten by anyone lucky enough to take part in it.

I was one of the staff in the Ops Room at Phantom Headquarters on Waterloo golf course when Operation Market Garden, the Arnhem drop, took place. The next ten days or so were traumatic. Towards the end the only messages coming out of the Arnhem pocket were from the Phantom patrol and there was a peculiar poignancy about them as the situation got more and more desperate.

I was still at Waterloo when, on 16 December, 6 SS Panzer Army and 5 Panzer Army launched an attack in strength and burst through 28 and 106 US divisions in an advance towards the Meuse. The stubborn gallantry of the Americans, especially at Bastogne, was sufficient to absorb the shock until the regrouped Allied Armies were able to attack the salient from north and south and eventually to restore the status quo. But it was a grim few days in which the Allied flags customarily displayed by each Belgian house were suddenly conspicuously absent. As the offensive lost its edge I was sent to join another Phantom officer at Eagle Tac, the forward headquarters of General Bradley. From there I was sent to take over the Phantom patrol with VII Corps of 1 US Army. I found them at Düren, on the Roer river, where the line had been stable for some time and there was no fighting, merely an occasional and desultory exchange between the artillery. The high command had eventually agreed on a frontal assault to clear the western bank of the Rhine and 1 and 9 US armies attacked on 23 February. We crossed the river without difficulty and during the next few days the only really uncomfortable enemy opposition was from newly encountered jet fighters, who did not seem to have mastered the technique of ground strafing. In the event they were more frightening than lethal and ten days later we duly arrived in Cologne with only minor casualties. The night after we had captured that part of Cologne which lies on the west bank I was astonished to receive a wireless message from Phantom ordering me to take my patrol to a town called Remagen, to cross the Rhine and to report to the Headquarters of XVIII US Airborne Corps at Siegen, on the southern edge of the Ruhr. This arose from the unexpected capture of the bridge at Remagen on 7 March by a platoon of 9 US armoured division, a military achievement of almost priceless value. On arrival we discovered, very much to our relief, that some thousands of American troops had preceded us into the bridgehead and that the only thing we had to worry about was interdictory fire on the bridge itself. A strong pontoon bridge was already being built alongside it. Just as well, because the original collapsed into the river a few days later. The military police with great coolness and skill got us across in hurried little convoys of three or four vehicles at a time, taking more casualties than we did. We then set off for Siegen where all was indescribable confusion, both sides being unsure of the whereabouts of the other and neither terribly anxious to throw away their lives at this stage in the game. On 23 March the British

Army crossed the Rhine in strength and began the encir-
clement of the Ruhr. There were about 300,000 German
troops between us. After the failure of an attempt to break
out, Field Marshal Model, who was in command of the
Ruhr pocket, shot himself and thereafter mopping up was
the order of the day. But not for me. I was ordered to take
over a patrol of XII US Corps, which was part of Patton's
Third Army and was on its way across northern Bavaria to
the Czech frontier. Memory gets a little dim, but I caught
up with them, I think, at a town called Viechtach and
remained with them until we reached the Czech frontier
facing a town called As. We were prevented from crossing
the frontier by the Yalta agreement but were later allowed
by Stalin to make a limited advance well short of Prague.

There was a lot of nastiness during this period on which
I will not dwell. The uncovering of a mass grave of murdered
prisoners of war. The continuous trail of murdered prisoners
by the roadside, each column marching pointlessly east
being accompanied by 'Teufelhenker', or 'Devil's hangmen'.
Occasional meetings with liberated prisoners of war and
more horrifying, with the survivors of the concentration and
extermination camps. Occasionally the Americans, ordinarily the most generous and kindly of troops, lost their cool
with some of the Germans, either guards accompanying
prisoners, or local officials who pleaded ignorance of obvious
inhumanities and cruelties. It was not just the beastliness
that was upsetting, it was the pathos. I remember trying to
tempt to the roadside four or five men and women crouching
under a hedge in concentration camp garb. We held out
chocolate and cigarettes but they didn't seem to understand.
They simply cowered like beaten animals. Finally we put
our offerings down by the roadside and drove on a little way,
then waited to see them come out to collect them.

I was glad to get a message summoning me back to 21
Army Group 500 miles away. Off I went, fondly imagining
that my days of military service were over. Not a bit of it.
They didn't have computers in those days but some wretched
clerk in the War Office had identified me as a former

policeman. Tom Reddaway, the field adjutant of Phantom, asked me, on arrival, if I was prepared to volunteer for service with military government. My answer was an unprintable version of 'Not on your nelly'. I should have known better. Within twenty-four hours I was presented with an order promoting me to Staff Captain and posting me to military government. This meant the compulsory freezing of my entitlement to demobilization. It was a bitter pill. From June 1945 until January 1947 I remained with the Control Commission at Bad Oeynhausen and Bunde doing a fairly pointless job. My time would have been much better spent in the field, helping to reconstitute local government. However, gin was two shillings a bottle, even if it did burn the varnish off a table top, and the time passed. Wastage, rather than military talent, ensured due promotion to the rank of major. I suppose if I had stayed there long enough I would have finished as a brigadier *faute de mieux*. Eventually, however, the high command decided that my services could be dispensed with and I returned to my native shore to resume my so far undistinguished police career. Incidentally, both my brothers and my brother-in-law survived, although the latter only weighed seven stone on his return from Singapore. My war had not been a particularly perilous one, but as a family, I think we were lucky.

# CHAPTER 4

# Return to Detection

I remember when I landed on the Normandy shore my total wealth amounted to £5. My parents-in-law were reasonably well-off, but my wife and I, with one child, had nothing. On my return from the army with the honorary rank of major I had a gratuity, which was so small I cannot remember how much it was, a demob suit which Max Wall would not have looked at, and my pay was reduced by about two-fifths. I was then twenty-eight. I reported to CID Headquarters with some apprehension. Returning warriors were not generally welcome at that time in the police service. The chairborne army, recruited for military government, were in a much better position, ordinarily having held fairly high rank before they left. But I was the lowest of the low. A detective constable who had the bad taste to return alive with field rank, however phoney. In fact one of the snags was that the police hierarchy of that time could not distinguish between genuine and phoney rank and it was always those who held the latter who made the greatest use of it, thus perhaps justifying the sense of resentment of those who had remained in the force during the war. People like Walter Stansfield, eventually chief constable of Derbyshire, who had risked his life for a lengthy period behind enemy lines and was awarded a thoroughly well-deserved Military Cross and Croix de Guerre never even mentioned that they had been in the army, let alone made use of military rank.

I was lucky. Valentine, who was the deputy chief constable of Manchester, had won the Military Medal in the First World War for bringing in the body of the brother of Sir Arthur Bliss, the former Master of the Queen's Music, under fire, and he felt no inhibitions about greeting returning ex-servicemen. I began duty in the latter part of January and by April had been promoted to detective sergeant. Special Branch had been enlarged during my absence but Pierpoint, my old friend, was still in charge. I soon became engrossed in a torrent of work, particularly the naturalization of former enemy aliens. In addition, we were closely concerned with a resurgence of the equally odious extremes of the right and the left. An additional problem was the exploitation of Zionism. One organization cheerfully defrauded both Jew and Gentile alike whilst urging the establishment of an independent Jewish state. Had it not been so serious, it was really quite funny to see them emerge with their collecting boxes in direct competition – and often conflict – with the members of Haganah at meetings held throughout Manchester. I can only hope that the genuine Zionists caught up with them in due course.

A particularly nasty problem at this time was the perfectly lawful exploitation by the Union Movement of the right of free speech. We had some sticky moments protecting one of its leaders, Jeffrey Hamm, from extremists of the left, whose counter arguments were often expressed by throwing bricks or other persuasuve impedimenta at him and his colleagues. One of my less happy memories is of one such meeting in Portland Street breaking up in disorder under a shower of missiles. It drew the most imperial rocket for the Chief Constable from the Home Office, and rightly so.

Soon afterwards I was to become involved in an incident on which I still look back with humour, albeit misplaced. The drunken Irish playwright, Brendan Behan, had been released from Mountjoy Prison under a political amnesty, having earlier been sentenced to a long term of imprisonment for shooting at three policemen. He was invited to address the Manchester cell of the IRA. At the time he was the subject of an exclusion order under the Prevention of Violence (Temporary Provisions) Act 1939. What the British public do not understand, of course, is that for decades the supporters of the IRA have been a mixed bag. Genuine idealists, perhaps one or two per cent. People dwelling on the undeniable hardships of Irish history, perhaps the majority. People naturally inclined to violence without rational cause, yet another ingredient. Last of all, a number of people taking part in the heady excitement of conspiracy for the thrill, the excitement and occasionally just for the fun of denouncing each other. This kind of thing is, of course, beyond the experience or imagination of the civil libertarians but anyone concerned with Irish affairs for any length of time will know exactly what I mean. Brendan was denounced by the very people who had invited him to Manchester. Pierpoint and I were detailed off to deal with the matter. Unfortunately, Pierpoint had rheumatism in his right shoulder so when we duly arrived to collect Brendan, he wasn't much use. This was before *The Quare Fellow* and Brendan was still quite a strong and formidable character. However, a police car drew up alongside us just in time and he gave in gracefully. We duly locked him up at Bootle Street. The next morning there appeared on his behalf an Irish barrister, who kept on referring to him as a 'love choild of the Oirish revolution'. He might have added with justification 'and a very smelly one at that'. However, the old stipendiary, whose hearing and sight were questionable, was understandably amused and gave him four months. Brendan was never proud of that conviction. It doesn't exactly fit the higher traditions of Irish folklore. But it is there in the records, for anyone to see. The Irish informer, needless to say, got his pound of flesh.

A sadder and rather more serious case was that of Marian Kaczmarek, an officer in General Anders' Polish corps, who had been demobilized, but whose wife and child were still in Poland. The assistant military attaché at the Polish embassy, Major Kajdy, picked on him as ideal for blackmail and told him that if he did not recruit agents in the US airforce base at Burtonwood his family would suffer. Inevitably, he picked on the wrong man, a Pole who was married to an English girl whose loyalties were entirely with this country. He reported the approach and thereafter a combination of the security service and Special Branch took over. The operation continued for three months because it was important to discover its extent. Information was supplied to Kaczmarek from time to time through our informer but it was of no real value, just enough to keep him interested. Eventually, we were satisfied that we had all that we wanted and the trap was sprung. Kaczmarek was caught redhanded and ought in the ordinary way to have pleaded guilty. Unfortunately, however, he did not agree. Some odd instinct prompted me to put in his cell a desk, writing paper, a pen and ink and he wrote, in Polish, of which I do not understand a word, the most complete confession one could hope for. The judge, Sir Fred Pritchard, gave him the merciful sentence of three years. But I am afraid the Poles were not so merciful, if our subsequent information is to be believed. In court he denounced Major Kajdy who was declared *persona non grata*. Kaczmarek was deported after serving his sentence and I was told that he was shot on arrival home. I hope that this is untrue. What impressed me most about the case were the lengths taken by the Director of Public Prosecutions personally to protect the informant from possible harm. With the help of a number of ministries and organizations he ensured that every single document relating to the informant's life in England disappeared. He was given a new identity with all the papers necessary to establish it, was found a job and, to coin a phrase, lived happily ever after with his British born wife and children. In fact, having served this country well, he is now a respectable pensioner.

As a Special Branch officer I was not, of course, known to the ordinary Manchester criminal in the same way as a detective dealing with crime from day to day. I was therefore sometimes lent to the CID on occasions on which it was thought that anonymity was an advantage. I admit quite frankly that there were some such occasions on which my hair stood on end when I discovered the difference between theory and practice in applying the rules governing police interrogation. First of all, let me make it quite clear that I am one of those who believe that if the criminal law and the procedures relating to it were applied strictly according to the book, as a means of protecting society it would collapse in a few days. There has long been an unwillingness in this country to define police powers. Rather has the tendency been to expect the police to run the risk of criticism or worse in dealing with suspected criminals, squatters and so on. It works reasonably well on the whole because the courts are quick to condemn any action they think excessive or unfair and such criticism almost invariably puts an end to any hope of a successful prosecution. But it means that the police are often in a very difficult position. Consider, for example, the problem with which we were faced in 1973 when we arrested the IRA London bombers at Heathrow. We were convinced we had the right people, but we had no evidence of sufficient weight to hold them. Already a lawyer not instructed by any of the prisoners was demanding access to them. If we had played the game strictly according to the rules we should have released them to return to Ireland. Of course there was no question of our doing anything of the kind. The bombers were held incommunicado at Ealing for four days and the police were castigated by almost every legal journal in the land and by many newspapers also. Not one of them retracted or apologized when the judge in the case ruled that the action of the police had in the circumstances been perfectly proper. There are cases almost daily in which the police are expected to run risks of that kind in the public interest. The difference between our behaviour in recent years and the pre- and early post-war period, is that we now tell the truth about it. There is another difference, too. Before, and immediately after the war, there was a willingness by the police to use violence against the hardened criminal which I believe now to be rare indeed, and perhaps more important, strongly disapproved of by most policemen if ever it does occur.

In the nineteen-forties, however, policing was still a fairly rough and tough business. I can remember a very successful, fairly senior detective in Manchester, who, when dealing with hardened criminals, had his own version of the Judges' Rules. It consisted of greeting the prisoner with the blunt enquiry, 'Will you talk or be tanned?' If the reply was in the negative, sometimes colourfully so, the prisoner was removed smartly to the lavatory where he was upended and his head jammed down the bowl. It usually took two to hold him, whilst a third repeatedly pulled the chain until a waggling of the feet indicated a more compliant attitude. He then signed a form headed by the usual caution against self-incrimination. My point in relating this is to make it clear that practices such as this were perfectly well known to solicitors, to counsel, to judges and to the Press but that no one did anything about them because there seemed no obvious way to achieve a fair balance between the public interest and the rights of wrongdoers. To pretend that knowledge of such malpractices was confined to the police alone, as people occasionally do, is sheer hypocrisy.

In the late forties or early fifties, when Wellesley Orr was the stipendiary magistrate, I saw personally a classic and unforgettable example of this kind of thing. An old lag, flat-nosed Taylor alias Thompson, who had spent most of his life in prison, was disturbed one Saturday afternoon by an off-duty sergeant named Cornish whilst breaking into a furniture store on Stretford Road with three companions. They set about the sergeant and fled after leaving him seriously injured. He was rushed to the Royal Infirmary and word soon got out that he had a bone splinter on the brain. His chances of survival were thought to be minimal. Reaction was typical of the police of those days. The search was immediate, extensive and ruthless. Anyone assaulting a policeman in Manchester could expect 'first aid to be rendered', the euphemism for a thorough hiding. Thompson was soon found and taken to Platt Lane police station.

I was in court at Minshull Street when he appeared for remand in custody. He was carried into the dock by two policemen and sat in a chair, in itself unusual. His head was swathed in bandages and his face was scarcely visible. The formal questions put to him by the clerk after brief evidence of arrest were answered by the grey-haired police gaoler in the dock without any reference to Thompson. After about two minutes he was whisked downstairs. It was perfectly obvious to the meanest intelligence that he was either unconscious or at least was unaware of the process in which he was taking part. The old stipendiary was notoriously failing in sight and hearing but the court was crowded with policemen, journalists, solicitors and counsel. Yet no one raised any enquiry or made any public comment. It was a disgraceful incident not to be forgotten. Cornish happily recovered and is still alive. Thompson got a long sentence. It is an indication of welcome change that such an incident today would have rightly caused an outcry, the withdrawal of the charge against Thompson, notwithstanding its gravity and the prosecution of the detectives responsible for what was a barbarous assault.

Such extremes were, even then, not common, but familiarity breeds contempt. It is not difficult to see how tolerance of that kind of thing could lead to total loss of discretion and to occasional incidents attracting a great deal of publicity, adverse to the police.

The Judges' Rules really originated in 1906 and arose from a doubt in the mind of the then chief constable of Birmingham following a ruling by one judge, criticizing a constable for cautioning a prisoner, whilst a brother judge criticized another constable for not administering the caution. The Lord Chief Justice, in consultation with the Queen's Bench, then formulated the original rules, which have been enlarged and modified since. The Rules are not binding in law but they are certainly binding in practice, because judges have the power to rule inadmissible any evidence which they think has been unfairly or improperly obtained. The Rules afford, I think, the classic example of the enormous gulf between those who enforce the law and those who administer it, between whom, incidentally, there has never so far as I know, been any joint consultation. They begin with the pious declaration that 'citizens have a duty to help a police officer to discover and apprehend offenders'. They do not, however, point out that this duty is not recognized by law except in very limited and special circumstances, or reveal that those same citizens may with impunity refuse to assist the police in any way at all. The legal correspondent of the *Security Gazette* in its October 1964 issue commented, 'The layman might be forgiven for thinking that the Rules themselves appear to have been designed for the specific purpose of protecting those citizens who regard it as their duty to thwart the police in the performance of their function.' He continues, 'The potential witness commits neither crime nor tort if, instead of giving information to the police he keeps his knowledge to himself. Indeed, the potential witness is generally not only under no legal obligation to answer questions, but, if the appropriate procedure for questioning him is not followed, such answers as he does give may not even be admissible in evidence. It must follow, therefore, as a general rule that the police officer investigating an offence is helpless without the co-operation of the ordinary citizen.' There is, in fact, a fundamental contradiction between the principle expounded by the judiciary and the lawful entitlement of every citizen to refuse to comply with it.

It is hardly surprising that the Rules, the conduct of police interrogations and the so-called right of silence should today be the subject of such controversy when, for the first time, the effectiveness and the fairness of our criminal justice system is being questioned. Many distinguished judges and lawyers have voiced dissatisfaction, whilst no less a number have voiced opposition to change. The quickest way to achieve long overdue reform would be for the police to agree throughout the whole country to apply the existing laws and procedures strictly according to the letter. The effect would quickly be disastrous. Only the weak, the spontaneous and the intellectually underprivileged would continue to be amenable to the law. The deliberate wrongdoer would, with the help of his legal adviser, be immune except in the comparatively rare event of being caught red-handed. I shall return to this theme later on. I touch on it now only because I do not wish either to mislead or to appear a humbug in disclosing frankly that malpractice of that kind did occur in my experience but that it ought to be seen in the context of policing at the time.

Whilst I was still in Special Branch my daughter Christina was born on 1 January 1948. Though both my father and father-in-law were generous in helping us, police pay at that time was disgracefully low and in my third year as a detective sergeant, I began to look around for another job. The family business, to which my eldest brother had returned from the RAF, could not afford to support another member of the family. My idea of a good time during that period was a rucksack full of books from Chorlton public library and two or three bottles of Tetley's beer. By 1950 I was near to the point of despair when, without warning, I was sent for by Valentine and told that I was to be promoted Detective Inspector. Promotions in Manchester were normally done in batches three or four times a year and my solo appearance astonished not only me, but the force generally. Even so at that time I found it necessary to stop smoking, not for fear of cancer but from poverty. It took some doing. I was still playing lacrosse and found it difficult to resist a cigarette with the usual pint after the Saturday afternoon game. But I made it, even though I used to wake up having dreamed that I had been smoking. Only when I had got to the stage when for days on end I no longer gave it a thought did I realize that I was immune.

I was not to continue on detective duties for much longer. I had realized for some time that if I were to have a chance of achieving high rank in the police I must somehow get wider experience than the CID. Transfers between CID and uniform were virtually unknown in those days and I could not see any real prospect of a move. It came without warning and only as a result of tragedy for someone else. Harry Flowers, the Chief Superintendent (Administration), died from a heart attack at an early age whilst on holiday in North Wales. He had been the head of a small but very important department known as the chief constable's office, through which the chief and his assistant controlled the three main departments of the force, uniformed branch, traffic department and CID. By long tradition men selected for service in that department never emerged from it except on pension. It was an unimaginative system because it meant that the men controlling force policy had no real experience of police work and no rapport with the men on the ground. The natural successor was an inspector, who, whilst a competent subordinate, soon showed himself to be unfitted for the chief superintendent's job. Next in line were two sergeants who were far too junior. Even so, I was surprised to be summoned by Valentine on 10 December 1951 and told that on 1 January I would assume responsibility for administration. He added almost as an afterthought, that I would be promoted to chief inspector to compensate me for loss of detective allowances. It was rather a daunting prospect. I knew nothing at all about the preparation of annual estimates of expenditure or the intricacies of force administration. Relationships with the local authority and the Home Office meant absolutely nothing to me at the time and there are not, oddly enough, any books of reference likely to be of much use to anyone facing this kind of problem. However, I needn't have worried. Once I had made it plain to the remainder of the staff that I was not going to stand for any nonsense the job soon became comparatively straightforward and, in fact, very interesting. I soon realized that Valentine was the *de facto* commander of the force. He was a very odd mixture. Far-sighted, intelligent, scrupulously honest, bitterly resentful at not having attained the highest rank, idiosyncratic, he could be kindness itself one minute and a bullying tyrant the next. But not to me. I sensed early that despite his status and achievements he had a massive inferiority complex and the best way to get along with him was to talk down to him without ever letting him realize what you were doing. I grew adept at feeding him ideas as if they were his own until I became quite shameless in the process. But we got on extraordinarily well and he was generosity itself to me. I was promoted to superintendent within a year and fifteen months later given the rank for the job, chief superintendent. This was handsome, indeed, since I was younger than the youngest inspector in the force.

He taught me one lesson of incalculable value for the rest of my police career. I was standing beside his desk one day as he was going through a report by a senior detective on a very serious crime. The detective was a former coal miner, scrupulously honest, hardworking and competent, but more eloquent with a pickaxe than a pen. In his account of interviewing the wrongdoer he had written, 'I told him it was a diabolical lie.' Valentine looked up at me with a quizzical grin, drew his pen through the offending sentence and wrote above it, 'I told him it was untrue.' All my subsequent police career was, in that context, devoted to the reduction of the diabolical lie to simple untrue. In other words, give free vent to all the adverbs and adjectives which police work naturally inspires, then go through your report and eliminate them all.

Life with Valentine was not, however, all beer and skittles. He could be an awful bully and I had some very trying moments diverting, not always successfully, his wrath from my fellow chief superintendents, Pierpoint in particular, whose procrastination went from bad to worse and used to drive Valentine into fury. There were also moments of humour. I remember persuading him to acquire some wireless-equipped general purpose vans to speed up our response time, despite his awful warning that the men would put them to all sorts of improper purposes. Sure enough, within a week of their introduction an attractive young woman complained of being seduced by a policeman in the back of one. It was all I could do to persuade Valentine not to withdraw them. A week or two later the girl came along and asked if she could withdraw her complaint. It turned out that she had feared pregnancy, needlessly in the event. Too late, alas! The policeman had already been sacked. Not for seduction, of course, but for using a police vehicle for an improper purpose. It was rather bad luck, but even I jibbed at the idea of asking Valentine to give him his job back.

I suppose the most valuable experience I gained in those

years was in watching Valentine deal with the Watch Committee, whom, not surprisingly, he detested. He followed the precept of rendering unto Caesar precisely, taking particularly good care not to render any more. In those days, the Watch Committee of a borough with its own police force exercised the power to appoint and to promote. It was the disciplinary authority. It also determined the size of the force and controlled its expenditure. All of these powers were to some extent subject to influence by the Home Secretary, whose Inspectorate of Constabulary determined the fitness of the force to receive the Exchequer grant of one half of its annual expenditure. Nevertheless the Watch Committee was in those days a power to be reckoned with and though disagreement between them and the force administrators was often bitter, there was no doubt that the senior policemen involved were all the better administrators for having to deal with them. There was, of course, a continual running battle between them, neither side missing an opportunity to score off the other. There was one happy occasion on which someone on the committee suggested that our police horses should be called after members. I can't remember whether it was Bell, the Chief Constable, or Valentine who put paid to that one by remarking airily, 'Well, I don't know, Chairman. It might look a bit odd on the agenda to see "Councillor Albert Bloggs to be shot!" '

By this time I was thirty-eight and had begun to think of applying for a job elsewhere in the service. It was not that I thought I was better than anyone else, but on looking round at some of the chief constables of those days I couldn't believe that I could possibly be worse. I was still playing lacrosse each Saturday, having in 1949 enjoyed the unusual distinction of playing for the only Rest of England side to beat England 14–9! We also won the Northern Senior Flags twice. For anyone not familiar with men's lacrosse in the North of England let there be no misunderstanding. Not only was it fast and skilful in those days, it was also just about as dangerous as ice hockey. At rugby the worst I ever suffered was a bent nose which was easily straightened. At lacrosse I was knocked out cold three times and my chin was opened to the bone. But it offered great enjoyment to the fit and the fleet, though not, I am afraid to spectators. There is little or no mid-field play and it is not really a spectator sport. It happens quite accidentally that a lacrosse memory reminds me of my point of greatest wealth whilst serving in Manchester. I recall that whilst turning out one Saturday to play Mellor in the Flags final at Wythenshawe, which we unexpectedly won, I looked at my Post Office Savings Bank book and found that I had three hundred and thirty pounds in it, not a lot for a chief superintendent with two children and no car but more than I could ever boast before. Our life was made much easier by the kindness of our parents. Christopher attended Hulme Preparatory School, the fees being paid by my wife's father. My father had long made up his mind that he wanted to give each of his children £3000 before he died, but that he also wanted to avoid death duties on it. His first cheque, for £250 soon after Christina was born, was the most money I had ever had in my life up to that time. Moreover he never asked me once what I did with it.

There was then no tradition in Manchester of applying for jobs. Twenty years before, Alfred Edwards, the only man I know to win as a Warrant Officer both the Military Cross and Military Medal, had escaped first to Burnley and then to Middlesbrough.

I began unsuccessfully with the post of assistant chief constable of Newcastle-upon-Tyne. The shock of receiving what Stella Gibbons calls 'the monkey's allowance' was unbelievably good for me, though I certainly did not think so at the time! It occurred to me that it might be a wise precaution to get myself on to a course at the Police College then at Ryton-on-Dunsmore if only because candidates having been there might stand a better chance. Valentine very decently let me nominate myself for a 'C' Course for superintendents which lasted only three weeks, was wholly without value of any kind, but did provide me with the label I wanted. Incidentally, I am almost ashamed to admit that apart from my initial training course at Manchester, that was the only course I attended in nearly forty years' police service. I must be the classic example of the man who beat the system. The College did, however, teach me one thing; how to write an application for a job. Its staff then consisted mostly of people who were doing very little else!

I then got down to it in earnest and appeared on six further short lists in reasonably quick succession. Preston, Oxford, Monmouthshire, Somerset, Manchester itself (for the post of second assistant) and finally Leicester, all but the last feeling that they could survive without my help. The Oxford experience was not without humour. Harry Plowman, the then town clerk, was a friend of Philip Dingle, Manchester's town clerk, who was lending me support. We were interviewed in the morning, the Watch Committee entertaining us to lunch to see if any of us ate with our feet. In those days the Oxford Watch Committee was required by law to include a number of members of the University. I sat at lunch on my best behaviour with a don on my left and a non-University member on my right. Over the soup the don remarked encouragingly, 'And where will you send your boy to school when you come to Oxford?' Even more encouraging, over the dessert the councillor dug me in the ribs and said, 'Got a lovely 'ouse for sale. Six thousand quid.' I really thought my ship was in. Imagine my surprise when the clerk, looking a little put out, came into the ante-room where we awaited our fate to announce, 'Mr Burrows. By one vote.' Monmouth was very pleasant. It developed into a contest between Bob MacCartney of Lancashire and me, and he, having county experience, had the edge. He was replacing Neil Galbraith as assistant to Ronald Alderson, the chief constable who sadly died in his car six months later. Galbraith, who had gone to Leicester as chief constable, thereupon returned to Monmouth as chief, and I took his place at Leicester, having failed to gain the Manchester appointment only ten days earlier. I very nearly didn't bother to go for the Leicester interview. It was on a Monday and the World Cup Final was on television on the

Sunday afternoon. The short list was crowded with chiefs and assistants and I didn't think I stood a chance. But when I put this to my wife she insisted that it would be impolite not to go and the label might stick. But this time it was roses, roses all the way. I still remember ringing up my wife and saying, 'Doubting Thomas.' The moral of all this, though I pitch it rather high, is that if you really want a job and do not allow yourself to be put off by disappointment, sooner or later you will get one. At least it was true of those days. It is in line with my belief that if you put 'A. Horse' on a parliamentary ballot paper it will get not less than 500 votes. My delighted father gave me a cheque for £1000 and my wife's father gave her £500. Even so, by the time we had bought a house and our first car, a second-hand Ford Consul, we found ourselves with an overdraft of £35 which offended my simple northern philosophy intensely. Still, we had made it. The only assistant chief constable in Leicester, Bernard Ecob, who was then in charge of the force, suffered a severe heart attack and I departed in haste to take over command on 1 January 1957.

# CHAPTER 5

# Chief Constable of Leicester

My brother John very kindly drove me to Leicester in my newly acquired Consul because I was not a qualified driver. I had been commissioned in the army before being graded as a tradesman and was not therefore entitled to a substantive civilian driving licence on demobilization. In any case, never having owned a car there seemed little point in learning to drive. By a fortunate coincidence, the British government had just recently decided to launch its abortive attack on the Canal Zone, which had the temporary side effects of petrol rationing and the concession that learner drivers could drive unaccompanied. He dropped me at the Midland Hotel, left the car in the hotel car park and made his way back north by train.

I was greeted on arrival at the Charles Street headquarters by the three senior serving officers, who made me welcome. My own office was rather a splendid room with an enormous coal fire, though I am afraid I found later that it was the only splendid room in the whole building. I sent for the last few years' Watch Committee minutes, always a good way to find out about current and past problems, and by lunchtime was beginning to feel quite at home. Imagine my perplexity when, about half past twelve, I walked into the general office to ask a question and found no one there. For one awful moment I thought they had all taken such a dislike to me that they had all gone home. In fact, they had, but only to lunch. As a Mancunian it had never occurred to me that people actually went home for lunch in the middle of a working day. I was quite relieved to see them reappear about two o'clock. This was, incidentally, a habit I never adopted. I used to eat in my office throughout my ten years in Leicester, unless I was entertaining visitors.

I soon found that the force was basically in good shape but suffering from the disadvantage of having been commanded for too long by the same person, Oswald John Buxton Cole, a fine old man and a very nice person who had held office for twenty–five years. Galbraith, his successor, had simply not been there long enough to implement the reforms he had in mind. After only six months, he knew he was returning to Monmouth. This was, of course, very much to my advantage because long overdue reform meant considerable improvement in the rank structure, and therefore the career prospects, for the force as a whole. Moreover, I knew that Bill Willis, HM Inspector of Constabulary, thought that reform was long overdue and that I could count on his support with the Home Office. Territorially, the force consisted simply of one division of just over 300 men. The CID, traffic department and women police made up a total complement of just over 440. There was only one assistant chief, three superintendents and a handful of civilians to cope with a city of almost 17,000 acres with a resident population of 281,000. The daytime population was increased considerably from the heavily populated surrounding dormitory areas. The salary of the chief constable, incidentally, was £2330, which was £1000 more than I had been getting as chief superintendent in Manchester.

By October I had obtained the approval of the Watch Committee and the Home Office to increase the number of superintendents to six, commanding respectively three territorial divisions, the CID, a newly created traffic department and the force administration department. This meant many promotions and a considerable boost to morale.

The operational problems of the force were easy to assess. Crimes amounted to only a little under three thousand a year, a very low figure. Violence against the person was almost negligible, two murders and less than fifty assaults of real severity. The detection rate was highly satisfactory, about 63 per cent. There were 57 vacancies in the authorized establishment but this was not surprising in a town which was then, in terms of income per family, the second wealthiest in Europe. Unemployment was about 1 per cent of the population and an abnormally high proportion of adult women then worked outside their homes for a living. It took no great intelligence to see that the two main problems were shortage of manpower and even more important, the motor car. Leicester is an ancient city with a market going back nearly a thousand years. Its roads all run to the centre dominated by an architecturally ugly clock tower. The trouble was that Cole was basically such a nice man that he simply couldn't accept the need to deal firmly with motorists, especially in a city where so many people knew each other. There was no question of corruption. He was a scrupulously honest and honourable man, but if anyone appealed to him against police action in trying to control the parking motorist, he simply could not find the heart to send them to court. Traffic was, therefore, chaos. He tried to avert the worst consequences of his kindness by putting men on point duty to ensure that the delivery vehicles of the most important local paper, the *Leicester Mercury*, were always given a free run at distribution times. It simply had to stop. I made it plain to the superintendent of the central division that there would be no exemptions from the parking laws, not even for the archangel Gabriel, never mind members of the city or county councils and told him to get going. I had also declined to receive any more free copies of the *Mercury*, placed a regular daily order, to be paid for by the police authority, and withdrawn all the pointsmen assigned for the paper's particular benefit. Looking back on it, the reaction was pure Clochemerle. Barthélemy Piéchut and his pissoir had nothing on me! In such a wealthy town most people had cars and had long been used to Cole's genial rule. The reaction was immediate and vociferous. It grew in strength when it became apparent that the city magistrates warmly supported me and that the chairman of the transport committee of the city council was using all his considerable influence to persuade his council colleagues that the city generally had everything to gain and nothing to lose. The police, of course, were delighted. They soon realized that they could enforce the parking laws without regard for wealth, politics or status and their self-respect rose immeasurably. The *Mercury* and its now defunct rival the *Evening Mail* were not, of course, quite so keen. In fact I think Attila the Hun or Genghis Khan would have received kinder treatment at their hands than I did. To the force, the policy became known as the Three Years War. At the end of that period many business people in Leicester had realized that strict but fair control of parking had benefited their trade. Even the newspapers had come to the private conclusion that traffic conditions were so much improved that they no longer needed preferential treatment. Gradually public opinion accepted the policy, acknowledged grudgingly that at least it was fairly applied and finally came to accept it with reasonably good grace and even with a touch of humour, for which Leicester is not noted.

I should add that in the meantime I had arranged for a driving examiner to be brought specially from Lincoln to give me a driving test, which I managed to pass.

By this time I think both the editors of the two local newspapers had reached the same conclusion that had belatedly occurred to me, that there really was no point in carrying on a pointless feud and that it might be best for all concerned if we achieved a kind of *modus vivendi*. Fortunately an ideal opportunity occurred to bring this about. The City Surveyor, John Beckett, had been selling the idea of parking meters to the city council and I had strong reservations about them. It seemed to me wrong in principle that the ability to park in the centre of a city on highways on which, in theory, all should enjoy equal rights, should depend on the ability to pay. Moreover, I suspected that the control of parking space by payment would require for success the disregard of any other factor such as the need for compassion in particular cases. It did not need a great deal of imagination to see that control of parking on the public highway by payment was objectionable in principle, unnecessarily arbitrary in practice and likely to rebound most harshly on those who had to enforce it.

I therefore set out to preach a different philosophy. It could be summarized by saying that traffic should flow, not necessarily fast, but freely on all streets, that all frontagers should have reasonable rights of access for the purpose of loading and unloading, but that subject to those considerations as much parking space as possible should be made available with the overriding consideration that it must be fairly shared. This meant making clear to the vehicle driver in every street just what he could or could not do. For those enforcing compliance with this system the emphasis should be on prevention, not on prosecution. I explained my ideas at length to the Watch Committee and the city council in a lengthy memorandum and though the argument waxed quite furious the police view prevailed. An order for several hundred parking meters was cancelled and approval was given in 1961 for the establishment of a traffic warden corps and the introduction of the fixed penalty system. Some women traffic wardens were employed at the outset and the council went to great lengths to determine the extent to which parking could be allowed in each street and to make this clear to the public. The instructions to the wardens were given to the Press and they included the comment that 'Your efficiency will not be judged by the number of tickets you issue, but by the freedom of your patrol areas from vehicles parked in contravention of the law.' In other words, prevention, not prosecution, was the primary objective. Copies of the whole scheme, with the reasoning behind it, were sent to Charles Collins, the clerk to the magistrates, who circulated them to all the members of the bench.

From the outset the scheme was a resounding success and gained immediate and widespread public approval. It allowed the virtual divorce of police from dealing with the parked car, did away with the need to devote two days a week at the magistrates court to deal with nothing but parking offences and increased police concentration on crime to the point that one in every seven arrests was being made at the scene of the crime or in pursuit. Both newspapers gave the scheme unqualified support and it offered the perfect opportunity to bury the hatchet, although the *Evening Mail* sadly folded soon afterwards. The two newspapers were soon commending the scheme to the nation as a whole. Some twenty or thirty other local authorities visited Leicester and many adopted it bag and baggage.

In the meantime, the town clerk, George Ogden and the leader of the Council Mark Henig had a brighter idea. They saw the obvious advantage of co-ordinating all traffic planning and persuaded the city council to appoint a traffic committee on which the chairmen and vice-chairmen of all interested committees, watch, transport, finance, general purposes and highways were represented. The police were also invited to take part. The beneficial effect of this was so quickly apparent that it flowered without opposition. We were careful, in the police, quite rightly to insist on much of the credit for all this going to the city council. It was they, after all, who were the final arbiters and who made the decisions. The success of the scheme, however, taught me some very painful lessons. First, I realized far too late that success in this field had made me the most crashing and painful bore in the whole of the Midlands. I still blush with shame at the extent to which, uninvited, I bent people's ears with the subject. Second, I learnt that success in a difficult field such as this is a guarantee of unpopularity with one's professional colleagues. Many, but not all, of my fellow chief constables faced with similar problems looked upon me with an unconcealed loathing for which I could hardly blame them. Third, neither the Ministry of Transport nor the Home Office was prepared to take the slightest notice of anything happening north of the Watford Gap. This was to prove true in other issues besides that of parking. However, from my point of view, whatever disadvantages of this kind I might have incurred, I was firmly established with the goodwill of my force, my watch committee, the city council and not by any means least important, the Press.

The disappearance of the *Evening Mail* left the *Mercury*

with a monopoly. It was a well-produced and well-edited paper exercising considerable influence throughout the county and the city. My relations with the editor, John Fortune, became even closer when he decided to devote a whole page on each of eight or nine consecutive days to reproducing a lecture I had given to the Leicester Literary and Philosophical Society on the Police, the Public and the Law. This was a new dimension in police-Press relations which thereafter continually improved on a basis of mutual trust and confidence.

This was followed by an invitation from the Chief Inspector of Constabulary, Ted Dodd, with whom I had a love-hate relationship, to give a lecture to the 'Crime-a-challenge' society at Nuffield College, Oxford. In that lecture, which was given in October 1965, I asked for four changes in the criminal law:

majority verdicts in jury trials;
pre-trial disclosure of defence alibis;
abolition of the caution against self-incrimination;
the requirement for the accused to enter the witness box.

Two of these changes were to be made much sooner than I had expected.

Tom Harper, then the editor of the *Law Society's Gazette*, having taken note of all this fuss about parking had started to ask me to do the occasional book review. In 1963 he had sent me a copy of *Crimes of Violence* published by the Cambridge Institute of Criminology and asked me to review it. I thought perhaps it might be better to read it first and on doing so found to my surprise two facts of which I had previously been unaware. The first was that half of all crimes of violence against the person are self-detecting in that the identity of the assailant is never in doubt. The second was that of all those tried on indictment for crimes of violence 39 per cent were acquitted. This second fact struck me as extraordinary. For years the Law Society had been arguing in its annual reports that the proportion of acquittals was so small that there could not possibly be any justification for shifting the balance of the criminal trial in favour of the prosecution. The two different views seemed irreconcilable. I therefore sent for my statistical expert, Sergeant House, explained the position to him and asked him what our acquittal rate was. His reply seemed to support the Law Society. Something then prompted me to say to him, 'But in how many cases was guilt contested?' and he replied, 'I can't say. We aren't required by the Home Office to differentiate between pleas of guilt and findings of guilt after a trial.' I then asked him to go through the records for the last few years, differentiating between those who pleaded guilty and those who were found guilty after trial. He came back, looking very surprised, and said 80 per cent pleaded guilty, 20 per cent pleaded not guilty and of those 40 per cent were acquitted. Then at last the great white light dawned. Eight acquittals of every hundred prisoners tried on indictment did not mean an 8 per cent acquittal rate in contested cases, but an acquittal rate of 40 per cent, *viz* 8 out of 20. The criminal justice system is not, of course, tested by those who plead guilty. Its efficacy can only be judged by those contesting their innocence. I soon found that the Home Office figures published annually were equally uninformative and misleading so I persuaded the Midland chief constables to research back for some three or more years to see if their experience was the same. One, Norman Goodchild of Wolverhampton, declined on the grounds that this was just an effort on my part to seek personal publicity, but Tom Moore of Nottingham, a much bigger city, agreed to take his place. The results were all that we could have hoped for and were published in detail in the *Guardian* in May 1965. The immediate reaction of the customary legal wiseacres on television and radio was that the figures were untrue and misleading, but the evidence was too strong to be dismissed so lightly. It so happened that the 1964 Police Act had required all chief constables to submit annual

73

reports to their police authorities and to the Secretary of State so. I sent each an appropriate form, designed by Sergeant House, and asked them from the next first of January to complete it in respect of every offence tried on indictment. The results, published by Tom Harper in the *New Law Journal* in mid-1966, were devastating and incontestable. For the first time the British public could see solid evidence in support of Lord Devlin's statement in *The Criminal Prosecution in England* that, 'If the success of a system of criminal prosecution is to be measured by the proportion of criminals whom it convicts and punishes, the English system must be regarded as a failure. Far too many people who have in fact committed crimes escape punishment. When a criminal goes free, it is as much a failure of abstract justice as when an innocent man is convicted.' Suffice it to say, that in 1966 Roy Jenkins successfully introduced legislation to require the pre-trial disclosure of defence alibis and to end for the first time in 600 years the requirement for unanimous findings of guilt by juries. Though hotly opposed at the time by both the Bar Council and the Law Society it is unlikely that reversion to unanimity would now find any favour. One in every eleven findings of guilt these days is by a majority verdict. The avoidance of hung juries, the saving of court time and public money, the absence of any serious contention of injustice arising from the change can properly allow it to be described as the most beneficial in criminal justice for many decades.

This was one of two changes brought about by Jenkins, despite strong and bitter opposition, which did more to improve and enhance the reputation of criminal justice than anything else in this century. The second change was the enforced amalgamation of police forces against the strong opposition of chief constables, local authorities and some civil servants. This took real courage and determination, reducing the number of forces by almost two-thirds, but proved so obviously right that Jenkins was quickly accorded the reward to which he was entitled, the enhanced respect of police and public alike.

The Great Train Robbery did not loom very large in our affairs in Leicester, apart from our arresting one of the perpetrators, but its after effect led to a disagreeable experience for me. Those convicted for the robbery were distributed around security prisons of which Leicester was one. Some idiot from Scotland Yard seconded to the Home Office came up to see me about security, masquerading, if you please, under an assumed name for no conceivable reason that I could imagine, unless he was being watched by his wife. Later there came the expected tip-off from the Yard of a breakout, possibly by tunnelling under the walls. This caused hilarity at Leicester as we were assured by city officials that the walls of the prison were so old that anyone tunnelling under them would certainly be buried in the debris. We didn't in fact take it very seriously. Then came the speculation by a northern chief constable about the possible use of small atomic weapons to effect their release. I think most policemen were not quite sure whether to laugh or cry at such blatant idiocy but it was followed by a summons to see Sir Frank Soskice, then the Home Secretary. The Chief Inspector of Constabulary at the Home Office asked if I would see him first with the chief constable of Durham. To my surprise, they both wanted me to join them in expressing the view that prevention of the escape of the train robbers was not a matter for police and that the army should be called in. I couldn't believe my ears and although I realized that my attitude would not enhance my popularity I told them, in effect, that they were talking nonsense, that prison breach was a criminal offence with which I was perfectly capable of dealing and that all I wanted was sufficient weaponry to enable my men to deal with revolvers, shotguns or at the worst, sten guns. We went to the meeting in painful disharmony. On being asked for our opinions we each stuck to our point of view, although I went so far as to say that law enforcement in Leicester was my responsibility and that I was not prepared to tolerate interference from anyone. I asked for a dozen up-to-date rifles with sufficient ammunition for training purposes and Home

Office approval for them to be carried in secure conditions on police vehicles. I got both. The chief constable of Durham formally abrogated responsibility for the safekeeping of the prisoners at Durham and was duly provided with troops for a short period. In the event, neither guns nor troops were needed. The incident made me no friends except perhaps the Home Secretary and the Permanent Under Secretary, Sir Charles Cunningham, both of whom had gone by the time I needed them most. The Watch Committee made no bones about giving its blessing to the proposal and the efficiency of our mobile fleet at that time was so high that morale was heartening.

We had also embarked on another undertaking which was to prove more worthwhile than we at first realized. The chief constable of Leicestershire and Rutland and I decided to exchange men and women regularly on a monthly basis, the idea being to become thoroughly familiar with each other's forces in case of the need to lend each other support. Detectives, beat officers, women police all performed a month in the sister force on a rota basis, this proving invaluable when amalgamation eventually came. Its value was to be demonstrated all too soon, though the result was not without tragedy. A gang of villains from London one day robbed a bank in London Road and got away after striking the manager over the head. Straight away the hue and cry was on. They never stood a chance. They were arrested before they could get out of Leicestershire, but sadly, one of our vans jumped the traffic lights though not in close pursuit. It struck a lorry, overturned and killed a young man by the roadside. A small force takes things like this very much to heart. The success of the chase was forgotten. He was an only son and we all felt desolate. I wrote to the parents and although no force order was issued scores of Leicester policemen lined the roads outside the church whilst the funeral was taking place to demonstrate their sympathy. For so long as I remained in Leicester a wreath was placed on the grave on the anniversary of his death and I hope very much that this gesture of sorrow and sympathy still continues. Incidentally, the case had one nasty aspect, a foretaste of things to come. I was in the detective office when we received a call from the Yard, the caller being a little elusive about his identity, but knowing sufficient about arrest and remand procedures to convince us that he was a policeman. He offered a thousand pounds cash in return for non-opposition to bail. He was told exactly where to go and for each remand hearing and the trial we made sure that armed men, dog handlers and ample reserves were constantly available. They had picked the wrong man. Eric Lacy who was then in charge of the CID is one of the most honest and conscientious detectives I have known in forty years' service. The robbers all got the long sentences they richly deserved.

I don't know why the word 'Tiger' should figure so largely in Leicester folklore. It is the nickname of the local regiment, now, alas, merged with the Royal Anglian Regiment and is, of course, the name by which its rugby club is generally known. Looking back on ten years I remember nothing tigerish about it. It was essentially a place of moderation, a little dull, perhaps, but kindly, hospitable and pleasant. The folklore about the girls of Leicester and Nottingham being prettier than those elsewhere had a quite simple explanation. They generally had more money to spend on clothes, make-up and jewellery than women in less prosperous towns and could therefore afford to dress well. Certainly fashions did not lag behind those in London.

The old assistant chief constable, Bernard Ecob, was a likeable old scallywag who had really outlived his time. He was rather like the old village constable who lived off the land without really offending anyone. He lasted for three years, alternating three months' duty with three months' sickness and I hadn't the heart to ask the Watch Committee to retire him on an ill-health pension, as I certainly should have done. But he died from a heart attack at the age of 56, whilst happily awaiting a glass of Scotch with an anticipatory smile on his face. Deservedly, Eric Lacy was appointed to succeed him, an appointment popular with police and public alike. Incidentally, in view of the controversy about lawyers I was to stir up later, I should perhaps put on record with some pleasure that in the whole of my ten years in Leicester I did not know of one lawyer, either barrister or solicitor, who could conceivably be described as dishonest or dishonourable. A fortunate town, indeed!

After ten years in Leicester I was 49. The Royal Commission and public opinion had compelled the government to increase police pay belatedly by 40 per cent and I was really having the easiest time I had ever had in my life. I think it was P. G. Wodehouse who said that it was always at times like this that fate sneaks up behind you and strikes you smartly behind the ear with a stuffed eelskin. In my case, it was Roy Jenkins and his enforced amalgamation programme. I had fondly imagined Leicester, which was then over 500 strong, to be immune but it was not to be. Oddly enough, I had earlier fought hard on a committee to prevent a shameless and dishonourable attempt by the Home Office to worsen the terms of compensation for chief constables displaced by amalgamation without ever imagining that I would be liable to benefit from our eventual victory, which led to a special section being inserted belatedly into the Police Act. When the amalgamation programme was announced the bottom fell out of my world. After ten happy years' association with a force I believed to be both contented and efficient I was to go out on my ear. The county force was larger, the rateable value of the county was higher, it was bound to have a majority of seats on the joint police authority and to support its own chief constable, even though he was then already entitled to retire. The prospect of serving as second-in-command is not attractive to anyone who has exercised command for ten years. I therefore reconciled myself to retirement, my pension, largely thanks to my earlier battle with the Home Office, being just about £3000 per annum as compared with about £1200, reducible on account of further earnings, if we had lost. It was a miserable period. It was not made any better by the defection of the chairman of my police committee with whom I had been on friendly terms for years. He agreed to nominate the county chief constable for the post, the understanding being that he would be made the chairman of the joint police authority with no less a figure than the Duke of Rutland as his vice-chairman. The poor chap fell for this ploy, but before it could be put into execution I had been appointed an Assistant Commissioner in the Metropolitan Police. However, more of that later.

The news was not wholly bad. I had been invited out of the blue to lunch with Jenkins and one or two other senior policemen at the Hyde Park Hotel. Nothing of note happened but a week or two later I was invited by the Home Office to join the Standing Advisory Council on the Penal System, as its only police member. Only a few days later George Blake escaped from prison, where he was serving a 40-year sentence and Lord Mountbatten was appointed to carry out an enquiry into prison security to still the mounting clamour. I was appointed an assessor with Roland Lees of the Royal Signals and Research Establishment, Farnborough and Granville Bantock, a retired prison governor. We began work in October 1966 and finished before Christmas. It was an interesting, enlightening and not unamusing experience. The secretary was Philip Woodfield who, apart from being able to play all the Beethoven piano sonatas, is an unusually gifted civil servant. We worked hard for weeks, arguing, discussing, persuading and generally thinking of nothing else. Even the spectre of unemployment faded for the moment. In the middle of all this Fraser Noble, the Vice Chancellor of Leicester, told me that the University had decided to confer on me the honorary degree of Master of Laws. I was deeply touched, and am to this day. It was the first really encouraging and kindly gesture in almost a year of unrelieved gloom and I was more grateful than perhaps the University could possibly understand.

However, back to Mountbatten. I had managed to achieve quite a rapport with the great man. I sensed just how far one could go in pulling his leg without overdoing it and I think he liked having it pulled occasionally. Unrelieved obsequiousness must get a bit sickening at times. One day, quite early on he conceived the idea of borrowing the Civil Defence College at Sunningdale and calling all the prison and Borstal governors there for a pep talk. Philip and I both agreed this might be disastrous. After all, on his own admission he had never set foot in a prison in his life and how could he possibly understand all the conflicting and complex arguments about punishment and treatment? We decided to dissuade him and tossed a coin to decide who should do the job. I lost. I began with something like, 'Sir, do you really think it is a good idea . . .' but got no further. He said, 'Bob, you're looking tired, very tired. You've been overworking. Can't have it. You need a rest. Philip, where can we send him that we can mention in the report but where we don't really need to go? Somewhere pleasant and restful. I know. Dartmoor! Saw the Governor the other day. Get him on the 'phone. I'll fix it.' So much for my attempt at diplomacy. The following Monday I was sitting forlornly alone in a first-class compartment of a train bound for Exeter. I had bought all the newspapers but put them folded in a pile on the seat beside me. A pleasant man entered the carriage with a lady who seemed rather elderly, perhaps about 75 or so. He said to me, 'I'm sorry to trouble you but do you think you could possibly keep an eye on my mother for me? It's a long time since she travelled alone and she will be met at Exeter.' Of course, I readily agreed and to my delight found she was a thoroughly amusing and lively old girl. I never looked at my papers and was a bit surprised to see the station at Exeter swarming with television and radio reporters. I said, 'I suppose there must be a member of the Royal Family on the train,' and began the procedure of handing her over to her waiting relatives when all of a sudden I realized with horror that they were all looking at me. A microphone was pushed under my nose, a television lens into my face and someone said, 'Have you any statement to make?' to which I replied quite truthfully, 'Not at this time.' I managed to get to the station exit where Roland Lees was waiting for me and asked him, 'What in God's name is going on?' To which he replied, 'Haven't you read your papers?' There in the headlines it all was. 'MAD AXEMAN ESCAPES.' 'MAD FRANK LOOSE ON DARTMOOR' and so on. That wasn't all. Talk about naval sang-froid. When Jenkins had called in Mountbatten to ask him as a matter of urgency to add this to his terms of reference he said, airily, 'Don't worry, Home Secretary, I've already got someone down there looking into it.' Needless to say, he then got the prison to keep a line open so that no one, not even the Home Secretary, could get to me before him.

I had nothing, not even a pen and pencil. I was travelling in a suit I had had altered and the tailor had been over generous round the waist so that I looked and felt like Bobby Bruin. Roland had to go back to London. I really felt that emigration had a lot to be said for it. I was fortunate in that the chief constable of Devon, Ronnie Greenwood, was an old friend. I rang him up and asked him for help. I got it in full measure. A fractious opposition had insisted that my report into the escape should appear verbatim within the body of Mountbatten's report. A nice, trustful lot, these MPs. It does, from paragraph 131 to paragraph 193 and it makes interesting and amusing reading.

Mitchell was 37 years old, a giant in stature and he had at various times in his life been described as mentally subnormal or actually insane. He had been both in Borstal and prison and at Pentonville had been flogged for attacking two prison officers. He was afterwards certified to be mentally defective and moved to Rampton. He escaped in 1957 and committed some violent crimes for which he was sent to Broadmoor. He escaped again, committed further violent crimes and was given life imprisonment. In 1962 he was birched for attacking a prison officer at Hull and was then transferred to Dartmoor. In May 1965 he was allowed to work under supervision outside the prison and in the following year was assigned to an 'honour party' which often worked some distance from the prison unsupervised.

My task of enquiring into his escape on 12 December involved a rapid assessment of the layout, organization and administration of the prison and an attempt to discover how the escape was made. The first part was more difficult than the second. Dartmoor was built to house prisoners from the Napoleonic wars and had not been improved very much. Part of its immense wall had collapsed from dilapidation and was temporarily replaced by corrugated-iron sheets!

The prison authorities were laudably trying to discover whether Mitchell would respond to treatment and encouragement rather than mere incarceration and showed some courage in assigning him to outside work. What was not realized until too late was that once outside he dominated the honour party and the prison officer in charge of it and did pretty much as he liked including visiting pubs in villages on the moor.

My enquiry showed also that the arrangements for supervising monthly visitors were such that nothing could have been easier than to arrange with an honour party member a rendezvous from which to take him to freedom. This is exactly what happened. Mitchell's gangland associates simply collected him by car when he was outside on his own and brought him to London. Unknown to me at that time he was put in a flat with a woman to keep him quiet but as soon as he seemed likely to become an embarrassment was killed. No one knows where his body is although legend has it that he is now part of a motorway flyover.

The ease with which so dangerous a man could escape caused quite an outcry. The common conception of Dartmoor prison was that it was a kind of Bastille or Château d'If. In reality it was nothing of the kind, but to establish the facts and assemble them in understandable form with a public and parliamentary clamour going on was quite difficult. I was actually on the Moor only two days, taking a further two days in the Cabinet Office to produce a coherent account of my rather hectic and unforeseen experience.

The Mountbatten report has suffered much unfair criticism, a lot of it to be expected. It is dubbed reactionary and so on. It is nothing of the kind. Its implementation would in the long term have spared the great bulk of the prison population a lot of unnecessary hardship.

It was after my return from Dartmoor that the Home Secretary, Roy Jenkins, sent for me in that little room behind the Speaker's chair. He came straight to the point. 'I have decided to appoint you an assistant commissioner in the Metropolitan Police.' Pregnant silence. I reflected that only one provincial policeman had ever been appointed to such high rank in the Met, Arthur Young, and he only lasted three years. I asked Jenkins, 'Do you mind if I ask you a question?' To which he replied, 'Of course.' 'Have you consulted the Commissioner and does he agree?' There was a lengthy silence whilst the Jenkins eyes surveyed the ceiling. At last, choosing his words with typical Jenkinsian skill, he replied, 'He has loyally promised to abide by my decision.' It could hardly have been plainer, but for me, of course, it was Hobson's choice. I therefore accepted with as good grace as I could muster.

I wrote to the Commissioner, Sir Joseph Simpson, to assure him that I would do my best to serve both him and the Met loyally and well and got back a lengthy letter in manuscript telling me that the appointment would not be welcomed by the Met and suggesting that I call on him. I did so, expecting that some of the immense resources of the force would lend me assistance in finding somewhere to live. Not a bit of it. He merely told me to try to be available by 1 February and that he would like me to resign from the Standing Advisory Committee on the Penal System. I paid a firm advertising in the *Sunday Times* £200 to find me a house at Oxshott and arranged to move in March 1967.

# CHAPTER 6

# Appointment to the Met

Having no home in London I left my wife in Leicester and begged the National Liberal Club to take me in from Mondays to Fridays, which they very kindly did. From there it was a short walk to Scotland Yard, overlooking the Embankment. I am familiar with the arguments about its architectural value and the desire to preserve it for posterity. As far as I am concerned it had the outward appearance of a giant mausoleum without, as I was to discover, any functional advantages. It had originally been intended as an opera house until some malign influence decided otherwise. Of course, I shall be suspected of prejudice, since my appearance there was scarcely a matter for rejoicing on the part of anyone. I felt rather like the representative of a leper colony attending the annual garden party of a colonial governor and was soon left in no doubt that I was not alone in that assessment.

I reported to the Commissioner's office and one of his two secretaries told me he was dictating and very kindly handed me a copy of *The Times*. After about half an hour I was admitted to the presence and after a short chat was handed over to the deputy commissioner, Jack Waldron, who took me on a walk around the first floor and then led me to my office, in which he left me. This was a gloomy Victorian hovel with a desk, a rickety table and a telephone switchboard which I never mastered. The table was for meals, since there was no communal mess. The only other feature was an ancient Victorian lavatory right outside my office door, which I gathered was for my exclusive use. Rank has its privileges, even in Scotland Yard. An attendant looked in on me each morning to enquire what I wished to have for lunch, which he brought to me on a tray. Otherwise, the only person I saw in my first week was a genial giant, Gordon Nockles, who was my personal assistant and the second friendly face. The first was my driver, Mick Malone, a former guardsman with hollow legs and an unrivalled knowledge of the quality and distribution of the various kinds of beer to be obtained in London. The politics of Scotland Yard meant nothing to him. He was a good and faithful friend from the day I met him until his retirement. My happiest memory of him is of being stationary at traffic lights somewhere in London opposite a building that looked like a mosque with a pub on the opposite corner. I said, 'Mick, that's an unusual-looking building,' and he replied, 'Yessir! And they sell a most unusual brand of beer there.' Mick was very devoted to his wife and proud of his daughter who was head girl of her school. His wife made him retire to Sussex a year or so later and I think she was very wise. He had been badly machine-gunned in the western desert and strictly speaking ought not to have been in the police at all.

For the first week I saw nothing and no one apart from Malone and Nockles, both of whom were kindness itself. On the Friday night, just as I was debating whether I might catch the train for Leicester, Joe Simpson looked in, dropped a letter on my desk and said, 'I wonder if you would be interested in this?' As it happened, I recognized the letter, a copy having been forwarded from Leicester. It was a circular from the Home Office exhorting chief constables to persuade their best men to apply for the job of chief constable of Lancashire, Eric St Johnston having been brought to London as chief inspector of constabulary. I was therefore able to say immediately that I didn't think that an application from me would be likely to be greeted with enthusiasm by the Home Office, to which Joe replied, 'No. I suppose you've burnt your boats.'

The Metropolitan force consisted at this time of about 22,000 police officers, of whom 600 were women, and some 11,000 civilians, including 2000 traffic wardens and cadets.

The authorized establishment for police was 26,500 but the deficiency of 4500 had remained unchanged for many years. The four principal police departments are styled not surprisingly, A, B, C and D. 'A' consists of all uniformed police not assigned to traffic duties, including the mounted branch, the dog section, the Thames division (which is older than the force itself) and all uniformed policewomen. Each departmental head, an assistant commissioner, is always given the letter of his department as a suffix and for brevity, in the case of 'A' department, is known as 'ACA'.

'ACB' had under command about 1200 traffic police, all traffic wardens and a large civilian staff.

'ACC' is in charge of about 3200 detectives, including Special Branch, and is one of the United Kingdom representatives on the executive of Interpol, for which Scotland Yard is the United Kingdom link to the headquarters at St Cloud, in Paris.

'ACD', the post to which I was appointed, had at that time a curious collection of mixed responsibilities: recruitment, postings, training, welfare, communications, buildings, dogs, and so on. Much of its staff, apart from the training schools at Peel House and Hendon, was civilian.

All civilian staff, though deployed in many cases to police departments, came under the administrative control of the Receiver, who, as the chief financial and administrative officer, alone had direct access to the Home Secretary in financial matters. He still retains this, even though the civilian and police staffs were formally merged into one comprehensive organization in 1968.

All personnel other than those at Scotland Yard and the several other headquarters buildings, are deployed to one or other of twenty-three divisions covering the whole Metropolitan Police district, always known simply as MPD. The number increased to twenty-four when we took over the policing of Heathrow Airport, a development I will mention later. Each division had its complement of uniformed and detective officers, civilians and special constables. Although Joe Simpson made all non-indictable crime, known as 'minor crime', or 'beat crime' the responsibility of the uniform branch there was a sharp division of responsibility for preventive and detective work, all detectives on divisions being controlled for practical purposes by the four area detective commanders at Scotland Yard. The CID then had its own promotion boards.

At Scotland Yard itself and at other headquarters buildings were housed the administration of the principal police and civilian departments and branches. Under the Receiver, for example, were large branches dealing with administration, finance, buildings, vehicles. The solicitor was supported by fifty lawyers with a complement of managing clerks and junior staff. The chief architect and the chief engineer similarly had large and highly qualified staffs. The number of people at Scotland Yard alone was around 4000 of whom the police were in the minority. The specialist detective squads were originally centred at the Yard but some dispersal became inevitable through shortage of space.

The whole organization was uncoordinated to a remarkable extent. There was only a nominal pretence of democratic management. The commissioner exercised unchallenged authority. There were five assistant commissioners of whom one, the deputy, was *primus inter pares*, having no actual authority over the others except in the absence or illness of the commissioner.

The autonomy of the four departmental assistant commissioners was extensive and traditional. Until 1968 the division between police and civil staff was tangible. An observer might have been forgiven for thinking that they were more concerned to oppose or frustrate each other than to attain a common objective. There were monthly conferences between the commissioner, deputy and assistant commissioners with the Receiver and secretary. I thought them so meaningless as to be an insult to the intelligence. Each departmental head was concerned to protect his own interests and of constructive and thoughtful discussion there was practically none.

Similarly at quarterly meetings of divisional commanders,

the stifling presence of senior officers between assistant commissioner and divisional commander (then a chief superintendent) ensured that discussion was non-controversial and innocuous.

However, for the present moment I was head of a department of which the components were scattered to the four winds of heaven, from the training centre at Hendon in the north, to the dog training centre at Keston in Kent. From my dingy office the complexity of my far flung empire was difficult to comprehend. All the more so since no one attempted to explain it to me and for the short time that we were to remain in the Norman Shaw building we had no communal mess so I never saw anyone. I thought it possible that they had probably forgotten that I existed. In view of the qualifications and qualities of some former assistant commissioners that is perhaps not quite so unlikely as it sounds.

It is perhaps necessary to offer at this point an explanation of what I believe to be the reasons for my quite extraordinary reception by the Metropolitan Police and why I came to look back on the whole painful experience with humour, rather than with resentment.

The Hendon College, founded by Trenchard in the thirties, had produced some very good and some very bad policemen. In the first category were Joe Simpson and Ted Dodd, the latter longtime chief constable of Birmingham and eventually Chief Inspector of Constabulary at the Home Office. Hendon was established by Trenchard because, after taking up appointment as Commissioner against his own inclination and in deference to a direct appeal from the monarch, he was appalled by what he found. His solution was to introduce into what had admittedly always been an artisan service an officer class through a newly created college to be known as the Hendon Police College, which was intended to be rather like a police Sandhurst. The 15-month course was, by modern standards, derisory. It can be summed up not unfairly by the ancient dictum that CAT spells cat. Admission was to be by direct entry from university or by competitive examination from within the service. In fact, as a temporary solution to an urgent problem it was not without its good points. The trouble was that its bad points tended to be overlooked. It was really a quite open attempt to attract men of good educational and social background to a service which had always been thought, even by Peel himself, to be inappropriate for those of gentle birth or upbringing. It was bitterly resented by the police service generally and by the Metropolitan Police in particular, because it limited the promotion prospects of those who were recruited in the ordinary way. What Trenchard overlooked was that almost all the decisions that matter in the police service, the decisions to be discussed in the courts or on the floor of the Commons, are made at the lowest point in the rank structure, the constable, sergeant or inspector who decides whether to arrest or not. The relationship of the police to the public is determined by the acceptability of the law, the limitation of police powers and police accountability. It has nothing to do with the creation of a socially acceptable status designed to equate the police with the armed forces. The bitter opposition to Hendon unevitably aroused a sense of group solidarity between those who were so fortunate as to be included in the chosen few.

Simpson joined the police before the Hendon College was even thought of. After leaving Oundle he had, I think, done one year at Manchester College of Technology before deciding to join the Met and he entered Hendon by competitive examination as a constable. On leaving Hendon he successfully read for the Bar and was soon appointed assistant chief constable of a provincial force. He was later an outstanding Regional Police Staff Officer during the war. Thereafter he was chief constable of two provincial county forces before returning to the Met as assistant commissioner in the knowledge that he was destined to be commissioner. He was, without doubt, one of the most valuable products of Hendon and with Ted Dodd could virtually be said to have justified its short life. Attlee, immediately after the war, pronounced its death sentence. The sense of group loyalty amongst the

Hendon 'graduates' was all the stronger because of the reaction of the force and service generally. The public did not realize that the mixture of which Hendon was composed ranged from university graduate to the public schoolboy with one 'O' level, or its equivalent, in woodwork or some other subject not requiring marked intellectual capacity. It was, however, doomed, not because of an unreasonable political antipathy to the conception of an officer class but because as time went on it became apparent that it simply did not meet the requirements of a social service which was clearly likely eventually to be no less important than the armed forces of the Crown.

Simpson and Dodd had always been very close, not surprisingly, because they were I think the two most outstanding products of Hendon. Simpson I knew hardly at all and he was not to know that I admired his integrity, his dedication, his moral courage and his intellectual capacity. Dodd, on the other hand, I got to know very well as chief constable of Birmingham when I was chief constable of Leicester. Chief constables confer with each other within a regional organization and at that time, unfortunately, Birmingham and Leicester were within the same region. It was known, understandably, as Dodd's Own Country. The arrangement, however, had no regard for operational police problems. There is no relationship between Birmingham and Leicester from the police point of view. Leicester is more concerned with Nottingham, Northampton and all points north, east and south rather than with the West Midlands. Indeed, the arrangement of regional conferences has now been changed to take account of this. But Dodd, whom I liked and admired greatly, objected to this view and saw me as a disruptive influence because I did not wish to dissipate my slender resources in activities centred on Birmingham. He formed a profound dislike for me, which was not reciprocated, but was heightened when he was asked why Leicester's parking control system would not work perfectly well in Birmingham, as, indeed, it would have done. This dislike was heightened by the incident I have described earlier involving the use of troops at Durham. Oddly enough, we seldom, if ever, disagreed on administrative or technical police procedures and policies. Had I been destined to work with him as one of his assistants I think we would have got along as well as I did with Valentine, but it was not to be.

Although Simpson and I hardly knew each other there is no doubt that his view of me was heavily influenced by Dodd. All this would not have mattered but for one incident. In my last year at Leicester, John MacKay, who had been an outstandingly successful chief constable of Manchester having long been Dodd's deputy in Birmingham, was appointed an Inspector of Constabulary, not surprisingly since Dodd was then the Chief Inspector. The inspector of constabulary for the Midlands was then Joe Manuel, a decent, amiable Metropolitan officer. He put to me persuasively that, having been chief constable of Leicester for ten years, I ought to apply for Manchester rather than retire prematurely. I was not keen. I had had lengthy experience of the Manchester Watch Committee and was not willing to renew it voluntarily. But as Joe pointed out, my friend, George Ogden, the town clerk of Leicester, was already the town clerk designate of Manchester and it seemed unreasonable not to apply. Rather unwillingly I agreed and sent off an application. About three weeks later Mark Henig, the Labour leader of Leicester Council, an impeccably honest and dedicated public servant, called on me and said, 'I thought I'd better warn you that you aren't going to get that job. I thought I'd tell you in case you want to withdraw.' I told him I couldn't very well withdraw and would go for the interview anyway. In the event I had a most entertaining interview and accepted my rejection with good grace. It was not until after Simpson died, and Ogden had long been town clerk of Manchester, that he told me that the previous town clerk had written to a number of elder statesmen in the police service in view of the success of that procedure in selecting MacKay, and that Simpson, whose advice had been sought, had recommended strongly against my appointment. He can only have done this on the advice of Dodd, since he hardly knew me and only a few months earlier had sent me a long congratulatory letter in manuscript on my receipt of the Queen's Police Medal. In retrospect it is quite obvious that when, only five months later, I was sentenced to the Met, Simpson must have thought that Ogden, who by then was town clerk of Manchester, must have told me of his recommendation. I don't suppose it occurred to him that Ogden would be too tactful to do that whilst he was alive. It is therefore perhaps not surprising that, having to accept me unwillingly into his own force five months later, he was anxious to keep me at a distance. He certainly succeeded.

The second reason was no less weighty. The Metropolitan Police had long felt itself pre-eminent in police affairs and resented comment or criticism from outsiders. The senior officers also tended to disregard the realities of life. The fact that the posts of commissioner, deputy and assistant commissioner were within the gift of the Home Secretary tended to be brushed lightly aside. The Met intention was that a Metropolitan assistant commissioner who had attended the Hendon College, preferably Peter Brodie, the assistant commissioner (Crime), would be the next commissioner. What was overlooked was that no one else, least of all the Home Office, was prepared to go along with the plan and that my arrival was the first overt indication of this.

All this, however, was at that time unknown to me and I found my reception all the more puzzling. The situation was alleviated to some extent when, only a month later, we moved from the Norman Shaw building to Victoria Street, where there was a communal mess, and where many of D department's branches were centralized. This at least gave me something tangible to do and life began to improve slightly. I made a number of changes in D department policy largely because I had got to the point of not giving a damn whether they met with approval or not.

The first related to a procedure known as 'assessment'. Officers living in married quarters were assessed by the Receiver, the chief administrative and financial officer of the force, for any damage or dilapidation, whether or not they were responsible for it. If children playing football broke a police window, the unfortunate officer occupying the house or flat was assessed for the amount of the damage. He could, of course, appeal, which meant travelling to the Yard in duty time, but his prospects of success were small. The same procedure applied to loss of police property. If a constable chasing a breaker, or a thief, lost a torch or a pair of gloves, he was 'assessed' for the loss. Tom Mahir, my predecessor as assistant commissioner D department, who got a George Medal for outstanding bravery during the blitz, put down a torch and a pair of gloves to apply a tourniquet to the leg of a man whose foot had been blown off. A second bomb blew Tom, his patient, his torch and his gloves all over the place. He was 'assessed' seven shillings and sixpence and one of his predecessors, George Abbiss, disallowed his appeal. The irony was that when Tom reached thoroughly deserved promotion to assistant commissioner, though he breathed fury whenever assessments were mentioned, it never occurred to him to abolish the system. I was more fortunate. In thirty years' police service I had never heard of assessments. When they told me what they were I said, 'Now, go away. Calculate the number and travelling time of appeals and come back and tell me how much we have recovered and how much it cost to recover it.' The answer was quite quickly forthcoming. It had cost us £2000 in twelve months to recover £200. The resentment arising from the process was not, of course, costed. Henceforth, in respect of every assessment of less value than £50 I automatically endorsed the file 'No evidence of wrongdoing or negligence. No assessment.' It was never challenged and so far as I know is still force policy.

The second related to the allocation of married quarters. For some odd reason the Metropolitan force had always equated matrimony with prison. Once contracted, or sentenced, there was no conceivable justification for departure from the norm. Thus, when a constable, deserted by his wife, sought to have a housekeeper live with him and his children in married quarters, he was sure of a pious refusal. One particular application gave me the first moment of pleasure I had experienced in the Met. A senior officer had endorsed the file 'This officer will never be given permission to occupy married quarters' to which I added the comment, 'Oh, yes he will.' And he was.

Another application related to a constable who, after fifteen years' loyal service had decided to try his luck in Australia and found that he did not like it. He applied for reinstatement at a time when the force was 5600 under strength and the chairman of the selection board refused, despite his unblemished record, endorsing the file 'You can see his attitude. He has even appealed against my decision.' To which I added, 'Yes. And successfully.' When you consider that refusal meant denial to him of the benefits of fifteen years' faithful service in terms of the pay scale and pension entitlement the imagination boggles at the intellectual capacity and inhumanity of men entrusted with decisions of that kind.

The third and fourth changes related to the remuneration of the staffs of the Convalescent Home and the Friendly Society. A survey of both taught me that nobody grinds the poor into the dirt more enthusiastically than the poor themselves. Largely owing to the tireless efforts of Tom Mahir, despite appalling ill health, the Convalescent Home at Hove had been rebuilt on the sea front at a cost of £¼m. Unfortunately, no thought had been given to ensuring a sufficient annual income to defray expenditure and to pay the staff reasonably well. This was not Tom's fault. He had achieved marvels, though he was a dying man. Not only had he raised the money to rebuild, he had negotiated a much improved charter of management which made it possible to persuade the service generally that this was their home and that they ought to support it. The staff wages would have been thought admirable by an early 19th-century Lancashire mill owner. There was, in fact, an excellent committee, consisting of police representatives and sympathetic local residents. It took little time to persuade all southern and some other

94

forces to contribute on a per capita basis, to double staff wages and to make essential repairs to the faulty construction of the home. I continued my association with it until becoming commissioner and I must say, few things have given me as much pleasure and satisfaction. If I had my way, I would rename it the Mahir Convalescent Police Home, but I appreciate that policemen generally are not a sentimental lot. At least it can today be said to be one of the most admirable and beneficial of all police institutions.

The Metropolitan Police Friendly Society was in much the same boat. With a capital of well over a million and an ever rising annual income it had employed police pensioners exclusively and paid them disgracefully. That, too, was rectified speedily. I noted quietly that when I let Joe Simpson have an account of these changes, after they had occurred, he never demurred and that his behaviour to me became distinctly less chilly.

The last change I made as assistant commissioner D related to women. This does not imply any need for alarm. I had always recognized that women were biologically necessary for the continuance of the force and were better able than men to persuade the public of our virtues as a service. In Leicester I had boldly ignored all the various Home Office exhortations and equipped them with court shoes, short skirts, air hostess tunics and shoulder bags. The effect was electric. Even in a town like Leicester, where women earned exceptionally high wages, our recruitment rocketed. So, alas, did our matrimonial rate of wastage. My predecessor in the Met had asked Norman Hartnell to do something similar for the women and we had a special Press showing of the result. It took time to bite, but gradually had an effect on recruitment. One of my happier achievements as commissioner was to double the strength of women police from 600 to 1200 plus. A particularly interesting aspect of this is that whilst the Met have an ongoing daily total of about 1500 complaints under investigation, practically none of them apply to women. It seems that their sex counteracts the natural abrasion of the police function.

During my time in D department I had made two friends for whom I was to form a lasting regard. One was Kenneth Parker, who was appointed Receiver soon after my arrival. A First at Cambridge, head of the police department of the Home Office, devoted to the police service and having played a major part in the establishment of the police college he was to prove a tower of strength throughout my time as deputy and commissioner. He was awarded a CB for his services at the Home Office but got nothing for his much more valuable services to the Metropolitan Police, in which he bore the responsibility for expenditure in the order of £250m annually and contributed to policy decisions on a major scale. No doubt he would have been better advised to go on the stage. His contribution to the development and efficiency of the police service is never likely to be adequately recognized. Most important of all, he devoted his considerable intellect to breaking down opposition to a realistic London allowance. The Metropolitan Police owe him a great deal, as indeed I do.

The second was Cappy Lane, the Metropolitan Police solicitor. He graduated in law with First Class Honours at Sydney, learned to fly privately, joined the RAAF on the outbreak of war and served in the Middle East and northwest Europe. He was awarded the DFC and AFC, the latter in recognition of flying experimental aircraft, including the first Meteor jet. Cappy was a real personality: effervescent, full of humour always excepting, of course, visits by the Australian test team, when he was unbearable, worse even than my father. I still remember his comment on the return of Brian Close, a great cricketer, to the English side. 'Christ! They'll be asking the Home Office for exhumation orders next!' He, Kenneth and I formed a tightly knit friendship. These two, with Henry Hunt and Ray Anning, of whom I will say more later, were the saving grace in an otherwise dismal prospect.

My time in D department was, however, coming to an end. Before my arrival in the Metropolitan Police the Home Office had, with the agreement of the commissioner, asked a firm of management consultants to advise on its organization and control. Opinions about this differ, especially after the publication of their report. In my view it was an expedient of the Home Office desperate to bring the Met under their control after ten years of failing to make any impression on a strong commissioner. The resultant report was costly indeed, far from impressive, but had some good points. It was quite obvious that the consultants, though expert in the commercial field, did not really understand the much more complex issues arising from law enforcement and public service. Parking control, for example, one of the costliest absurdities of Metropolitan Police activity, was dismissed in a line or two. However, once committed the commissioner had to go along. The four Districts into which the Met was divided, were abolished without the least justification whilst one really valuable recommendation, that a Policy Committee should be established to co-ordinate central management, was ignored. The key recommendation, which was to affect me, was that the Director of Personnel should be the third most important person in the force. Since that was me it meant my immediate removal. I was told abruptly that I was to become Assistant Commissioner (Traffic) without further ado. Andrew Way, all 22 stone of him, was moved from traffic to A department, responsible for all uniformed activities except traffic, and John Hill became Assistant Commissioner D Department. I didn't mind. I liked traffic, loathed the London parking system, with its political expediency, lack of foresight and moral cowardice but unfortunately, before I could really get to grips with it, Joe Simpson died. He had given his all in the face of countless difficulties, two heart attacks, senior colleagues who were mediocre or worse, though admittedly chosen by him, and innumerable crises in which he stoutly defended his force, right or wrong. The Committee of One Hundred, the visit of Queen Frederika with the resultant Challenor enquiry, the Eastmond and Brian Rix affair, these and many other controversial incidents kept him under immense pressure. It is necessary only to see the film of the

St Pancras rent riots to gain a vivid impression of the strain he must have undergone. Moreover, his dedication to his men and his personal commitment to them made him unwilling to delegate, though this was perhaps just as well in view of the calibre of some of his senior colleagues. At any rate, it all proved too much and he died, as I suspect he would have wished to do, in harness. He was deeply and sincerely mourned both within the Met and outside. Whatever his problems, and shyness and inarticulacy were two of them, his innate integrity shone through. This is not hypocrisy on my part. Though circumstances never allowed me to get close to him I never doubted that feeling for his force excluded all other considerations and that this governed his relationship with those around him. I suspect, indeed, have good reasons to believe, that he had become quite reconciled to my presence in the Met, but he could not bring himself to say so. Instead, his frigidity gradually thawed, though not having been brought up in the Met I could never expect to get beyond a certain limit. Westminster Abbey was filled to overflowing for his funeral, a tribute he richly deserved.

However, do not imagine that so moving an event stifled altogether the innate cynicism of the police. The King was dead and the most pressing question was, 'Who is to succeed him?'

# CHAPTER 7

# Crooked Policemen

On 28 March, eight days after Joe's death, I was sent for by Jim Callaghan, who had changed jobs with Roy Jenkins four months earlier, following devaluation. He had Philip Allen and, I think, his personal private secretary with him. Choosing his words with obvious care he said, 'I am now considering the appointment of a Commissioner to replace Sir Joseph Simpson. I would like you to consider yourself as one of the candidates for the job and let me have your reaction.' It did not take me long to decide on my reply. I told him that I thought I was no less well qualified professionally than any other candidate, and perhaps better than most, but that to appoint me would be mistaken, if not disastrous. I explained that I knew very little about the Met, had not a single friend or ally amongst its police members, that my appointment would be bitterly resented by the very people I would need to make a success of the job and that I had no doubt that some of them would lend all their endeavours to ensure the opposite. I made it perfectly clear that as much for the sake of the men and women in the Met, as my own, I did not wish to be considered. Callaghan thereupon said, 'Well, what would you do in my shoes?' I told him I thought he had no choice but to appoint the deputy, Waldron, on a caretaker basis, that he was 58 and could depart gracefully at 60, having given the Home Office a better opportunity to consider the field. He thanked me courteously and I withdrew. I then went home and told my wife that I had probably cooked my goose so far as the Met was concerned but that I had no doubt that it was the right decision. I was soon to learn that it was the wisest decision I ever made. Joe's funeral was on 29 March and the succession remained in the balance for a few days longer. On 5 April I was sent for again and Jim Callaghan didn't waste any time. He said, 'I've decided to take your advice. Waldron is to be appointed for two years. You are forthwith deputy commissioner and I propose to tell him that you are to be given every opportunity to familiarize yourself with the administration of the force. This is not to be taken as an indication that you will succeed him but at least you will have the chance to show what you can do.' I thanked him and withdrew with mixed feelings. A few minutes later Waldron was summoned and told of his appointment. By the time he returned to the Yard we were all at lunch. As the only person in the mess who knew, I rose to congratulate him, omitting to mention my own appointment. Just as well, perhaps, since the only people likely to welcome it were Kenneth Parker and Cappy Lane. Thus began four of the most unpleasant years of my life which might have ended more happily for those who sought my departure had they not provoked me so far as to arouse an overpowering determination to withstand all that they could do.

At that time the status and effectiveness of the deputy commissioner depended entirely upon the support of the commissioner. The deputy had no authority over the other four assistant commissioners except in matters of discipline or in the absence through sickness or leave of the commissioner. Even in matters of discipline he was emasculated if the allegation amounted to crime. In such cases his authority was overridden by that of the assistant commissioner (Crime) who, since 1879, had been given absolute authority under the commissioner for dealing with criminal investigation. True, the deputy had a Management Services Department, consisting of branches dealing with Research, Forward Planning and O & M, but this was remote from the actuality of policing. He also had an Inspectorate of four deputy assistant commissioners, but since they were outranked by assistant commissioners and could not report to the Home Office direct it was largely an academic arrangement disliked by the inspectors themselves. My total staff consisted of two secretaries, a driver and a part-share in a groom. It was, as Waldron told me truthfully at the outset, the worst job in the force. It need not have been so, but earlier commissioners had done nothing to rectify the position and I could well understand that Waldron had no intention of doing so. After all, the other assistant commissioners were his friends and colleagues of long standing, all of them with a Hendon background, and two of them resented my appointment bitterly.

There were, however, some activities in which I had a right to intervene, the most important of which was discipline not amounting to crime. Others included participation in selections for promotion and recommendations for honours. The latter did not last very long, but I was determined to exercise my statutory right in respect of discipline and very early found staunch support in the persons of Henry Hunt, then Deputy Assistant Commissioner 'A' (Admin) and his Chief Superintendent Ray Anning. These two taught me early that the worst of the Metropolitan Police were no fair representation of the countless number of honest and well-intentioned men at every level. My first discovery was that policemen convicted of criminal offences were allowed to remain on the payroll, suspended, until their appeals had been heard, often many months or over a year later. I stopped that forthwith. Conviction was henceforth followed immediately by the sack, with reinstatement in the rare event of a successful appeal. It cleared the decks and saved quite a lot of money. We then began a close scrutiny of cases in which the Director of Public Prosecutions had declined to prosecute or in which prosecution was followed by acquittal. In most of these we had little difficulty in formulating disciplinary charges involving suspension from duty and eventual dismissal or a lesser penalty. More ominously, I invoked the provincial system, hitherto unknown in the Met, of returning to uniform any detective involved in disciplinary enquiries who was thought no longer fit to work unsupervised. My most surprising discovery was that the uniform branch, led by such stalwarts as Jim Starritt, who had borne the main burden of the Challenor affair, Colin Woods, John Hill and many others, warmly approved of what I was doing. The Joint Executive Committee of the Police Federation, the Metropolitan, as distinct from the national, representative body, made no secret of their whole-hearted support. It soon became plain that of the increasing number of officers being suspended, the majority were from the CID and that the uniform branch were only too pleased to see someone deal with a department which had long brought the force as a whole into disgrace.

At this point I had better explain the basic problems of police wrongdoing and discipline. It needs no great brain to appreciate that the two classes most immune from the criminal law are lawyers and police, if only because they know most about it. The function of policing, being one of regulation and control, involves an inevitable temptation to corruption, sometimes petty, sometimes serious. The extent of petty and routine corruption, however, can be restricted or virtually eliminated by sensible laws, such as the legalization of betting shops and the independent control of gaming. More tolerant and sensible laws relating to prostitution, homosexuality, abortion and changing attitudes to petty wrongdoing have in thirty years virtually eliminated corruption from the uniformed branch of the police. It is not that they are essentially different from the CID, so much as that the basic police principles of honesty and decency are not put to the much more severe test and temptation faced continually by the detective, particularly in London, the centre of lucrative crime and vice. Moreover, the uni-formed officer does not suffer the inevitable disillusion of the detective, as he sees the law fail continually where it is most necessary that it should succeed, with consequent high profits for lawyer and criminal alike. Maintenance of a high standard of probity in the uniform branch since the war has therefore been comparatively easy, though this is not to say that uniformed officers do not do wrong. Far from it. But it does not compare in scope and gravity with that which, in the case of the Metropolitan CID, had become routine and so accepted as to become a source of bitter resentment between the two branches and of disharmony and distrust in the police service generally.

Dealing with allegations of police wrongdoing is not easy. The problem arising from a very large proportion of complaints is that until they have been thoroughly investigated it is not possible to say whether they allege criminal wrongdoing, misbehaviour amounting only to a breach of discipline, or both. The situation is further complicated in that if the allegation turns out to be a crime, any departure from the judicial rules governing police investigation of crime will inevitably preclude a successful prosecution and expose the investigating officers to suspicion of partiality, or cover up. Indeed, such suspicions were sometimes only too well-founded in cases of investigations of complaints against detectives by their own colleagues. There are, however, literally thousands of allegations annually and though most are trivial the only organization with the numbers, training and skill to investigate them with any possibility of success is the police. All reports alleging crime, however, go to the Director of Public Prosecutions, who decides whether to prosecute or not. The great disadvantage under which he labours is that juries dislike convicting policemen on the evidence of criminals and many of the worst cases are naturally reliant on just such evidence. A senior member of the Director's staff told the Birmingham Institute of Judicial Administration in 1976 that 59 per cent of police officers tried on indictment were acquitted, as compared with 17 per cent of the Director's other cases. Quite obviously, therefore, the system of criminal justice is not effective for the purpose of maintaining an honest police force.

The next corrective measure is the police discipline system, embodied in regulations made by the Home Secretary after consultation with the police and local police authorities. This is a very different kettle of fish. The accused, though allowed a friend, is not allowed legal representation and the more dubious malpractices of the criminal courts are thereby avoided. He has a right of appeal to the Home Secretary against all convictions and punishments and the Home Secretary frequently takes legal advice before deciding the issue. Properly used, this can be a most effective procedure, not only for dealing with wrongdoing, but for inducing in the worst wrongdoers a willingness to depart without awaiting the inevitable. A police tribunal of experienced officers knows very well that policemen do not meet prisoners on bail or suppress knowledge of their previous convictions without good reason. They know the regulations inside out, as no jury can, and are not likely to be taken in by what Lord Devlin calls 'the world of fantasy created by a defence lawyer at a loss for anything better to do on behalf of his client'. Perhaps the best evidence of the effectiveness of the discipline system, is that during my four years and eleven months as Commissioner 478 men left the force following or in anticipation of criminal or disciplinary proceedings. Only 76 of them had been subjected to formal proceedings, 50 of them by way of prosecution. 402 had therefore anticipated their likely fate by resignation. I would have liked nothing more than to have been able to make every one of the 428 cases not involving prosecution available to an independent reviewing authority. It was a matter of conscience for all those concerned with this process that not one man could claim to have been treated harshly or unfairly. The figures are, however, necessary to an understanding of the scope of the problem. I should add that departures in the previous decade had averaged about sixteen a year.

As I mentioned earlier, the third corrective measure was the arbitrary removal from CID to uniform duties of anyone thought to have forfeited the confidence of his seniors. In some ways, this is perhaps the most formidable corrective of all. At any rate, with the help of Hunt, Anning and their colleagues I began to apply the second and third of these measures with vigour and, even when prosecutions failed, to go through the papers, to which I then had access for the first time, with a fine tooth comb. All this, of course, took time and was played out against the background of force activities generally. Nevertheless, it is important to understand that behind all the events of those four years there was an implacable war fought by a comparatively small number of men, widening the rift between the CID and some of the Hendon old guard, on the one hand, and a significant body of the uniformed branch led by me on the other.

Before the end of 1968 there occurred two events, both of which were helpful to Waldron and the Met. The first was the making by the BBC of a film in the television series 'Cause for Concern'. It was intended to show that the Met were prejudiced against coloured people and must have been one of the most inaccurate and distorted films ever to find its way on to a BBC screen. It nevertheless afforded me one of the most amusing evenings for years. The BBC did not consult us in the making of the film. The producer decided we were guilty and then set out to prove it, the very sin, in fact, of which police are so often accused. Unfortunately for him he got so many of his facts wrong as to destroy its credibility. The film began with a man describing how badly he had been treated by the police. It omitted to mention that he had twice been convicted for carrying offensive weapons and that a City of London policeman had received £100 from the Criminal Injuries Compensation Board arising from his last arrest. It went on to portray a number of alleged injustices suffered by coloured people, omitting to mention that no one in the film had failed in the end to achieve justice. The mistakes were unbelievable, including one allegation of acquittal which related in fact to a conviction quashed on appeal only for compassionate reasons. Representatives of the Met were only allowed to see the film after its completion. They were horrified. The commissioner objected to its viewing and the BBC got cold feet. Then of course the civil libertarian Press began to rage about censorship and to make matters worse the commissioner gave a brief interview to ITV. The BBC therefore decided to go ahead. Clearly, we had to be represented in the subsequent discussion and there were no volunteers. The day before it was due to be shown the commissioner told me that since

I had more television experience than anyone else in the Met I was to do it. I had no illusions about the task or about the good wishes I took with me. Fortunately, with the help of Cappy Lane, I had done some swift homework. I had identified the City policeman who had been injured and managed to trace some of the more glaring inaccuracies in the film. The City commissioner let me borrow his constable and I turned up at the studio with him, Ray Merricks from our Community Relations Branch and Reg Gale, representing the Police Federation.

The BBC were slightly puzzled by the London constable. I told them not to worry. He was merely being called to prove that one part of the film was false and defamatory. At this they looked worried and said, 'Which part?' to which I replied, 'I'll tell your viewers, not you. After all, you didn't consult us about its accuracy during the making of the film.' There was a hurried conference in a corner. They came back and said, 'We're sorry. You can't produce your witness. The studio has already been arranged to take a specified number of participants,' to which I replied, 'No bother, one of my chaps will make way for him. After all it's important to expose falsehood.' Another pause and then the rather terse message, 'We've decided to cancel the programme' to which I replied, 'Very sensible of you. I'm now going to Scotland Yard to explain to the Press that the decision is yours, not ours, and I think, in the circumstances, very wise.' A hasty conference followed, after which a legal adviser was produced. By this time I was getting a bit fed up and said, 'I don't mind telling you, as an act of generosity, that your first performer is a violent, convicted criminal and I am prepared to prove it to your audience.' They then tried the ploy that the mixed bag of the opposition taking part in the programme would walk out if we called our witness to which I replied, 'Good. I'm sure it will improve the programme.' To cut a long story short, we finally entered the studio about twenty-five minutes late. Some sixth sense prompted me to say to my colleagues, 'In no circumstances whatever leave your seats unless I do.' Sure enough some bedraggled and harassed character said to me, 'Do you insist on calling your witness?' to which I replied, 'Yes,' whereupon he waved his arms and said, 'The programme is cancelled, ladies and gentlemen' (of whom there were remarkably few, if any, there that night). We sat tight and, surprise, surprise, there we were on the monitor. The programme had started.

The film was shown in its entirety. It lasted about 35 or 40 minutes but it turned out to be just the appetizer before the meal, which consisted of the discussion, or free-for-all, between the invited panel, representing immigrant groups and political activists and the three police representatives. I don't think anybody won but as general Press comment was to show, the contents of the film, coupled with the behaviour of the panel, was such as to swing public opinion away from the critics to the criticized. I was relieved but not happy. Confrontations on television are not the best way to promote good race relations, even if you appear to win, and I had a feeling that the film and the panel had done the coloured community less than justice. My only dubious consolation was that the confrontation was not sought. It was literally forced upon us.

My reception back at the Yard was mixed. The force generally were glad someone had done battle for them, but some of my senior colleagues were undoubtedly sorry that it had not ended in disaster. Needless to say, a tactful veil was drawn over the pressures by the Press, the NCCL and other pressure groups to have the film shown in the first place, nor was any word of apology for this disgraceful piece of journalism ever made public. I must, in fairness, add finally that the chairman, Magnus Magnusson, gave me the impression that he had no prior idea of the basic inaccuracy of the film and he seemed thoroughly ashamed of it. Moreover, Charles Curran, newly appointed Director-General, whom I had not met, had the decency to ring up as soon as the programme finished and make sympathetic noises.

The other noteworthy event was the so-called October Revolution, the anti-Vietnam war demonstration, which attracted very large numbers of people and finished as the biggest non-event of the year. Waldron nevertheless deserved great credit for not allowing himself to be stampeded. Not for years had there been so much fuss and apprehension about a demonstration and he stoutly resisted any suggestion of panic measures. In fact, although we were not to know it at the time, it was his finest hour and one for which he deserves an honoured mention in Metropolitan Police history. Not since the late 19th century had a commissioner faced so potentially dangerous a situation and conducted himself so well. The event exposed critical weaknesses in our resources for surveillance and communication and it is also to Waldron's credit that he set in train the steps to remedy this. As a result, the Metropolitan Police have probably the most sophisticated equipment for dealing with major emergencies that any European police force can boast.

Whilst all this was going on I decided to learn to ride. I lived near Imber Court, the Metropolitan Police riding school, and needed exercise. But that was not my main reason. I had been struck by the fatuity of compelling policemen reaching high rank to undergo an equitation course. Most of them hated it and some had suffered serious injury. The age of 50 is a little late for riding. Moreover, nowhere in the order of proceedings of any state ceremonial is the commissioner mentioned on horseback. They all rode because they liked the sense of importance it gave them. My decision was strengthened by a photograph of the commissioner and deputy of some years earlier riding together in all their glory being totally ignored by the troops lining the route, who were standing easy despite cocked hats, feathers and all. I decided if ever I became commissioner to put an end to all this childish nonsense, but I realized that before I could do so, I must have qualified as a horseman if I was not to be suspected of cowardice. I therefore began the course and to my surprise enjoyed it immensely. In fact, so much so that after one over-enthusiastic session I lost a lot of skin off my backside and couldn't sit down on a train journey to Manchester. When I rang up and asked the mounted branch what to do about this I got the sympathetic response, 'Blanco it, sir!' I went on riding, off and on, until my last year in the Met and to the great pleasure of the chief instructor actually managed to get four paws off the ground at the same time. But I never rode on a ceremonial occasion for which, I have no doubt, my successor is profoundly grateful.

I had the impression by the end of my first year as deputy that the commissioner's stock with the Home Office was up and mine was down. After all, I had declined to stand and he had scored a thoroughly well deserved and major success. Moreover I did not lack friends who were willing to question my fitness to hold senior rank in the Metropolitan Police. By that time I was not unduly worried. I was quietly perversely proud of being easily the most senior undecorated officer in the whole police service and I was pensionable. I was also making some inroads into police wrongdoing. It is perhaps worth mentioning that against the opposition of the CID and without the support I was entitled to expect, with the help of Hunt, Anning and their colleagues in my four years as deputy I actually managed to achieve the premature departure of 20, 40, 60 and 80 men in successive years, a statistical accident, but a feat I think in the circumstances rather more remarkable than that more easily achieved when I was in command.

The winter of 1968 slipped by without any particular event of note. In the spring of 1969 I was surprised to receive a call from the chief constable of the newly amalgamated Leicester force to tell me that my old chairman was seriously ill in the Middlesex hospital. I was a little surprised but thought I ought to go and see him. I am glad I did. He was obviously dying and I was glad to part with him on the friendly terms we had enjoyed for so long, before the pollution of politics intervened.

In mid-August, when I thought my stock was probably at an all time low, and didn't care very much if it was, I was sent for by Callaghan and told that the army was going to aid the civil power in Northern Ireland that very night and that I was to go there with Douglas Osmond from Hampshire forthwith if not sooner. We were to wear plain clothes, had no authority and were to act as observers. I left Northolt in a tiny aircraft that afternoon and picked up Douglas on a dismal airfield somewhere in Hampshire, arriving at Aldergrove late that evening. It was like Dante's *Inferno*. We were taken on a circular tour by the RUC in which we counted something in the order of 100 fires, none of which was being attended by the fire brigade for fear of reprisals. It was an eerie occasion. We got very little sleep in the next few days and were not surprised when Douglas was called to the Cabinet Office for consultation. Whilst he was away, I continued my sightseeing and was appalled by what I saw. I asked a lot of questions, particularly about shots fired by 'B' Specials at cars which did not stop. I had the feeling that Peacock, the Inspector-General, thought me unnecessarily curious. In fact, as I was to find later, there was a good side to the 'B' Specials, who were a natural target for anti-Stormont propaganda. Many of them did duty unarmed, in Belfast in particular, and throughout the province they probably had better knowledge of terrorist deployment and potential than the RUC itself. It was nevertheless a paramilitary organization whose continuance was clearly incompatible with democratic government, but that is not to say that many of its members did not give valuable, unselfish and courageous service.

Osmond and I left on 22 August full of admiration for the rank and file of the RUC and without any admiration at all for most of its leaders. With the noteworthy exception of Graham Shillington it seemed to be the policy of most of the senior officers at headquarters not to worry too much about what was going on outside Belfast. Conditions in Derry had been appalling, the police there behaving with great bravery throughout days of violence of a kind not seen for generations on the mainland.

On my return I was not particularly pleased to be told that I was to return to serve on an Advisory Committee to be chaired by Lord Hunt of Everest fame, with Sir James Robertson, Chief Constable of Glasgow, as the other mem-

ber. I was told that only the identity of the chairman was
to be announced initially because Stormont had objected to
my inclusion. It did neither them nor me any good. From
26 August until 3 October I served on the committee,
meeting people of every kind and at all levels in Ulster,
returning home for an occasional weekend by courtesy of
the RAF. We were working against the background of the
report by Lord Cameron, a fearless, impartial and admirable
document, which should be compulsory reading for everyone
with an interest in Irish politics. I should perhaps mention
that I am not a Roman Catholic and so far as I know,
neither is John Hunt nor Jimmy Robertson. As time went
on we became more and more aware of the colonial system
which had administered the province for years. Only its
association in law with the United Kingdom and its representation at Westminster prevented it from being seen in
realistic terms as in no different relationship to Great Britain
than Cyprus, Aden or any other of the countless colonial
territories from the great days of empire. This is, of course,
a very hard and distasteful conclusion against the background of the magnificent service given by Ulstermen for
generations to the Crown, both in the armed forces and
elsewhere. It is nevertheless an inescapable conclusion for
the impartial observer. The complexity of the subject and
the composition of the committee meant that hard argument,
occasional disagreement and some very difficult moments
were inevitable. However, the result was not a bad balance.
The final report still makes very sensible reading given one
seemingly unattainable factor, the willingness of the people
of Northern Ireland to accept the concept of government by
consent in the manner acceptable to Great Britain. No
society in which a sufficient minority dissents from that
principle can be controlled by an unarmed police force
operating in the conventional manner. In the case of Northern Ireland neither the minority nor the majority wants it
and all that can therefore be done is to try to keep opposing
factions from eliminating each other or the one dominating
the other by virtual dictatorship. The eventual solution must

be political. The efforts of the committee were not however wholly to be wasted. We seized the opportunity to drag the RUC by the scruff of the neck into line with the mainland forces so far as pay, leave, allowances, pensions and conditions of service were concerned. In particular, we managed to give them negotiating machinery with real teeth, so that they were no longer dependent on the patronage of Stormont. The long-term benefit of this is likely to be very important. It has already demonstrated its value by encouraging a steady flow of recruits of high standard, even though the force continually faces more danger and discomfort than any other in Britain.

I found on my return that Hunt and Anning had been carrying on the war without me. Tension between the CID and the uniform branch was high. This was to be given increased impetus at the end of the month when *The Times* published very serious allegations against some Metropolitan detectives, a most unusual step for a paper of that kind to take. The method of revelation bordered on the sensational. 'London policemen in bribe allegations. Tapes reveal planted evidence.' It read more like the *People* or the *News of the World* than *The Times*. Nevertheless the article bluntly charged a detective inspector and two detective sergeants with taking bribes for dropping charges, with giving false evidence in return for money and with allowing a criminal to pursue his activities. Moreover, references in a leading article to 'a firm within a firm' made it clear that *The Times* thought the case to be merely the tip of an iceberg. There are disadvantages arising from public disclosure on television or in newspapers of matters likely to be subject to criminal investigation and trial. A very important one is that a fair trial may not thereafter be possible. Another is that even if the allegations are true, the wrongdoer is forewarned and is given the opportunity to take evasive or other action. As a generalization it can fairly be said that such disclosures are rarely in the public interest and that they are almost certain to impede, rather than assist, the process of justice. Why, then, did a newspaper with a worldwide reputation to sustain behave in this uncharacteristic manner? The answer was quite simple. The editor and his legal advisers did not believe that if the allegations against the detectives were disclosed privately to the Metropolitan Police they would be properly investigated. He decided, therefore, to bring the matter into the open even at the risk of prejudicing a fair trial for the accused, if, indeed, there were to be any accused. At the time and in hindsight I thought his decision was absolutely right. Admittedly, I was prejudiced. I had, with my closest colleagues, long been critical of the way in which complaints of crime by Metropolitan detectives were investigated, or not investigated, and I was encouraged by the realization that there were people outside the force who knew this and were willing to say so. I was, too, in the happier position of knowing that in the event of an enquiry or a Royal Commission there was plenty of evidence on our files to justify the action of the editor. It was for me rather like the throwing down of the gauntlet. What was rather less satisfying was the ineptitude with which, as it seemed to me, the affair was handled, in particular by the Home Office, who are ultimately responsible for the administration of the Metropolitan force.

What should have happened is that the Secretary of State should have immediately exercised his power under Section 49 of the Police Act 1964, and insisted that the matter be investigated by a suitably senior chief constable assisted by a specially selected team of provincial and Metropolitan officers. The Home Office, however, decided to follow a different course. The enquiry was left in the hands of the Metropolitan Police, with Frank Williamson, HM Inspector of Constabulary (Crime), being assigned to the task of advising and overseeing the operation. Inspectors of Constabulary are not police officers and have no police powers. They are not able to give orders to police officers at any level. Their duties are inspectorial and advisory and their authority depends entirely upon the willingness of the Home Secretary to support them on a particular issue, if necessary, in extreme cases, by threat of withholding the Exchequer grant of half the cost of the force. It can hardly have come as a surprise to Frank Williamson that in circumstances of this kind he was not likely to see the enquiry conducted in the way in which he would have wished. He did, however, fight tenaciously and was able to insist on the inclusion of provincial detective officers in the investigating team. It is largely to his credit that it ended, but not before March 1972, with the conviction of two detectives and their subsequent imprisonment. A third fled the country and has not been seen since.

The revelation had, however, served one useful purpose. It had disclosed to the world that there was widespread and, as events proved, justified lack of confidence in the way in which allegations of crime by Metropolitan detectives were investigated. This lent great weight to the activities that I had been pursuing with Hunt, Anning and their staff and must have convinced the Home Office that although there was clearly something badly wrong there were also people within the Met who knew it and were anxious to do something about it. From that point on, I never felt alone. Rightly or wrongly, I was convinced that the Home Office had at least realized that all was not well and I was in the happy position of knowing that any kind of enquiry could only redound to my advantage and the exposure of a situation which had already lasted far too long.

# CHAPTER 8

# The Battle for Control of the CID

1970 should have seen the departure of Waldron and the appointment of a successor and in hindsight it would have undoubtedly been kinder for him had that happened. In fact, however, the Top Salaries Review Committee had reported, with a consequent belated increase for the commissioner from £8600 to an eventual £12,000 per annum. The Home Office generously and rightly thought that it would be unfair not to give him the opportunity to attract the consequent higher pension and his service was therefore extended for one year. On the surface it was an unremarkable year, the general public being unaware of mounting internal tension arising from increasing pressure upon the CID, not only from the continuing *Times* enquiry, but from a number of other related disciplinary enquiries, the cumulative effect of which was to cause the CID to close ranks against everyone, uniform branch, the Press, the Home Office, in fact anyone whose conduct or comment might be thought harmful to its morale or reputation.

Early in the year I had given a lecture to the Medico-Legal Society under the heading 'Thoughts from a Psychological Ghetto' and in April I was warned by Philip Allen not to book a summer holiday since I would probably be required to go to Victoria to look at the police there. It appeared that the government of the State of Victoria was so dissatisfied with its assessment of the efficiency and integrity of its 4600 strong police force that it was contemplating a Royal Commission of Enquiry into it, for which Whitehall approval would be necessary. It needs no great intelligence to suspect, against the background of Australian politics and police, that a reconnaissance might be desirable before adopting such an extreme measure. In fact, the Home Office omitted to tell me that it was later decided to send St Johnston prior to his retirement at the end of the year. However, there were compensations. In July I was elected a Visiting Fellow of Nuffield College, Oxford, a distinction enjoyed by, amongst others, Edward Heath, William Whitelaw, William Rees Mogg, Alastair Hetherington, James Callaghan, Campbell Adamson, Shirley Williams, Jack Jones and quite a number of other interesting people from public life. No less rewarding was the relief offered to me by the Home Office from the unattractive situation in which they had placed me by my inclusion in a working party set up by the Ministry of Defence to review the army's policies in respect of aid to the civil power. The travelling part of the working party consisted of Major-General Anthony Deane-Drummond, CB, DSO, MC and Lt Colonel Desmond Bastick, MBE and me. Between September and the following February we travelled the world first class at the expense of the Ministry of Defence, my part in the operation being particularly easy in that it merely consisted of saying 'No' at frequent intervals. Desmond and Tony did all the actual work whilst I enjoyed myself and tried to look useful. We managed to get to Ulster, Berlin, Paris, the USA and Canada, Rome, Singapore, Hong Kong, Tokyo, Cyprus, Holland and, not least amusing, Lancashire.

Tony was the legendary figure who not only escaped from Italy, after having been dropped by parachute in 1941 to blow up an installation, but hid himself in a cupboard for thirteen days after the fall of Arnhem. He was a helicopter pilot, parachutist and at one time British national glider champion. He had commanded 22 SAS and 3 Div and amongst other activities had been injured to the point of death by rioters in Cyprus. He and Desmond, who had won the Sword of Honour at Sandhurst, were congenial travelling companions and I eventually got to the stage at which I resented seeing a plane in the sky without me in it. However, all good things come to an end and the resultant report did not recommend any change in our well-tried and funda-

mentally sensible and reasonable arrangements for co-operation between the army and the police in the homeland. The
exercise was not only valuable in affording an insight into
police methods elsewhere, it was also a welcome relief from
the mounting tensions at Scotland Yard.

*The Times* investigation had been lumbering on and a
number of others were in train. The Drugs Squad was the
subject of a number of allegations, a number of members
of the Flying Squad had been suspended and there was
continually increasing interest by the Press in the state of
the CID. It did not, of course, lack friends, but too much
was known to too many people about the situation and there
was a feneral feeling of uneasiness, like the calm before the
storm. I was not allowed to see the papers and was not
consulted by the commissioner or the assistant commissioner
(Crime) in any of these cases.

Some of the internal disagreements, though in themselves
petty, were cumulatively an indication of the state of affairs,
only possible because the force had operated so long as if
each department or branch was a separate entity with no
communal interests or loyalties. I was asked, for example,
by two very senior officers to quash the suspension of a
detective for alleged corruption on the ground that he was
a key witness in five or six criminal prosecutions. I not only
declined but asked the commissioner to consider obtaining
the consent of the Home Secretary to the enforced retirement
on pension of the two senior officers on the grounds of
general efficiency of the force, a procedure authorized by
the Police Pensions Regulations. He felt unable to agree.
The suspended officer was eventually sacked. His appeal to
the Secretary of State was dismissed. One incident, in
particular, annoyed me intensely. A Temporary Detective
Constable on an outer division had asked his own Detective
Chief Superintendent if he might buy a house about a mile
beyond the force boundary, where his mother particularly
wanted to live. The Chief Superintendent, who himself lived
about three miles over the boundary, assured him it would
be all right so he paid a deposit of £600 to a building society.

He then moved from single men's quarters to live with his mother only to be told by C department that he must move back into the Metropolitan Police district or face a charge of disobedience to force orders. He declined and the papers duly arrived on my desk with a demand that I issue the order or institute proceedings. The TDC was, of course, only a pawn in this particular game. The intention was to embarrass me. My reply was to mount a rapid survey of the number of uniformed and detective officers in the Met and in that particular division who were living over the force boundary with official permission. As I expected, there were scores, including many in the division to which the TDC belonged. I therefore replied rather tartly that I had no intention of following either course since the effect would inevitably be to bring discredit upon the administration of C department. By way of reply, C department transferred the young man back to uniform, which, in accordance with the system at that time, they were entitled to do. I therefore endorsed the file to the effect that I thought the young man had been treated unjustly and that should the opportunity occur, I would ensure that it was rectified. There was a sequel. On appointment as a commissioner designate, much later, I had the pleasure of offering the young man reinstatement in the CID, with seniority to count as if he had never left it. Greatly to my surprise, he accepted.

Relations with the CID reached an all time low as a result of a case involving a provincial force. Two Metropolitan detectives had arrested two men, both of whom had bad records, for breaking into premises outside London and stealing property worth several hundred pounds. They charged the two men and notified the provincial force who undertook to send two officers to court on the following day. When they arrived, they found that the charges against the two men had been withdrawn, the storekeeper to whom they were trying to sell the stolen goods having pleaded guilty to a charge of dishonest handling, a previous conviction for dishonesty not having been revealed to the court. Needless to say the two provincials were speechless with rage. Withdrawal from the court of a charge for an indictable offence requires the consent of the Director of Public Prosecutions and he had not been consulted. The provincial chief constable complained to the commissioner and an enquiry was mounted by CID, the deputy commissioner, of course, having no status in the matter because the allegation was of crime. The resultant report was a classic of its kind. The Metropolitan Police solicitor to whom I sent it described the report as so partisan as to be virtually worthless. No gloss favourable to the two Metropolitan officers had been omitted, however fatuous. He described the investigation as a travesty and said that the investigating officer had shown himself to be unfit to conduct any future investigation into allegations against police officers. He emphasized that if ever the report was disclosed to a court it would bring our system of investigation into contempt and went on in much the same vein. It is important to understand that he was not assuming corruption on the part of the two officers and that there might have been a satisfactory explanation for what they did. In the event neither they, nor anyone else, proffered one and the investigation was such as to pre-empt the possibility of criminal or even disciplinary proceedings. C department were asked to answer many pointed questions but replied immediately and simply with an assurance that there was no question of corruption. The investigating officer was even promoted from chief inspector to chief superintendent!

I thought this case so bad that I recommended to the commissioner in the strongest possible terms that it demanded executive action of the most stringent kind which only he could authorize. He declined to take any action and, in fact, a few days later, following my departure on leave, one of the two detectives was promoted! It was significant that following that decision one of the most senior officers in the CID remarked to Henry Hunt, 'I see your governor's been kicked under the carpet!' It was also noticeable that thereafter corruption in the CID seemed to run wild. I considered very carefully what I ought to do in the light of this particular case, which was the worst in the whole of my experience. Should I, in the public interest, put my duty to the commissioner on one side and go to the Home Secretary? If I did, what would be the likely result in view of the Home Office performance in *The Times* case? Should I have a showdown with the commissioner? What good would that achieve, since he had already disregarded overwhelming proof of the need for action? In the event, I decided to do neither, because I suddenly realized that the file was now a kind of time bomb which could blow Scotland Yard apart and that for the first time I was armed with a weapon with which to deal with the situation. I was to use it sooner than I thought.

Unknown to me *The Times* felt very strongly about the Metropolitan Police situation. It had quite properly had dealings with Frank Williamson and the team investigating its own allegations and knew that other newspapers in Fleet Street were showing a lively interest. No one but the chief managing editor, the editor and their closest colleagues will, I suppose, ever know the truth, but events were to make it possible for the informed observer to make an intelligent guess.

The election of a Conservative government had resulted in yet a further extension of one year for Waldron; Maudling quite understandably not wishing to decide the issue of his retirement on such brief acquaintance. *The Times*, however, must have had other ideas in mind. On 16 August 1971, the assistant editor and a senior reporter came to lunch at Scotland Yard and invited the assistant commisioner (Crime) to give an interview with the permission of the commissioner, who agreed. I was not invited to the pre-luncheon drinks and only joined the lunch when it was half-way through. That afternoon, I was asked on the telephone if I would lunch with *The Times*'s representatives and I agreed. On 19 August I fulfilled an engagement made weeks earlier lecturing at the Police College on 'Social Violence'. It had originally been written for the Royal College of Defence Studies and was adequate, but certainly not inspiring. *The Times* had been given an advance copy on request. It certainly did not deserve to be reprinted almost in full, taking up most of a page of *The Times* in the process. It seemed rather odd to me at the time but apart from feeling faintly pleased I thought no more about it. On 24 August, by way of sharp contrast, there appeared on the front page of *The Times* an interview with two anonymous senior Scotland Yard officers in which they freely criticized the judiciary, the Home Office, Parliament, Old Uncle Tom Cobley and all. For a day or two, of course, it got the usual reaction from the 'get tough' brigade until a little more careful thought suggested that it might be rather intemperate and not supportable by evidence. The interview was described as taking place in a red-carpeted office on the fifth floor of the Victoria Street building. They might as well have given the name of the assistant commissioner (Crime). All Fleet Street knew perfectly well that there is only one office fitting that description. If the intention was to underline for the public a sharp contrast between the lecture and the article it certainly succeeded. Whereas Fleet Street generally was having great fun and selling lots of newspapers speculating about a battle for succession at the Yard, *The Times* alone had appreciated that this was utter nonsense. I do not mean by that that I was assured of the commissionership. But what was quite certain was that if I were not to be appointed there was no question at all of the job going to anyone else at the Yard. The real issue, in which I suspect *The Times* was at one with the Home Office, was the need to bring the CID under proper control for the first time in nearly a hundred years. The Press generally followed up the story with zest not lessened by the arrest of some Flying Squad officers by officers of the Lancashire constabulary. The assistant commissioner (Crime) had departed abroad to an Interpol meeting and for a well-deserved holiday and was to be away for about six weeks. From the point of view of C department he could not have chosen a worse time for so long an absence. During that absence, in the course of a routine conference, the commissioner unintentionally opened the door through which so many of us wished to walk. Showing signs of despair at the continually increasing number of suspensions he said, 'What can the explanation be? It must be lack of supervision,' which enabled me to reply politely, 'Nothing of the kind. There isn't a person in this room, except perhaps the C department representative, who doesn't know perfectly well that the answer lies in the thoroughly unsatisfactory way in which the CID investigates allegations of crime against its own members. There is ample evidence on the files to prove this beyond doubt, one of the worst cases being . . .' (and here I cited the file I have mentioned earlier). The obvious agreement of the others in the room, with one expected exception, clearly shook him and he said, 'You are the *de facto* disciplinary authority. Why don't you do something about it?' To which I replied, 'Am I to understand that you are giving me the authority to devise, with my colleagues, a means of putting an end to all this?' To which he replied, 'Yes.' That was enough for me. With Jim Starritt, then assistant commissioner 'A', who probably knew as much about police wrongdoing as anyone in the force, Henry Hunt and Ray Anning, two of his senior officers, I could not have asked for more. Within ten days they had produced the blueprint of what was to become known as A10 and the commissioner had been sold the idea and taken it to Philip Allen for approval a day or so later. We all realized the importance of getting it off the ground before C department could recover its balance and when Allen told us that the Home Secretary was delighted with it we knew that at last we were going to get the tool with which to do the job.

But the birth was not to be without complications. The Home Office had very charitably allowed me to escape once again from the unpleasant atmosphere of the Yard by sending me off on a lecture tour of the United States and Canada at the request of the Foreign and Commonwealth Office. I set off with the comfortable feeling that on my return battle would be joined for the bringing of the CID under proper control. I should perhaps add briefly that the proposal for A10 contemplated a hand-picked team of officers drawn from both uniformed and detective branches and commanded initially by a senior uniformed officer. It was to operate under the Deputy Commissioner for twenty-four hours daily with supradepartmental authority and in particular would deal directly with all allegations of crime against members of the force. In other words, the century-old tradition was reversed. The CID were excluded from the investigation of crimes alleged to have been committed by police, unless, of course, the deputy commissioner decided that their assistance was necessary, in which case they operated under his authority. There was no doubt in my mind that the experience and wisdom of Starritt, Hunt and Anning had produced the ideal solution to the problem. There was also no doubt that the CID would fight it all the way. The autumn and winter looked like being exciting.

The lecture tour was exhausting but very enjoyable. It began with three days' briefing in New York, from where I progressed in reasonably easy stages to St Louis and Kansas City, Missouri, Minneapolis, Seattle, Pittsburgh, Washington and Atlanta. I was due thereafter to go on to Hartford, Connecticut, New York, Edmonton, Calgary, Montréal and Toronto. Alas, it was not to be. On arrival in Atlanta, which was an attractive place but a sad disillusionment for readers of *Gone with the Wind*, the desk clerk at the hotel handed me a 'guest telephone message' with an obsequious bow not in the American tradition of hotel desk clerks. The message, which I still have, read 'Ring Whitehall 8100 before 7 p.m. England time. Philip.' All was immediately clear and I said to the clerk, 'No, it's not that Philip.' In fact I waited until the morning until I rang Sir Philip Allen at the Home Office. He said, 'We think you have been away long enough. I've booked you a seat on the Saturday night flight from New York. Be on it. I'll phone your wife.' I felt distinctly aggrieved at being done out of my week in Canada, which I like, but I sensed that this was no time to argue and agreed. I managed to get to Hartford and finished my tour with a lecture to a large audience of uniformed policemen, all armed to the teeth, at the New York Police Academy. I then caught the plane home.

I went to the Yard on the Monday morning following my return expecting that I would be given some explanation for this sudden change of plan, but not a bit of it. A whole week passed before I was sent for by Maudling with Philip in attendance. His words did not remind me of the accession of the youthful Victoria. He merely said, 'Are you going to do this ruddy job for us?' or words to that effect. This time I said, 'Yes. But I am afraid I must ask you to accept one condition.' He said, 'What is that?' I replied, 'I must be given authority to switch assistant commissioners from one department to another.' He didn't ask for any explanation, he simply said, 'Done.' He then asked me who I wanted to replace me as a deputy and I replied without hesitation, 'John Hill.' And so it was agreed. This took place on 1 November and the formal announcement followed on the 3rd. All that remained, therefore, was for me to agree with my senior colleagues the changes we had in mind, get them agreed by the Home Office and sit tight.

Waldron had been given some latitude in choosing the date of his departure and he chose 16 April, for what reason I know not. This left me with about five months to survive in circumstances of considerable embarrassment, but at least the future was clear. It was marred only by one sad event. Frank Williamson, who had served with me in the Manchester force before becoming Chief Constable of Carlisle and then of Cumbria had suffered every conceivable frustration during the long drawn out *Times* enquiry. He was thoroughly disillusioned and depressed by continual disagreement with, and obstruction by, policemen who did not share his very high standard of personal and professional integrity. He therefore decided to resign notwithstanding the utmost persuasion by Philip Allen, Jimmy Waddell and Jimmy James, now the Receiver for the Metropolitan Police, not to leave a service to which he had devoted his life, as had his father before him. I did my best to dissuade him. He had considerable experience, exceptional ability and unquestioned integrity and his continued potential value to the police service was considerable. Moreover, all his battles were on the point of being won. He knew that the old guard were on the point of being swept away and that all the reforms he had in mind were in the immediate offing. But he had had enough, and it says much of the conditions under which we both laboured that a man of his calibre had reached such a point. He left the service at the end of the year, an honourable man unable to accept any longer the frustrations and difficulties militating against the fulfilment of the ideals for the police service in which he deeply believed.

# CHAPTER 9

# Commissioner

No one ever explained to me the reason for the unseemly haste of my return from America. One eventual suggestion was that the assistant commissioner (Crime) on returning from leave had dissuaded the commissioner from pursuing the creation of A10. Another was that one or two influential newspapers had decided in concert to demand a Royal Commission into the Metropolitan Police. I never discovered whether there was any substance in either story but I found it necessary early to make my views on A10 unmistakably clear. After about a month of uneasy peace as commissioner designate a file reached me en route from C department to the commissioner expressing willingness to discuss the formation of A10 'with a view to saving the time of CID officers'. This was just what I needed. I sent the file back through each assistant commissioner to the commissioner with a minute making it clear that A10 had nothing to do with saving anyone's time. It was a necessary innovation because no one had any confidence in the way in which C department investigated allegations of crime by its own members. More important, I made it plain that no one at any level of command, no matter how senior, would be allowed to obstruct the implementation of A10 in the spirit as well as in the letter. The message could hardly have been spelt out more clearly. Even the dumbest detective must have understood that if he was obstructive his days in the CID were numbered.

A number of vacancies in the senior ranks of the force occurred about this time and Waldron, who had not consulted me about anything to do with the force for a long time, thought it appropriate to make recommendations to the Home Office with a view to filling them. However, this was tactfully overcome by a gentlemen's agreement with the Home Office that I should be consulted informally before each was considered. In the event, however, the last few weeks of Waldron's reign were neither smooth nor relaxed. They were more like a minor Götterdämmerung. The Press were having great fun with continued headlines about dissension at the Yard, most of the stories being inaccurate or imaginary. Then the *People* splashed a story about the commander of the Flying Squad holidaying abroad with a Soho pornographer and their respective ladies. This inevitably led to a real showdown. The CID argument was that suspension would undermine CID morale, encourage criminals and do irreparable damage to the reputation of the force. Tell me the old, old story, in fact. My reply was that failure to suspend would confirm the public's worst suspicions and, whatever the outcome, was inevitable. It resulted in a final trial of strength between C department and me, with the unfortunate commissioner in the middle. But this time, as commissioner designate, I was not prepared to stand any nonsense and took such action as to leave the commissioner no choice but to suspend. Nine days later the assistant commissioner (Crime) went to hospital for observation having obviously suffered a long period of excessive strain. He never returned to duty, though we were all relieved to hear that there was nothing fundamentally wrong with him. The trouble was that he believed too many of his subordinates to be untainted by corruption or other wrongdoing. He was incapable of seeing or believing the failings of many of those on whom he relied for advice. He was, too, the inheritor of a tradition of solidarity which had been fostered by C department and some of the Press for their own ends. No one could possibly suggest that he was moved by other than proper motives. The assistant commissioner's misfortune was to be in office at a time when change was literally inevitable and to feel that it would be disloyal to subordinates to go along with it. I am not without sympathy for that view. I was to resign in similar circumstances five years later, though in my case, the predominant emotion was disillusion rather than resentment.

I assumed command of the force on 17 April 1972, having first agreed with the most senior officers, police and civilian, all the principal changes I had in mind after lengthy and helpful discussion with the Home Office. Looking back on that moment I realize that though my appreciation of the problems confronting me was basically correct it was also skeletal. In fact, it reminds me of a comment by a friend of mine that if we had been aware of the relative strength and weakness of Germany and Great Britain after the fall of France every sane instinct would have prompted immediate surrender. Unawareness of the truth, the resilience of the British in adversity, the incredible folly and incompetence of Hitler as a military leader, these and other unpredictable factors allowed our survival in circumstances in which there seemed initially little or no hope. Tackling the problems of the Met in 1972 was hardly to be compared with facing those of a European war, but from the point of view of those responsible for their solution seemed just as difficult on a minuscule scale. There was not only a lack of adequate co-ordination between police and civilian departments, there was longstanding and traditional ill-feeling between the CID and the uniformed branch to an extent unknown in any other British force. The uniformed policeman in London bears the brunt of violence, whether political, industrial, criminal or from hooliganism and he had long resented the airs and graces of the CID, generally known as 'the department'. The CID regarded itself as an elite body, higher paid by way of allowances and factually, fictionally and journalistically more glamorous. It also, unlike its provincial counterpart, enjoyed an immunity from external supervision and investigation.

This facilitated for many decades three kinds of wrongdoing. The first, institutional corruption, of a comparatively minor kind but affecting a significant minority of detectives, such as 'charging' for bail, suppressing additional and sometimes more serious charges and failing to bring previous

The Mark children and some friends. Robert Mark is sitting second from the right.

A Manchester street scene with a police box at the time the author joined the police.

1–6 The release of Sheila
Matthews: a surrendering
gunman helps his hostage to
safety, covered by an armed
police officer.

7 Spaghetti House siege,
September 1975.

8 The IRA bomb explosion at
the House of Commons, June
1974.

9 A Special Patrol Group
covering the Matthews's flat in
Balcombe Street.

1

4

7

8

Robert Mark with his wife and daughter outside Buckingham Palace, 15 February 1977.

Robert Mark's farewell speech at Central Hall, Westminster, 4 November 1976. The Home Secretary is on the author's right.

convictions to notice. Very often, the dubious cover for this kind of malpractice was 'the need to cultivate informers'. The second, more spectacular corruption affecting fewer but more specialized or senior officers, such as those concerned with major crimes like bank robbery, illegal drugs and obscene publications. The third, quite different, a widespread general acceptance that in London, at least, the system of justice is weighted so heavily in favour of the criminal and the defence lawyer that it can only be made to work by bending the rules. In fairness to the CID that view is not confined to them. Ever since Jeremy Bentham a variety of people without vested interest have been making similar suggestions. As an organization the CID was, and is, nevertheless professionally and technically highly competent and rightly proud of this. It also cannot be over emphasized that notwithstanding its defects it always contained a considerable number of thoroughly honest, dedicated and skilled detectives at every level and that the whole of Special Branch was never at any time involved in or suspected of this kind of wrongdoing. Few things in this world are simply black and white. The reputation of the good was sullied by the bad and the department as a whole was therefore distrusted by its own uniformed colleagues, the Metropolitan solicitor and his department, provincial police forces, the Home Office Inspectorate of Constabulary, by lawyers and by the Press. It is only fair to add that very few people in the department trusted many people in either of the latter two categories and too often with good reason. To pretend that this was not the general situation in the post-war years in London is nothing but hypocrisy. It was well enough known to lawyers, journalists, policemen and criminals but no one seemed anxious to rock the boat. There was a tendency to argue the need to 'set a thief to catch a thief', or that exposed wrongdoers were only 'the occasional rotten apple', the scarcity of exposure being hardly surprising in a system designed to prevent it. The relationship between the Press and the force as a whole was of mutual distrust and dislike sometimes amounting to hatred. The consequent denial of information to the Press encouraged clandestine association between crime reporters and detectives seeking favours either by way of image-building publicity or in more material form. There was no interchange between CID and the uniformed branch and the force had no sense of corporate identity. It is an eloquent comment on our communications industry, on our criminal justice and on the difference between the theory and reality of political control and accountability that the system should have survived as long as it did despite its fairly frequent crises and adverse publicity. To the world in general, and even to the Metropolitan Police, the words Scotland Yard imparted an aura in which they took pride. No one really wanted, or perhaps thought it possible, to separate fiction from reality. It had gone on for so long that everyone concerned tended to accept it as unchangeable and, in any case, better than anything that might replace it, much the same view, in fact, that many take of British justice and Parliamentary democracy.

No one could possibly doubt the need to preserve belief in, and support for, the desperately undermanned police force of a capital city which had long managed somehow to contain problems, ever increasing, some of them giving rise to public anxiety. The argument in favour of turning a blind eye to wrongdoing, or the closing of ranks in face of justified criticism was therefore only too easy to accept. Indeed, I suspect it was accepted by many honest policemen, lawyers and politicians who saw no solution that might not have disastrous consequences for the public as well as for the police. But one very important factor was overlooked for far too long. It was that this situation did not apply to the provincial police generally. I had served in two provincial police forces for thirty years and though I had known wrongdoing, I had never experienced institutionalized wrongdoing, blindness, arrogance and prejudice on anything like the scale accepted as routine in the Met. Clearly, therefore, the problem was not insoluble. It was one of cutting out a major cancer without killing the patient.

I might have been forgiven for thinking with Hamlet

> The time is out of joint: O cursed spite
> That ever I was born to set it right

but it was not like that at all. In the first place, in addition to Kenneth Parker, the Receiver, and Cappy Lane, the solicitor, I now knew well and had the solid support of many of the most senior officers, including John Hill, Jim Starritt, Colin Woods, Henry Hunt and others. Secondly, something like 90 per cent of the force, including a large part of the CID, and in particular the Joint Executive Committee of the Met branch of the Police Federation were as anxious for change as I was and were desperately keen to improve its tarnished image. Thirdly, I had the solid support and wise counsel of Jimmy Waddell and Philip Allen at the Home Office, who not only lent encouragement but protected my flank against interference by both politics or vested interest. With the Home Office, many senior colleagues, the Police Federation and the bulk of the force firmly behind me, there was no reason to doubt that radical changes could be made and would even be welcomed. They posed no constitutional or legal problems. But they did involve the abandonment of attitudes which had dominated the force for many years. They were also certain to impair vested interests, particularly those of the detective and the crime reporter, and thus were likely to be deliberately misrepresented to an already confused public. Paradoxically, the more wrongdoing brought to light, the more adverse publicity to be exploited by the supporters of the status quo. Much depended, therefore, not just on deciding and making the changes but on the way in which the need for them was explained to public and police alike. My last few days as deputy commissioner were therefore spent in careful consultation with the Home Office not so much about what to do but about how best to do it. The result was to rock the Met to its foundations, to enforce more significant change in five years than in the preceding century and to put the Met almost continually in the fore-front of the news.

# CHAPTER 10

# Putting Our House in Order

> If it were done when 'tis done,
> > then 'twere well
> It were done quickly
> > *Macbeth*

The overall strategy for which tactical planning was necessary was quite simple. First, our house was to be put in order firmly, quickly, ruthlessly but without undermining the confidence of the honest and dedicated detective required to run risks in the public interest. Second, to give the public the opportunity to satisfy itself of our willingness to be accountable and of the effectiveness of our corrective measures. Third, from experience of those measures to introduce changes in the system of selection, deployment and promotion so as to make institutional wrongdoing very difficult, almost certain of discovery and conviction and therefore much less likely to occur. Fourth, from the platform of our newly acquired respectability to gather evidence to enable us to satisfy the public of the need for change in other areas of the criminal justice system. Whilst all this was in progress it was essential to convince the whole force that they would be supported to the full in every incident in which they acted in good faith in the public interest and whether or not they made mistakes so long as they admitted them truthfully and readily.

Before the introduction of the tactical changes dictated by this strategy it was necessary to convince the force, policeman and civilian, that they now belonged to one corporate body under a system of management in which everyone had a voice. Full disclosure of information was to be obligatory at the highest level. Allocation of resources and priorities was to be agreed communally and complaints and suggestions from any level would be carefully considered. For this purpose a Policy Committee, recommended by the management consultants in 1968 but never set up, was introduced. It began to operate from my first week as commissioner and consisted of the six senior policemen and three senior civilians. It did not include representatives of specialist technical departments who were available as advisers. From its first meeting no major change in organization or policy was made by any departmental head without approval of the Policy Committee. Its decisions or proposals were communicated through force orders and orally at Commanders' conferences three times a year. Commanders were required to hold similar discussions with the representatives of the staff associations three times a year, and to complete the circle the staff association representatives met the Policy Committee with the same frequency. Far from being formal occasions, freedom of expression was encouraged and there rapidly evolved a feeling of communal participation in forward planning and in the running of the force.

Before all this could come about, however, the initial drastic changes agreed by the Policy Committee and approved by the Home Office – the surgeon's knife – had to be applied. A special meeting of the staff associations was convened at the Yard on Sunday, 23 April. I did not want the representatives of the force to be the last to know! On the following day, at a Press conference attended by well over a hundred journalists, the following changes were announced:

1. All detectives serving on divisions, about 2300 of the total CID complement of 3200, were placed forthwith under the command of the 23 uniformed divisional commanders for all purposes, including discipline and assessment for promotion.

It was the latter part of this order which was significant because although detectives would necessarily continue to have regard for measures against crime devised at the Yard, the divisional uniformed commander would be responsible for their implementation.

2. The four Area Detective Commanders at the Yard, who had hitherto exercised great power, were deployed to the offices of the four uniformed Deputy Assistant Commissioners who comprised the Force Inspectorate.

These officers, who had long exercised great influence over the CID as a whole, were thus deprived of operational command and were subject to the control of the Inspectorate in discharging advisory and supervisory duties.

3. Responsibility for the investigation of all complaints, *including allegations of crime*, was placed upon the Deputy Commissioner, who was given a newly created department, A10, commanded by Ray Anning of the uniformed branch and consisting of a hand picked team of CID and uniformed officers.

The branch operates 24 hours daily. Service in it is limited to two years, experienced members being deployed to divisions as uniformly as possible to 'spread the gospel'. All allegations of crime by police are passed initially only to A10. This put a sharp stop to forewarnings from the CID at the Yard to their colleagues outside that meetings between bent detectives and their potentials victims, usually criminals, were likely to be 'covered'. The arrest of detectives attempting routine extortion and blackmail rose sharply and the risks of such behaviour were quickly and effectively demonstrated.

4. It was announced that responsibility for dealing with pornography would be transferred from C to A depart-

ment as soon as the necessary arrangements could be made.

The advantage of this was only too plain. Responsibility was to be distributed over a much wider field, subject to very much closer supervision and allowing frequent and regular change of those assigned to this duty. Moreover any allegation or suggestion of harassment by police or of 'protection' would come under examination by the divisional uniformed commander.

5. In the longer term, plans were to be agreed with the staff associations for routine interchange between CID and uniform on a regular basis.

The intention behind this change is, of course, that within ten or fifteen years every divisional commander shall have had experience in both uniform and CID and thus be better able to control and supervise the activities of his divisional detectives. For the intelligent, it was obvious that the CID stood to gain more than anyone else from this change because their opportunities for promotion were to be extended to the uniform branch. On the other hand, the widened field of promotion was thought likely to attract better men to the CID, ambitious for ultimate promotion to intermediate and higher command. In fact, from 1 January 1977 every detective constable and detective sergeant who passes the competitive examination for promotion is posted to uniform duties with the opportunity to return to the CID after a minimum period.

Perhaps the most significant change in personnel was the appointment of Colin Woods, assistant commissioner (Traffic), to the post of assistant commissioner (Crime). An experienced uniformed officer of outstanding managerial skill, great determination and the moral courage to do the job without any previous detective experience, he proved quickly and not surprisingly to be the most efficient and effective head of C department in living memory before promotion to deputy commissioner four years later.

It has been suggested that these measures were not enough and in particular that provincial officers should have been filtered into the CID to provide a new element. The suggestion ignores insuperable practical difficulties. The London allowance at that time was a derisory £50 per annum and compulsory retirement ages for senior Metropolitan officers are much lower than in the provinces. In the absence of a national force, officers cannot be directed to serve in London, where, in any case, local knowledge would take some time to acquire. Advertisement of a post as senior as deputy assistant commissioner in 1975 produced one applicant from the provinces. No one in his right mind could at that time have been expected to move voluntarily from the provinces to London, bearing in mind the difference in the lot of the provincial and Metropolitan policeman and the inadequate financial recompense for the extraordinary vicissitudes of the latter. Enforced retirement at the point of highest earning capacity eight years before the provincial equivalent is hardly likely to be regarded as an inducement to transfer voluntarily to the Met.

These measures constituted the first tactical operation. They clearly had to be given time to take effect before the second operation to increase public accountability could be mounted. A little house cleaning, in fact. To the reader they may seem unremarkable. To the Met and much of the Press they were little short of sensational and were the subject of extensive articles and speculation. They were also bitterly opposed by some detectives and their journalist associates. Every kind of device was tried to mislead and alarm the public and diminish their acceptability. It made good headlines for a time, but got nowhere, largely because it was all much as expected. After a week or two I thought the time had come to dispel any lingering illusions. I asked Colin Woods to call the representatives of the CID together and went to see them. They thought they were in for a placatory discussion but they were wrong. I told them simply that they represented what had long been the most routinely corrupt organization in London, that nothing and no one would prevent me from putting an end to it and that if necessary I would put the whole of the CID back into uniform and make a fresh start. I also made it plain that I was not witch hunting. Anyone who henceforth did his duty honestly and efficiently had nothing to fear so long as evidence of past wrongdoing was not forthcoming. But woe betide anyone found doing wrong in future. I left them in no doubt that I thought bent detectives were a cancer in society, worse even than the criminals and some of the lawyers with whom we had to deal. I did not ask for questions. Having told them quite plainly what the situation was I left them in silence. Needless to say, my brief talk was taped on a recorder concealed in a briefcase, a ploy I had anticipated by considering with some care what I proposed to say. It was being hawked around Fleet Street the same afternoon, but surprisingly enough the effect was the opposite to that intended. It convinced the editors of the honesty of the intentions of the new management and we got a sympathetic reception from the Press generally. The message got over loud and clear. The century-old autonomy of the CID had ended.

This particular experience ended on a graceful note, when I received the letter from Jim Callaghan shown on p. 140.

During the next few months the impact of A10 was considerable. Suspensions from duty averaged about fifty and very few suspended officers ever resumed duty, least of all in the CID. In the meantime, the commander of the Flying Squad resigned rather than appear before a disciplinary board. A number of reputable senior officers retired on pension during this period, giving the mistaken impression of an enforced exodus. But, on the whole, the changes worked efficiently and fairly and were soon generally accepted, except of course by the corrupt. They attempted one or two rather fatuous counter measures by spreading false reports of disaffection, working to rule and even of my mental breakdown. One such effort in particular amused me. I was told that during my first attendance at the annual general meeting of the Met branch of the Police Federation in the Central Methodist Hall, Westminster, there would be a walk out or worse. Some humorist predicted a lynch mob! I went to it undeterred and, of course, nothing happened. I was not to know until a little later that one of the prime movers, who got cold feet when he sensed the favourable reaction of the audience, was expecting suspension for alleged corruption, rightly as it proved, and eventually decided on a change of career.

It did not take Colin Woods long to get a grip on C department. He had been given the toughest job and did it magnificently. He soon made it clear that C department headquarters was to undergo a radical review. I should mention that about this time I was astonished to find that the force had been in the habit of sending long, detailed reports in answer to complaints by the National Council for Civil Liberties, a small, self-appointed political pressure group with a misleading title. I ordered this to be stopped immediately and issued instructions that the NCCL were to receive the same courtesy and consideration as any ordinary private citizen, no more, no less. This was a widely popular move with both CID and uniformed branch alike. It is, of course, tempting for both politicians and public servants to accord organizations of this kind a status they do not deserve, because of the fondness of the Press for exploiting the news value of minority views. This tends to obscure the reality that they have no mandate from anyone and are usually trying to usurp the function of the democratically appointed agencies for the achievement of political or other change. During my time as commissioner I would have no truck with that or any other similar political pressure group.

Just as the furore over the initial changes was settling down, John Hill was appointed HM Chief Inspector of Constabulary. He was replaced as deputy commissioner by Jim Starritt. John had done an excellent job and was a natural for Chief Inspector. But Jim, too, was tailor made for his new job. A strict disciplinarian with a sharp and

**HOUSE OF COMMONS**
**LONDON SW1A 0AA**

3 May '72

Dear Commissioner,

Quick, Decisive, & Right!
All I hoped you would do.
Congratulations!

Jim Callaghan

pungent wit, he was a force 'character'. He had spent most of his time in central London, knew a lot about the villains of Soho and their backers and was a constant source of support and strength for Ray Anning. He was, in fact, ideally qualified to become the *de facto* disciplinary authority of the force and he was to perform his task energetically and with considerable distinction, gaining a well-deserved knighthood in the process.

In July, Reginald Maudling was replaced as Home Secretary by Robert Carr, with whom my relationship was to be no less cordial. By September, I felt ready for the second operation, the proposed increase in our public accountability for which the help of the Press was essential. This was a very difficult matter requiring careful handling if we were not to be suspected of currying favour or worse and it meant unilateral abandonment of longstanding prejudice.

I was fortunate enough to learn a valuable lesson in reaction to newspaper stories early in my time as a chief constable. A much loved doctor at Leicester had told a Rotary luncheon that he had allowed a patient with a painful terminal illness to die. He did not realize that the press were present and the following day there were massive headlines followed by demands that I should arrest him for murder! In something of a quandary I sought the advice of Toby Mathew, the Director of Public Prosecutions and will never, never forget his reply which read, 'It is not incumbent upon a chief officer of police to take formal notice of anything he may read in a newspaper.' It is not bad advice to have framed on the office wall.

On 15 September we invited all the principal editors to Scotland Yard: Press, radio and television. Thirty-seven of them responded. I told them that relations between the Press and the police had been appalling for as long as anyone could remember. They all agreed. I told them that 95 per cent of the fault was ours. Not surprisingly, they agreed with that also. I pointed out that since implementation of one of the management consultants' recommendations in 1968 we had an excellent Public Relations Department with a first-class Public Relations Officer, who was not allowed to meet the needs of the Press because of lack of co-operation from the force and direction or support from senior officers. I told them that as a unilateral matter of policy this was going to change dramatically. The force were to be instructed that information not subject to judicial restriction, the privacy of the individual or the security of the state could be released to the Press at police station level so long as it was factual. Matters of policy or its interpretation would remain the responsibility of the Public Relations Department or of senior officers at the Yard, who would, however, be authorized and encouraged to speak much more freely than in the past. Generally speaking, force policy was to change from 'Tell them only what you must' to 'Withhold only what you must'. Every member of the force was to be told that this reversal in longstanding policy would inevitably lead to mistakes and embarrassment, if not worse, but that no one need fear adverse consequences, if, having made an error of judgement in good faith he told the truth about it. In addition, taking a leaf out of the army's book in Ulster, training in the techniques of public interview would be given to members of the force at every level. I emphasized that this change in policy was not in expectation of any favours, such as restriction of adverse criticism or comment, and that in no circumstances would we withhold information which ought to be made generally available from a journalist or newspaper against whom we thought we had grounds for complaint. Nor did the policy mean that we accepted the Press at their own evaluation. It arose from my belief that the acceptability of the police in a free society depended, amongst other factors, on our willingness to be an accountable and open administration. A free and open relationship with the Press was, in my view, the best way to demonstrate this.

A similar meeting with representatives of the regional Press was held in November. The minutes of the meetings were circulated to the editors for comment and from the result a revised force-Press policy was drafted, put into effect and circulated with the agreement of the Home Office to every Member of Parliament by way of an appendix to my annual report. Looking back, I think this was one of the most important changes in my time at the Yard. It was full of risks and potential friction. It might have involved us in unpleasant situations with ministers, civil servants, Members of Parliament, the courts and private individuals. It was likely to be all the more difficult because of the healthily competitive nature of the Press. But in fact it was the only way to convince the Press and the public of the changing climate of police feeling and to gain public support. It succeeded beyond our most optimistic hopes and I must say that this was largely because the Press, whilst initially finding the change hard to believe, were obviously determined to give it a fair chance. There were occasional difficulties and disagreements, none of them insuperable, and relations between the force and the Press underwent a gradual but far-reaching transformation.

I feel bound to emphasize that the Home Office deserve much credit for agreeing the change to open administration, knowing, as they must have done, that some of the issues to be aired in public for the first time would be controversial, some would be opposed and some would, in any case, establish firmly the practice of police communicating direct to the public matters some of which had hitherto been regarded, rightly or wrongly, as more within the province of the Home Secretary, as policy authority for the metropolis, than the commissioner, as leader of the force. The effects, of course, were not felt immediately. Words and good intentions are one thing. Actions are another. But without any doubt relations between the force and the media were transformed to the benefit of both but, more importantly, to that of the public interest.

Whilst all this was going on, Colin Woods, in consultation with his colleagues, both CID and uniform, was drastically revising CID priorities, free from the constant worry of the fast dying friction between CID and uniformed branch. Some forms of serious crime, notably bank robbery, had got out of hand, and a concerted effort was needed to direct our combined resources to the best advantage. The arrest of one or two detectives, including a detective chief inspector, was making it clear to criminal and police alike that the change was here to stay and that the leaks which had for so long impeded our crime-fighting effort were soon to be plugged.

It is one of the more engaging aspects of the police job that whilst so much of extreme gravity is going on there is always some interesting sideshow to relieve the gloom. This was provided by a Mr Raymond Blackburn who applied unsuccessfully to the High Court for an Order of Mandamus directing me to enforce the laws relating to pornography. Five years earlier he had pursued a similar action against my predecessor in relation to gaming. That action lapsed when my predecessor withdrew an Order in relation to enforcement but did not vary his policy in any other way. This time I was determined to air the issue more fully. I arranged for the research necessary for an affidavit to satisfy the Court that the fault lay as much with unsatisfactory laws and pusillanimous courts as much as with the pusillanimous police to whom Lord Denning had referred in the case five years earlier. The application was dismissed by the High Court and Mr Blackburn appealed unsuccessfully to the Court of Appeal, where we were not allowed the costs to which I thought we were morally entitled. I had instructed the Metropolitan solicitor to take the case to the Lords, if necessary, because I felt that the accountability of chief officers through their police authorities to the Home Secretary, embodied in the Police Act 1964, was being overlooked and it seemed to me open to objection that a court should seek to direct a chief officer to prosecute matters in respect of which it might have to sit in judgement. However, this was not to be. I was looking forward, in the event of an Order being issued, to enquiring plaintively of the Court from which duties I was to withdraw police already swamped with burglaries and other crime to deal with this matter of seemingly such great public importance that it could be given precedence in a Court already weighed down with serious business. However, all's well that ends well, though it would have ended better if we had got our costs. But then, as we were to find years later in the Red Lion Square enquiry, courts are inclined to generosity in handing out public money, especially if the recipients are lawyers.

# CHAPTER 11

# Public Relations

In retrospect I suppose 1973 could be said to be the most critical year for the Metropolitan Police since the century began. The changes of 1972 were gradually beginning to show results. Two men were leaving the force prematurely every week as a direct result. Opinion within the force was slowly solidifying behind the new management and morale, if not high, was beginning to recover. All our problems – and there were many – were, however, aggravated by a steady and continuing loss of manpower, mostly because of insufficient pay and allowances. We suffered a net loss of 487 men and 26 women, a very serious situation for a force having to deal with 72,750 burglaries, 2680 robberies and 450 demonstrations during the year. Our total strength at the end of the year was 20,953 as compared with an authorized establishment of 26,055. Such manpower as could be attracted to the police in a competitive society was going to the provinces where the pay and allowances were much the same and the work was a great deal less arduous. If indeed the evolution of the Royal Navy and the army could be said to have been marked by lack of ministerial and Civil Service foresight it is perhaps not surprising that the police were not to escape the same fate. Unfortunately, however, we ourselves were as much to blame. Control of police pay did not pass to government until the Police Act of 1919 and exploitation of policemen by the many local police authorities before that Act prompted the Police Federation, created by the Act, to regard a uniform rate of pay throughout the country as being of paramount importance. They did not, until many years later, appreciate that their insistence should have been on a minimum *basic* rate of pay, augmented to attract manpower to the areas where it was most needed.

Pay and conditions of service are negotiated by the Police Council, on which the government, local police authorities and police are represented. But the council bears no responsibility for the efficient policing of Great Britain. That is placed squarely upon the Home Secretary by the Police Act of 1964. No Home Secretary has so far thought it necessary in the public interest to overrule the Police Council but there is no doubt that the justification for doing so is long-lasting. On 9 August 1966, whilst Chief Constable of Leicester, when I had no idea that I would one day serve in London, I had argued in *The Times* that policemen should be paid most where they are most needed. In fact, when, after bitter dissension, a London allowance was agreed, it was fixed at £10 per annum, a very bad joke indeed. I commented to the Federation that it was like inviting a man to dinner and giving him bread and water. It was later increased to £50, augmented by a small 'undermanning allowance' and in 1973 increased to £74. The achievement of a meaningful London allowance was therefore of great importance, not just to obtain the rate for the job, but to show the force that the management was willing to stand up and fight for it rather than leave that kind of thing to the Federation which could scarcely be expected to achieve a result satisfactory to London against the opposition of their provincial colleagues, who enjoyed a majority on the Joint Central Committee, the national representative body. To make matters worse, there was a steady flow of young policemen who, after being trained in the Met, realized that they could transfer to the provinces without loss of seniority or pension rights and work where the grass is greener, where living conditions were pleasanter and, in particular, where their children would not have to attend the schools of Inner London.

It did not take me long to appreciate that the only way to win was to go over the heads of the politicians and the Civil Service and appeal to public opinion in moderate and persuasive terms, backed up by irrefutable statistical evidence. Kenneth Parker, the Receiver, brought the full weight of his considerable intellect to this particular cause and was more than anyone else responsible for a partial victory, an increase of £201, in the following year. Henry Hunt gave him stout support during this battle. I suspect, too, that the civil servants at the Home Office were far from unsympathetic. They had already devised of their own initiative a skilful means of increasing the tax-free rent allowance, to which all policemen are entitled if they do not live on police premises, without breaking the pay code then in existence for everyone. Owing to the complexity of the situation and the need to avoid even the suspicion of privileged treatment, the change was introduced so quietly that they never got the credit for this considerable achievement, which I gladly, though belatedly, acknowledge.

Increased remuneration was therefore a principal administrative preoccupation during the year. No less important was preparation for the third part of the initial plan, to begin to persuade the public of the difference between fictional and real police work. Throughout the year for this purpose I worked on the Dimbleby Lecture to be given in November, seeking advice and reaction and consulting many people, including lawyers and legal executives. But I will deal more fully with that topic later. I mention it now only to explain that whilst staving off difficulties such as arrests of police for wrongdoing, publicity arising from allegations by James Humphreys, the pornographer, and accusations of colour prejudice, we were coincidentally preparing, if I may use a thoroughly inappropriate analogy, to carry the war to the enemy and express our own views direct to the public itself.

In March, the first four major London car bombs were planted by the IRA, a particularly big one being left outside Scotland Yard. Fortunately, there was a rail strike and it needed no genius to guess that the bombers would use Heathrow or Gatwick to return home. This they obligingly did and were duly put in the bag.

The bomb outside Scotland Yard had been spotted by the same two constables of the special patrol group who had been involved in an incident at India House a few weeks earlier. This was the kind of tragic mishap it is impossible to foresee. Three Pakistani youths armed with a cutlass and imitation firearms burst into the Indian High Commission, slashed one person across the throat, made others lie on the floor and terrified the occupants. The special patrol group on arrival were greeted by what seemed to be a terrorist outrage. They entered the building, fired warning shots, called unsuccessfully on the youths to surrender and then shot two of them dead. It was only then that they discovered that their firearms were imitation. There was only one possible thing to do. Tell the truth and tell it quickly. This we did, and although the Press were sympathetic, it did not lessen our genuine regret and sadness at our unwitting part in this tragedy. The two constables, in particular, were much affected by it.

In April the CID began a major breakthrough against bank robbers and began a series of arrests which was to lead to a 60 per cent fall in the annual number of bank robberies. The Flying Squad, No. 9 Regional Crime Squad and the Robbery Squad, brought under one command, began to achieve very encouraging results against what the Yard calls 'top class villains' and morale rose steadily.

The year was marked also by a second Cause for Concern, this time by the Runnymede Trust, whose objectives include the promotion of good race relations, but who published a report by a Dr Stanislaus Pullee on police relations with the immigrant community in Ealing which they knew to contain inaccuracies, to be misleading and quite certain to provoke racial disharmony. I offered the trustees a detailed list of proved inaccuracies which they declined to accept. With their agreement, I then went through the Report with them, page by page, pointing out the errors and unjustifiable assumptions. It made no difference. They went ahead with publication some months later. On this occasion, however, we did not turn the other cheek. We issued a statement

149

pointing out the inaccuracies and making it clear that whilst the Report might contain a little that was worthwhile it was mostly tendentious and harmful nonsense. I suppose that the trouble was that the Trust, having commissioned the Report, felt in a difficult position in that to back down might have been thought a breach of faith on their part by the coloured community. However, the Report did us no harm, if only because we gave our evidence to the Press and told them to judge for themselves. Of course, the ethnic Press, *Time Out* and that kind of periodical made the most of it, but from our point of view that was not a bad thing. With critics like that you hardly need friends! Relations with the Trust were a little strained for a time but were happily to be improved later. The Report did, however, illustrate the continual dangers facing those engaged in the race relations industry of jumping to conclusions before considering all the evidence. In fairness, I must say that the police have not always been as willing as they were on this occasion to produce the evidence which they alone have. There has long been a tendency, now happily diminishing, to regard the race relations industry as interfering busybodies. Whilst this was true of some, it was certainly not true of all. Proper liaison, not polarization, is the only sensible path to tread in that particular field.

A significant event during the year was the arrest of the pornographer, James Humphreys, in Holland. He was arrested by us, not the Dutch police, and a long drawn out extradition process followed. In the meantime, of course, his wife was able to extract maximum Press publicity for his revelations and allegations, both real and otherwise, about police corruption in Soho. The difficulty was that without real evidence, which was not likely to be forthcoming without a conviction and custodial sentence, there was not a great deal we could do other than to bring him to court with, we thought at the time, not a very optimistic prospect before us. However, Fleet Street generally was aware of the extent of the cleaning up process within the force and was rather considerate about the Humphreys affair. Publicity, though occasionally lurid, did not lessen growing public confidence in the force or harm our relationship with the Press. Indeed, before the end of the year I was rather touched and encouraged to be invited as guest of honour to a rather splendid lunch given by Lord Thomson in the editorial boardroom of the *Times* newspapers. A number of distinguished outsiders were there and it was made quite clear that this was not so much a burying of the hatchet following the notorious *Times* case, as a spontaneous demonstration of trust and goodwill.

All in all, it was a year of consolidating change, of withstanding occasional shocks and public pressure, but also of gradually mounting public sympathy arising from our success in catching the bombers, our obvious willingness to deal effectively with our own wrongdoers and our successful containment of political demonstrations and industrial disputes. By the end of the year we were making progress and by a fortunate coincidence the opportunity to give the Dimbleby Lecture on BBC television allowed me to explain to the British public for the first time what policing London is all about. The event was to cause shock waves which have not yet subsided.

CHAPTER 12

# Criminal Law and Crooked Lawyers

On 3 January 1973, during the course of a routine lunch with Charles Curran, Director-General of the BBC, and some of his senior colleagues I remarked plaintively that it was a pity that so much of the television screen was given up to fictional police activities, Dixon, Z Cars and their American counterparts, whilst no space at all was devoted to the reality of policing, which was now arguably one of the most important social activities in this country. On 26 January, whether as a result of that remark or not I do' not know, I received a letter from Eddie Mirzoeff of the BBC inviting me to give the Dimbleby Memorial Lecture in the autumn. I pondered this awhile and decided I would like to do it. It occurred to me, however, that my feelings might not be shared by the Home Office, or indeed, by anyone else. The relationship between the commissioner and the Home Office, or, in particular, with the Home Secretary, is an odd one. The commissioner is appointed by the sovereign on the recommendation of the Home Secretary and on appointment ceases to be a policeman. He loses all his police powers and in my day was sworn in as an *ex officio* justice of the peace for London and all the surrounding counties. The latter no longer applies since Lord Hailsham persuaded Parliament to abolish all *ex officio* justices, other than aldermen of the City of London, who, of course, were sacrosanct. The commissioner controls the force by virtue of the Metropolitan Police Act 1929, as amended, and not being a police officer enjoys no security of tenure, unlike provincial chief constables who enjoy a measure of protection from arbitrary dismissal under the Police Act 1964. Dismissal for any reason would, however, be likely to attract the attention of Parliament, but if the Home Secretary felt that he was on strong enough ground there is no doubt at all of his right to dismiss the commissioner if he thinks fit. The commissioner's orders for the *administration* of the force are, too, subject to the approbation of the Home Secretary, though in practice such approval is rarely sought. *Operationally*, however, the commissioner, like a chief constable, is not subject to orders from anyone. His freedom in his operational role, in other words, is matched by his unusually high degree of accountability.

Far from disagreeing with this, I think the balance is absolutely right. The commissioner commands an enormous organization of some 36,000 people requiring an annual budget not far short of £300 m yearly and including a number of men trained in the use of firearms. It is right in a democratic society that someone in a position of such power should be the most accountable of all chief police officers. Nevertheless, it occasionally poses some nice problems. The commissioner is not a civil servant. He has a right, indeed a duty, to speak out on behalf of his men even though what he has to say may not be entirely to the liking of those to whom he is accountable. He cannot lead his force successfully without being aware of, and willing to exercise, that right. Furthermore, he must be strictly non-political. His operational actions must never be thought to reflect the wishes of the government in power, as distinct from his own professional judgement. It is really a question of rendering unto Caesar, or, in this case, the Home Secretary, whilst jealously preserving the independence of the police, essential if they are to enjoy the respect of men of all political beliefs. I never found this difficult, but, of course, I was reared for thirty years in the provincial tradition of greater independence still. In no other force, for example, are the administrative orders of the chief officer subject to the approval of the police authority. When, therefore, I became commissioner I had no intention of surrendering the freedom to express myself publicly on matters within my province if I thought that the interests of the force or the public required it. I am bound to say that in this attitude I received the most generous consideration from all the four Home Secretaries under whom I served, although at times I have no doubt they could each have wished me elsewhere. Commenting bluntly, for example, on the disgraceful failure of every government since the war to attempt a rational distribution of police manpower can hardly have enhanced my popularity. Yet it needed saying and the word disgraceful is far from inappropriate.

On many issues, of course, it was better to make representations privately. Only in the last resort was it really desirable to push one's luck at the risk of rocking the political boat. There was, however, one golden rule from which I never departed. Although I might voice criticism or urge unpopular policies, never in any circumstances would I do anything clandestine. If I intended to say something publicly or privately that I thought likely to displease the minister I always gave him forewarning. There might on occasions, therefore, be disagreement, but never distrust. When, for example, the Police Bill was published in 1976 I made it clear that I would oppose it in every way open to me and would go rather than administer it. On reflection, I erred in not making the reasons for my opposition public until it was too late.

When, therefore, the invitation to give the Dimbleby Lecture arrived I thought it only right that the BBC should address themselves to the Home Secretary rather than to me and told them so. A little later the BBC wrote to say that the Home Secretary had agreed, so the way was clear. From my point of view it could not have come at a better time. Public ignorance about the policing of Great Britain is appalling and the metropolitan force, after so many shocks, was in some doubt about its role. I therefore went to some trouble in preparing the lecture. I consulted some of our fifty lawyers, the chief legal executive for the Met at the Central Criminal Court. I sought the opinions of the senior detectives I trusted. I consulted outsiders, including a barrister. I read carefully, not the least helpful article being a brilliant lecture by Lord Cross of Chelsea. I then wrote the lecture, circulated it for critical opinion and took careful notes of the replies. I realized that never again in my life would I be able to talk to so large an audience, which was in the event estimated to be 8·8 per cent of the adult population of the United Kingdom, without censorship or subediting. It was therefore essential to be accurate, moderate, intelligible, but above all, fair.

I gave the lecture at the BBC Television Centre before an invited audience on the evening of Saturday, 3 November, and was not in the least surprised to be heckled by two barristers from the front row. They were noticeably less displeased when I passed from the subject of bent lawyers, about whom I was perhaps excessively mild, to that of bent detectives about whom I was brutally frank. I realized by the end of the evening that the public showing on the following Tuesday evening would cause a furore, and I was not mistaken. The outraged spokesmen for the legal trade unions were on the air almost before the lecture finished. The most interesting aspect, to me, was that although the lecture contained a logical sequence of very important issues they were all disregarded by Press and commentators alike. It was not so much that someone had said there were crooked lawyers. After all, Dickens and others had done that already. It was that a policeman should have the unspeakable temerity to do so. Looking back on the week that followed I cannot recall so many people making such idiots of themselves publicly in so short a time over one issue.

Whatever the lawyers may have felt about it – and I received some generous and encouraging letters from quite a lot of them, including judges, barristers and solicitors – was as nothing to the effect on the police. It is not too much to say that whatever reservations remained in the Met CID were dispelled overnight. I really had no idea how much some of the criminal lawyers in London were disliked and distrusted by the police and it did not take me long to realize that this did not always arise from malpractice on the part of the lawyer, who was often only doing his job, sometimes with his heart not very much in it, but was the price inevitably to be paid for the adversary system of which the policeman is too often the victim. Of course, as I said earlier, few things are simply black and white. I had made it clear that the CID was every bit as bad as the minority of lawyers I was describing, but the CID did not resent those comments. They knew perfectly well that they were true. The same reaction was hardly likely to be expected of lawyers. Speaking seven months later in a lecture, no less a legal luminary than Lord Salmon said, 'I cannot think why Sir Robert thought it worthwhile to make an allusion to the small minority of criminal lawyers whom he vividly described as dishonestly inventing spurious defences and alibis for their clients, suborning witnesses and doing very well out of highly paid forensic trickery.' To which *The Times* in a leader on 28 June replied succinctly, 'There is a very simple reason. It is true.'

The real truth of course is that our besetting national sin of complacency is seen at its worst in our attitude towards criminal justice, largely because so few people know anything about it and we all want to believe that it is as good as we are told by those who have a powerful vested interest in maintaining the status quo.

The Dimbleby Lecture was the first occasion on which a senior policeman had publicly voiced at length comment about the reality of criminal justice in London. It was not unlike opening Pandora's Box. Public reaction was so intense that it continued to attract heavy Press coverage for a week. I received literally hundreds of letters and had to set up a special team of typists to deal with them. Apart from the inevitable number of cranks and mentally unbalanced writers, or people who had a personal axe to grind because of some grievance, real or imagined, against the law, they were about 99 per cent pro and about 1 per cent anti. I had obviously touched on a very sensitive public nerve. The police as a service and the Met as a force were clearly delighted that someone had broken the traditional silence which for so long had made things easy for their traducers.

Some of the more significant themes are I think worth repeating, especially since the original lecture sold out and is now out of print. Moreover, nothing has really changed since it was given. The same corrupt practices continue and no satisfactory machinery exists to prevent them. Only the police have made progress in preventing or dealing with the wrongdoing of which the lecture accused them. The other participants in the criminal justice process are only too willing to let sleeping dogs lie.

One of the first controversial points was on the power of the police. During the lecture I said:

> Power is an emotive word, particularly in relation to the police. It suggests a right to punish at will, free from effective control. In fact, of course, we have no such power. Our development has always been conditioned by two conflicting needs. One to maintain order and protect people, the other to ensure that we ourselves do not act unreasonably or oppressively. For this reason the police have always remained few in number and answerable to the general law. We have no special immunities. A policeman who breaks the law is prosecuted and punished just like anyone else. The only power we possess is the power to inconvenience by bringing people before the courts, and even then we are at risk if we use that power improperly, or unfairly. The fact that the British police are answerable to the law, that we act on behalf of the community and not under the mantle of Government, makes us the least powerful, the most accountable and therefore the most acceptable police in the world.

This view has been repeatedly attacked by, amongst others, Lord Gardiner, the former Lord Chancellor, who favours the idea of a national police force accountable to a minister and has on several occasions described the British police as being the most powerful and the least accountable in the world. I have never been able to discern the evidence or logic which could give such an assertion even momentary credibility. The most essential factors governing the relationship between police and public in Britain are the limitation of police powers under the law, their high degree of accountability, unequalled anywhere else in the world and most important of all the confident awareness of the public that the police are politically independent in that they serve the people collectively and are not influenced in their operational decisions by any minister, political party or pressure group. I do not mean to give offence when I assert that in matters of public order, demonstrations, political, industrial or racial, the public trust the police a great deal more than politicians in government or opposition and I think it significant that all the Home Secretaries I have known have been only too glad to disclaim any responsibility for police operational actions in that sphere. Contrast that for a moment with the situation in those countries with a national police force and any momentary attraction which Lord Gardiner's suggestion might have is soon dispelled. Of course, if the intention is to undermine the independence of the police and make them a tool of government, that is another matter but I hardly think that idea would have much appeal either for police or public. At the very least, its implementation would produce a very different kind of police force from the present one.

A second theme was, I think, no less important because it outlined a glaring failure in the process of making laws, which, if anything, has got worse rather than better, since the lecture was given.

Of all the problems with which the police have to contend, undoubtedly the most continuous is the prevention and investigation of crime. But you must remember that this is only one part of our system of criminal justice. You should think of it as having four successive stages. First comes the enactment by Parliament of the criminal laws, secondly the task of the police to enforce them. The third stage is the criminal trial, where the question of guilt is decided. Finally, there is the problem of what to do with the guilty. Each of these four stages has usually been considered in isolation. Each tends to be the province of a different group of people. Politicians make the laws, police enforce them, lawyers run the trials, and the prison or probation services deal with the convicted offenders. None of these groups is obliged to give much thought to the problems of the others or to consider the working of the system as a whole.

Now this is unfortunate because the different parts of the system are intimately connected. It's no good Parliament passing laws if the police can't enforce them. There's no point in catching criminals if the system of trial is so inefficient that it lets them go free. Savage punishments serve no purpose if very few offenders are actually caught and punished. Equally, Parliament and the police are wasting their time if penalties are so small that it pays people to go on offending. Put like that you may think these points self-evident, but in practice, people often fail to make the necessary connection. That's why I'm going to have quite a lot to say (and I ought to make it clear that I am saying it on my own responsibility) about aspects of justice which you may think are strictly not the business of the police – the criminal law, the system of trial and the question of punishment.

There is still no machinery to correct this deficiency. It is true that the views of the police are sought through the Association of Chief Police Officers but it is no less true that they can be, and are, safely disregarded if they do not accord with ministerial wishes, since the legislators can rely upon the traditional silence of the police. The unwillingness of police chiefs to make their views public means that the staff associations, the Police Federation and the Superintendents Association rush gladly into the breach and express views to the Press or on radio or television on matters of which they have no experience or knowledge and for which they have no responsibility. Much harm has been done in recent years to the police image by irresponsible and ill-informed comment by police spokesmen whose only real concern is with the negotiation of pay and conditions of service and who, in many cases, have not had any practical experience of police work for many years. Thus issues like complaints, bail, terrorism and the death penalty are discussed in public by those who are in fact the least qualified or competent to express an informed view whilst the chief officers remain silent for fear of departing from a tradition of questionable value. The police know more than anyone about the practical application of the law and whilst their views should not necessarily be given undue weight they ought to be known.

One interesting example of the need for this arose when Michael Foot produced his original proposals to amend the law on picketing. The intention was to give pickets the right to stop vehicle drivers or to require the police to do that for them. I told Jimmy Waddell in no uncertain terms that if there was any danger of this proposal reaching the statute book I would declare in *The Times* that this was an unjustifiable infringement of individual liberty and an inexcusable requirement for the police to abandon the impartiality in industrial disputes to which they had always been dedicated. We were fortunate indeed in our Home Secretary, Roy Jenkins. He clearly must have shared our feelings to some extent because the Home Office arranged a meeting between representatives of all chief officers and Michael Foot's senior civil servants at which we left them in no doubt that the proposals would be publicly opposed by every chief officer. Happily, they were abandoned and no harm was done. But the prospect caused every senior policeman to reflect on the differing interpretation of freedom. To some of us, the Shrewsbury pickets had committed the worst of all crimes, worse even than murder, the attempt to achieve an industrial or political objective by criminal violence, the very conduct, in fact, which helped to bring the National Socialist German Workers Party to power in 1933. Murder usually involves the death of only one person, which is bad enough. But conduct of that kind kills freedom, and there are still people who feel that freedom is more important than life itself.

No one disputes the right of the party in power to push through its own legislation, but it is certainly arguable that all the relevent facts and factors, even the unpopular ones, should be known before the decision is made. The likelihood of this is still far too uncertain. Concealment is not always the tactic. Mere failure to do the necessary research, as with the Police Bill and the Bail Bill, is all that is necessary to ensure a comparatively easy ride. When the Prime Minister told the House that the Police Bill was the will of Parliament he tactfully omitted to mention that if every member of the House was compelled to sit an examination paper consisting of ten simple questions about the working of the police disciplinary system and the pass mark was set as low as 20 per cent not 5 per cent of them would be likely to pass. So much for the will of Parliament!

The third theme was predictably likely to stir up the liveliest controversy because it offered a realistic view by someone other than a lawyer about the process of criminal justice.

The object of a trial is to decide whether the prosecution has proved guilt. It is, of course, right that in a serious criminal case the burden of proof should be upon the prosecution. But in trying to discharge that burden the prosecution has to act within a complicated framework of rules which were designed to give every advantage to the defence. The prosecution has to give the defence advance notice of the whole of its case, but the accused, unless he wants to raise an alibi, can keep his a secret until the actual trial. When the police interrogate a suspect or charge him they have to keep reminding him that he need not say anything. If he has a criminal record the jury are not ordinarily allowed to know about it. Most of these rules are very old. They date from a time when, incredible as it may seem, an accused person was not allowed to give evidence in his own defence, when most accused were ignorant and illiterate. There was no legal aid and, perhaps most important, if someone was convicted he would most likely be hanged or transported. Under these conditions it's not surprising that the judges who made the rules were concerned to give the accused every possible protection. But it is, to say the least, arguable that the same rules are not suited to the trial of an experienced criminal, using skilled legal assistance, in the late twentieth century.

The criminal and his lawyers take every advantage of these technical rules. Every effort is made to find some procedural mistake which will allow the wrongdoer to slip through the net. If the prosecution evidence is strong the defence frequently resorts to attacks on prosecution witnesses, particularly if they are policemen. They will be accused as a matter of routine of perjury, planting evidence, intimidation or violence. What other defence is there, when found in possession of drugs, explosives or firearms, than to say they were planted? Lies of this kind are a normal form of defence, but they are sure to be given extensive publicity. In many criminal trials the deciding factor is not the actual evidence but the contest between a skilled advocate and a policeman or other witness under this kind of attack, often part of what Lord Devlin calls 'The world of fantasy created by a defence counsel at a loss for anything better to do on behalf of his client.'

The advocates for the defence are, for the most part, only doing their job. They are there to get their client off. In a hopeless or unpopular case this can be a distasteful task. To be a criminal lawyer needs professional knowledge, integrity and, when acting for the defence, moral courage. Whatever his personal feelings about the case the lawyer must devote himself to the cause of his client with all the persuasion and skill at his command. At the same time he also owes a duty to the cause of justice and the ethics of his profession. He must not put forward a defence which he knows to be false. It is not for a defence lawyer to judge his client's case. However unlikely his story may sound he is entitled to have it heard. But it's a different matter for an advocate to say things which he knows to be deliberate lies. To do this is not to take part in the administration of justice but to help to defeat it. Most lawyers observe very high standards. They manage to serve both their clients' and the public interest honourably and well. So much so that most of them tend to be frankly incredulous when it is suggested that there are some other lawyers who do not. The kind of behaviour I have in mind is often easy for the police to recognize but almost impossible to prove.

I cannot obviously discuss identifiable cases, but I can describe the practices I mean.

We see the same lawyers producing, off the peg, the same kind of defence for different clients. Prosecution witnesses suddenly and inexplicably change their minds. Defences are concocted far beyond the intellectual capacity of the accused. False alibis are put forward. Extraneous issues damaging to police credibility are introduced. All these are part of the stock in trade of a small minority of criminal lawyers. The truth is that some trials of deliberate crimes for profit – robbery, burglary and so on – involve a sordid, bitter struggle of wits and tactics between the detective and the lawyer. Public accusations of misconduct, however, have always been one-sided, with the result that doubts about the criminal trial mostly centre upon police conduct, as if the police alone had a motive for improper behaviour. Let there be no doubt that a minority of criminal lawyers do very well from the proceeds of crime. A reputation for success, achieved by persistent lack of scruple in the defence of the most disreputable, soon attracts other clients who see little hope of acquittal in any other way. Experienced and respected metropolitan detectives can identify lawyers in criminal practice who are more harmful to society than the clients they represent.

A conviction said to result from perjury or wrongdoing by police rightly causes a public outcry. Acquittal, no matter how blatantly perverse, never does, even if brought about by highly-paid forensic trickery. Of course I speak in general terms. I would like to be more specific but for obvious reasons I cannot. I'm conscious too that people who make general accusations can be said to be willing to wound and yet afraid to strike. This doesn't mean that such general accusations ought not sometimes to be made. They are often made against the police, no doubt for similar reasons, nor are they always without substance.

I ought perhaps to give you two examples to illustrate what I mean. The first is a form of questioning to smear a member of the Flying Squad of unblemished character giving evidence in a strong case. 'Are you a member of the Flying Squad? And is it not a fact that four or more members of that Squad are presently suspended on suspicion of corruption?' Before the Judge can intervene the damage is done. The Jury is influenced by the smear in direct contravention of the principles governing the criminal trial. That kind of theme is played extensively and with infinite variations.

The second example is what Conan Doyle would have called 'the Curious Case of the Bingo Register'. This was a case in which a hardened criminal burgled a flat and wounded one of the elderly occupants very badly. He was identified, arrested, denied the offences and was remanded to prison. A month after committal for trial his solicitor disclosed an alibi defence which suggested that he was playing bingo at a club on the night of the offence and had signed the visitors' book. Enquiry showed that the prisoner had actually signed the book at the foot of the relevant page but that unfortunately for him the two preceding and the two following signatures were those of people with different surnames who had visited the club in one group and signed the book together. The signature could, therefore, only have been entered later and, it would seem, must have been written in prison. The prosecution notified the defence of their findings. Defence counsel thereupon withdrew from the case, as indeed did the instructing solicitor. The prisoner, on the advice of his new solicitor and counsel, pleaded 'guilty' and the matter rested there. It was not, of course, possible to prove who had taken the visitors' book to prison, although the prison authorities pointed out drily that only a visit by a lawyer or his clerk would be unsupervised and such visits had occurred. This was, in fact, a painstaking attempt to establish a false alibi for a dangerous persistent criminal. The police looked upon the case as remarkable only in that they were able to prove the falsity of the alibi.

Needless to say these comments to an audience of several million people provoked a vociferous reaction none of which was quite so much to the point as a series of imaginary letters from lawyers written by Bernard Levin in *The Times*, which were not only very funny but which must have caused as much displeasure as the original lecture. The whole incident was most instructive. The pompous, self-justifying nonsense that swamped the radio, television and the newspapers probably did more than the lecture itself to convince millions of people that there really was cause for concern, as, indeed, there still is. The reaction of my own solicitors at the Yard was perhaps the most amusing, if the most cynical. Their general attitude was, 'What's the matter? Did you get cold feet?'

Looking back, however, I am sure I made a tactical error in not dealing with the subject of bent policemen before that of bent lawyers. So incensed were some members of the legal profession that they failed altogether to notice that I had some very harsh things to say about dishonest policemen. I put it like this:

Because of its technicality and its uncertainty, the criminal trial has come to be regarded as a game of skill and chance in which the rules are binding on one side only. It is hardly surprising that a policeman's belief in its fairness should decline as he gathers experience, or that he should be tempted to depart from the rules. The detective is the person most affected because it is he who regularly bears the brunt of the trial process. In theory he's devoted only to the cause of justice. He likes to think of himself as having no personal interest in acquittal, conviction or sentence and that his career is not affected

165

by the outcome of his cases. In practice this is a gross over-simplification. Most detectives have a strong sense of commitment. It would be unnatural if they did not feel personally involved in some of their cases and it would be untrue to suggest that they are not sometimes outraged by the results. All are under occasional temptation to bend the rules to convict those whom they believe to be guilty, if only because convention has always inhibited them from saying how badly they think those rules work. A few may sometimes be tempted also to exploit the system for personal gain. A detective who finds general acceptance of a system which protects the wrongdoer can come to think that if crime seems to pay for everyone else, why not for him? The next step may be to demand money for not opposing bail, for not preferring charges, for omitting serious charges, for a share in the stolen property, and so on. Not many, even of those who regard the system with cynical disillusion, give way to that kind of temptation, but it's no help to pretend that it doesn't happen. As a policeman I believe in the virtue of confession for ourselves no less than for our customers. In the past we have paid heavily and unnecessarily in loss of public confidence by trying to conceal or minimize the wrongdoing of a very few. I think it absolutely essential to expose it and to deal with it ruthlessly. Even a little corruption of that kind does untold damage to the reputation of a service which little deserves it.

Some of you may have heard of the new A10 Branch that we in the Metropolitan Police have created to deal with complaints against policemen. I think that most people who have had any dealings with A10 will agree that it has demonstrated beyond any doubt our willingness and ability to deal swiftly and effectively with our own wrongdoers. Well over 100 officers have left the force, voluntarily or otherwise, since the change of system for investigating complaints.

So intense was the interest and publicity following the lecture that the judge conducting the trial of the IRA bombers at Winchester thought it prudent to warn the jury against being influenced by it, especially in view of my comment about the standard legal procedure for accusing the police of planting drugs, explosives or firearms. Much of the comment amused me but to this day I think the most interesting reaction was that of the Home Office, who did not utter a single word to me, or, so far as I know, to anyone else. I was happy to insert into the text at Jimmy Waddell's suggestion the words 'and I am saying this on my own responsibility' because, indeed, I was and did not wish to give any other impression. But there was no doubt that the Home Office, like the proverbial ostrich, got its head well down into the sand and did not bring it out until the storm had subsided. I can't say I blame them. The division of responsibility for police, criminal law and courts between Home Office and the Lord Chancellor has never been marked by close identity of interest and the Attorney General as head of the Bar could hardly be expected to rejoice at being told by a common policeman that his slip was showing. In fact he exercised his prerogative as Attorney to demand the file on the Bingo case, but took no action on it. I suspect because I had carefully chosen the case from about ten years back because I did not want to give anyone grounds for civil action and out of a number of cases of malpractice this was not a bad one to illustrate my point.

Perhaps it is only fair to end the subject with a selection of Press comment. After all, virtually every paper made it the subject of a leader and some diversity of opinion could therefore reasonably be expected. *The Times* pronounced as follows:

Sir Robert Mark's views on the inadequacies of the present criminal trials system are well known. He believes that both during the stage of police interrogation and at the trial itself, a defendant is protected by laws and rules which place the prosecution at a considerable disadvantage and ultimately result in the acquittal of many defendants who are in fact guilty of the crimes of which they have been accused. Last night, during the course of his excellent and lucid Dimbleby Lecture on BBC television, he repeated these views but added a new dimension to them.

After reaffirming his support for trial by jury the writer supported my proposal that impartial research into the deliberation of juries was not impossible and might well be advantageous. He also suggested that, in view of the relaxation of qualifications for jury eligibility, a literary test for potential jurors might be worthwhile.

The liberal *Observer* was sympathetic:

Reactions to Sir Robert Mark's trenchant television lecture have been absurdly shrill: this is particularly true of the barrage of indignation it has evoked from lawyers and their organizations. The idea that the legal profession might nurture a number of black sheep may be outrageous to lawyers: to everyone else it will seem a perfectly reasonable proposition.

As for the suggestion that it is somehow wrong to make generalizations about lawyers (any more than about policemen or politicians), unless the alleged malefactors are named, this is particularly disingenuous: lawyers are in the best position to know that the libel laws prevent this and that the privilege that attaches to their consultations with their clients makes it practically impossible to produce the sort of evidence of collusion in concocting alibis or false evidence that would secure convictions.

Sir Robert Mark is right to insist that any system of justice worthy of the name must be even-handed: the conviction of the 'guilty' being as important for justice to the victims of crime as the acquittal of the innocent is for those who are wrongly charged. He is a remarkably able and clear-minded reformer and deserves a more intelligent response than the legal profession gave him last week.

Finally, I think the following three comments, by the *Guardian*, by W. F. Deedes, MC in the *Sunday Telegraph* and by Paul Ferris in the *Observer*, complete a fair representation of Press reaction.

The *Guardian*:

Crooked lawyers as well as bent coppers? In a country which is supposed to have one of the world's soundest systems of law enforcement, the mind staggers. But the allegation applies to no more than a small minority of lawyers or policemen; and it is probably well justified.

When our foremost policeman speaks in this way, it is time for the Law Society and the Bar Council to take notice. Will they? Their reply is likely to be on two levels at least. One is to say that our courts depend on the adversary system – which means that defence counsel must do their utmost to get their clients off. Sir Robert Mark readily accepts this but objects to deliberate lying, to fabricated alibis (which the defence lawyers have helped to fabricate), and to persistent attacks on the honesty of police officers. The Law Society and Bar Council may then ask why the Commissioner or his representatives have not brought particular cases of misconduct to the professional bodies.

W. F. Deedes, MC:

By the time the commentators who smell blood and the lawyers who smell heresy have had their way with the Dimbleby Lecture delivered by Sir Robert Mark, there is every likelihood, such is the mental confusion engendered by modern communications, that the clarity and importance of the Commissioner's message to us all will be lost.

169

He has been delivering the message with minor variants, to my knowledge for upwards of 10 years. His only innovation on this occasion was a relevant and well-merited attack on certain lawyers, Nearly everyone in the business knows they exist, and that what Mark says of them is true. And if respectable institutions protest too much on their behalf they will diminish not the Commissioner's credibility and integrity but their own.

Paul Ferris:

With one 45-minute appearance on television, Sir Robert Mark has ended the long British tradition that the police are defensive about their role, and has gone over to the attack. For better or worse, the police have begun to show their hand.

The Commissioner's Dimbleby Lecture last week was the tip of an iceberg. He argued forcefully that our legal system, too lenient to professional criminals, is exploited by all lawyers and abused by a few. He suggested that the nature of the game might provoke detectives to play dirty or even to act corruptly.

The two sides are utterly opposed. They have been grumbling at each other, more or less in private, for years. Now they have collided in public. Mark is a clever, rational man who acts deliberately. Without a doubt, he meant this row to happen.

I did not employ a Press cutting agency but the *Police Review* a few weeks later sent me a collection showing that the lecture had provoked comment in almost every newspaper.

I have dealt with the Dimbleby Lecture at some length because the principle it raises is of immeasurable importance both to police and public. Are chief officers of police in future likely to contribute from evidence and experience to public debate on law and order issues before legislation is passed, or are they, as in the past, to remain the silent and sole possessors of relevant information from a mistaken belief that they have no right or duty to speak? If the latter, the public interest will be ill-served. There can be no doubt at all of the freedom of a chief officer of police to express opinions publicly about matters within his sphere of responsibility. The difficulty in the past has been that some have been intellectually or otherwise incapable of doing so, some have thought their own personal interests might be adversely affected and some have been content merely to draw their pay and not stray outside the limits of management. Traditionally, of course, the way of the reformer is hard and goodness knows a police chief's lot is hard enough already. But both police and public deserve more information and better-informed debate about police affairs than that likely to be forthcoming from the Palace of Westminster, the Law Society or the Bar Council.

Of all the guardians of freedom the police are now in practice the most important. If that sounds rather difficult to accept, reflect for a moment on conditions before a professional force was established, when the rulings of both Parliament and the Courts all too often had little or no effect and when men had to band together, both for protection and law enforcement. Lord Radcliffe said over ten years ago, that we were becoming an ungovernable country and today I doubt whether anyone would seriously dispute his assertion. The most important single factor which has contributed to bad government, bad legislation and bad administration is not doctrinaire politics, which will always be with us, but lack of information and communication which could do more than anything else to improve our lot, economically, socially and above all in the system of justice. If the police really want to escape at long last their status as an artisan service, dominated excessively by politicians, civil servants and unthinking observance of outdated customs, they must be willing to play a more constructive part than hitherto in the debate of public affairs. Only time will reveal whether they have the courage and the willingness to do so.

# CHAPTER 13

# *The Turn of the Tide*

1974 was a hopeful year. The CID, despite rising crime and inadequate numbers, was arresting more real criminals than at any time in its history. The 98,326 arrests during the year represented an increase of 11 per cent over the previous year. Hardly a sign of discontent or low morale. Bank robberies were reduced dramatically from 65 in 1972 to 26 in 1973 to 17 in 1974 and a specially formed Robbery Squad took a heavy toll amongst people who had been practising that activity for years. 150 persons were arrested for robberies going as far back as 1965 and involving almost £3 million. The 27 worst got a total of 315 years' imprisonment. Success was not by any means complete. However, a number of those faced with honest and trustworthy detectives for the first time in their experience, began to sing. The age of the supergrass had arrived. The problem was how to protect them. Informers in cases of this gravity are heavily at risk. If in prison they have to be kept continually in their cells and even then receive frequent threats along the prison grapevine. They fear for themselves, their wives and children. That they had been willing for the first time to trust the CID marked a significant change. It was known that a contract for several thousands of pounds had been let for the killing of one of them. Bert Wickstead, the head of the Serious Crimes Squad, had a bullet through his window one night as a reminder of his vulnerability. It made no difference. The arrests continued. With the consent of the Home Office a police station was adapted as a 'grasshouse'. The arrangement worked well.

A purged Drug Squad operating with the newly created Central Drugs and Illegal Immigration Unit was also making encouraging progress and was rebuilding our bridges with HM Customs and Excise after the disastrous period culminating in the trial of some of the former members of the squad. The Flying Squad, the Regional Crime Squad, the Robbery Squad and the Serious Crimes Squad were all achieving successes on a scale never before experienced, largely because at long last they enjoyed the trust of CID, uniformed and provincial colleagues alike. Behind them the Bomb Squad was slowly and painfully gathering the experience and acquiring the techniques which were later to make it the most successful anti-terrorist unit in any capital city in the world.

A particularly significant event occurred in April when James Humphreys, the Soho pornographer, was sentenced to eight years' imprisonment for unlawful wounding. By this time the responsibility for dealing with obscene publications had been handed over to the uniformed branch and the way was now clear to investigate the allegations of police corruption by Humphreys and others. It was the beginning of the most complex, difficult and protracted criminal investigation in Metropolitan Police history. It was carried out by Gilbert Kelland, a deputy assistant commissioner with a hand-picked team specially chosen by Jim Starritt, the deputy commissioner. The arrest and conviction of Bernard Silver, another prominent personality in Soho pornography, for conspiracy to live on the earnings of prostitution added further weight to our efforts. A major effort against another prominent pornographer, Ronald Mason, was frustrated when he fled abroad. Not until late in 1975 were we to get our hands on him in Guernsey. Not many people can be expected to realize that although we were making such strenuous and unrelenting efforts to catch up with the porn kings and those they corrupted not one of us put the chances of success higher than one in a hundred. Convictions in porn cases are always unlikely. It is a quirk of human nature that jurymen faced with a choice between a pornographer and a do-gooder will usually choose the former. There is nothing less appealing to the ordinary mortal than unattractive virtue. Even if convictions were achieved they were followed, until the 1973 Dimbleby Lecture, by derisory sentences. The real fear of the pornographers was not of the courts but of harassment, either by strong-arm men seeking protection money or by police doing, in effect, the same thing. The sorry, sordid tale was not to be told in full until 1977, after my retirement, because of the difficulty and length of the investigation, but it is interesting that by 1974 police corruption in Soho had virtually ended. A year or two later, by way of contrast, two members of the porn squad were to be awarded exemplary agreed damages approved by the court after having been libelled by the publishers of a pornographic magazine. However, other events were to enliven the immediate future.

Late in the afternoon of Friday, 4 January, John Gerrard, the deputy assistant commissioner in charge of public order, called on me with the Head of Special Branch. Without going into detail it appeared that there was a possibility that terrorists had undertaken a reconnaissance of Heathrow and that they might be in possession of one or two ground to air missiles. It required no great intelligence to appreciate that such a weapon in those kind of hands would most likely be used near the point of take-off or landing, this being the only place where aircraft can easily be identified from the ground. The likelihood of finding a small team of determined men can never be high. The chances of finding and killing them after using the weapons are much better if adequate preparations are made, and this itself is a useful deterrent. All that is necessary is protective armour, weapons capable of penetrating buildings and adequate manpower. In other words, the army. I tried to reach the Home Secretary and Permanent Under Secretary, but without success. I had no better luck with the Minister of Defence. There was nothing else for it but to cross the Rubicon. I asked the GSO1 of London District to get the GOC's agreement to move troops into Heathrow by first light on the following morning and he readily agreed. During the night we managed to find the Home Secretary who gave us his blessing. The following day the operation took place. Happily it was uneventful, but we learned many lessons from it. It was to be repeated quite often, but with more sophistication, and less cabinet ministers claiming credit for it. It was nevertheless to arouse angry comment from what Mr Bernard Levin describes as 'Vanessa's loonies'.

In February the government fell and Roy Jenkins returned to the Home Office. Though I was not to know it at the time, this was to have unhappy consequences for me. On the evening of 20 March I was due to speak at the Reform Club to their Political Committee and its guests. In retrospect I call it my Francis Drake night. As I was about to address my soup one of our more colourful Yard waitresses, Magnolia, who must have been hired for the evening, leant over me and said, 'I suppose you know Princess Anne's been kidnapped, sir?' I replied rather tartly, 'Don't be an idiot. This is no time for jokes.' To which she replied rather haughtily, 'It's on the tapes.' At my insistence she brought me the tape outlining the now well-known incident in the Mall. I excused myself for a few moments, went to a telephone, and discovered from Colin Woods, the assistant commissioner (Crime), that the Princess was safe, her assailant had been arrested and the four injured men were all in hospital. There was nothing I could do for the moment and there were 200 people waiting to listen to me. I told Colin to come and pick me up in an hour and returned to talk to the gathering through muted champing. As the hour ended Colin's head appeared round the door and off we went, first to see the Home Secretary at the Commons and then to see the injured. It was a miracle that no one was killed. Inspector Beaton, the Princess's protection officer, who was shot three times, got a richly deserved George Cross and the Princess herself was deservedly decorated by the Queen personally.

At the end of April the government made known its intention that the Met should take over the policing of Heathrow, primarily to ensure unity of command in dealing with terrorism. This opened an entirely new prospect to the force. We had long ceased to police ports and dockyards and generally regarded private ground as being beyond our province. The airport already had an efficient little private police force but its police authority was the British Airports Authority whose primary concern was understandably to keep the airport operating. I could foresee difficulties in reconciling the unions to impartial law enforcement, especially in view of the known high rate of crime, most of it by their members, and I wrote to Roy Jenkins asking for an assurance that the government would not attempt to interfere with the enforcement of criminal law at the airport after we had taken over. This was readily forthcoming. A committee was then set up to organize the takeover and I arranged a meeting with the representatives of the various unions, who, though initially rather cagey were eventually co-operative, though they looked a bit askance when I told them firmly that crime was not negotiable.

Planning for the change continued smoothly but my attention was turned elsewhere following a demonstration in Red Lion Square on 15 June by the National Front which clashed with a counter demonstration by a mixed bag of organizations calling themselves 'Liberation' but not a whit less odious than the National Front. A deliberate attack on the police by the International Marxist Group led to quite a battle, in which, though a non-participant, an unfortunate young student fell amongst the crowd, was kicked or struck, and later died from his injuries. There was an immediate hullaballoo. Liberation predictably accused the police of murdering the dead boy, for whose death they were in fact indirectly responsible. Political activists cannot, after all, afford the luxury of evidence, or conscience. Nevertheless the public uproar was such that even though the lies were blatant, they could not be ignored. It is at times like this that a commissioner really earns his pay. His men are smarting both from physical injury and from unscrupulous, politically motivated liars. A weak, minority government is hanging on to office by its eyelashes unable to run the risk of offending its extreme left in case it should bring it down. Nothing is more certain than that an enquiry will be held if only to placate criticism and defuse the situation. The inquest will clearly not be sufficient because it will be confined to enquiring into the death. From a police point of view nothing could be worse than to appear to have an enquiry imposed upon the force. There remains only one sensible course of action, to get in first and demand an enquiry, though well aware that it will almost certainly be a waste of money, time and manpower. This is in fact what we did and precisely what happened. Lord Justice Scarman sat for a total of twenty-seven days to establish with infinite patience and courtesy, notwithstanding the ill manners of some of the participants, that Kevin Gately had met his death by misadventure and that the International Marxist Group were primarily to blame for it because they had deliberately attacked the police. It is a great pity that the proceeding could not have been televised. It was a field day for the lawyers. Those representing the Warwick University Students' Union and the National Union of Students were paid £9582, the Liberation lawyers were paid £9563. Even the representatives of the International Marxist Group received £8227, with the National Front coming last with a modest £6270. All these sums were paid from the Metropolitan Police Fund or, in other words, by the ratepayer and taxpayer. The judge approved them as reasonable but happily in this country it is open to every citizen to disagree. One quarter of these sums would, in my view, have been gross overpayment. The only tangible effect of the enquiry was to relieve an embarrassed government of harassment by it own extremists. It had no effect for the police at all, other than to waste a great deal of time and money.

It did, however, have a useful spin-off. I had been concerned for some time about the cavalier treatment of assaults on the police by the stipendiary magistrates of central London. We were sending three men off duty every two days after being assaulted and yet the fines being imposed by the magistrates did not even defray the cost of sending a police officer to court and this at a time when we had only three uniformed officers for each square mile and were suffering

177

some hundreds of burglaries and autocrimes daily. I therefore had some research done into the outcome of court proceedings during the last three years and prepared a lecture for delivery after the publication of Lord Scarman's report. Put very simply, the evidence showed that it was simply not worthwhile to prosecute in the lower courts for violence at disputes and demonstrations. The average fine was derisory and a positive encouragement to the unruly. It might therefore be worthwhile to abandon all prosecutions for this kind of offence before London stipendiaries and proceed only in those cases intended for a higher court. This bland but thoroughly justified statement had an immediate impact on the Press. Every single national newspaper wrote a leader on the subject, all of them, with the obvious exception of the *Morning Star*, lending strong support to the police view. An unexpected bonus had been the discovery that a letter published in a national newspaper, commenting more in sadness than in anger on police conduct in Red Lion Square, had been found on enquiry to be a forgery. It was so well written that it was treated as a complaint against the police. The investigating officer found that both the name and address of the writer were fictitious. It is incidentally both interesting and encouraging to note that although the lecture did not exactly enhance my relationship with the magistracy the penalties for violence and hooliganism in central London rose dramatically.

An event of rather less importance but of some interest had been under investigation during this period. During April the body of an Irishman, Kenneth Joseph Lennon, had been discovered in a ditch at Park Road, Banstead, Surrey. He had been shot in the head. Three days later, the National Council for Civil Liberties issued a 'statement' supposedly made by Lennon accusing Special Branch of a variety of malpractice or neglect. This did not cause any particular anxiety at the Yard, who knew only too well that for the NCCL this was about par for the course. The Home Secretary rang me from his country home when the story was published and was I think rather surprised when I told him straight away that I wanted an impartial and preferably a judicial enquiry. I told him that we had nothing to fear and everything to gain by openness and that in dealing with people of this kind it was the best tactic. He rather surprised me by asking me to wait until I saw him later that morning before taking any action. I went to see him with the Head of Special Branch later that morning. He was surrounded with a variety of advisers. I pointed out sweetly that in any other of the 42 police forces in the country I would not need his consent for an outside enquiry and that I felt sure that he, as an advocate of police accountability, would agree. To my surprise he was distinctly unforthcoming and the upshot was that I was told that we would have to do the investigation ourselves. To give him credit he sugared the pill as best he could by saying, 'Commissioner, there is no organization I would rather trust with this difficult and delicate enquiry than the Metropolitan Police', to which I replied, after making sure I had heard aright, 'Can I have that in writing?' The enquiry was undertaken by the deputy commissioner, Jim Starritt, who did a very thorough job but could not, for obvious reasons, carry the same conviction as a high court judge.

Lennon was a thirty-one-year-old Irishman who had offered himself as an informer on IRA affairs for money in July 1973. This is by no means unusual and the value of this kind of informant is rarely high. He did in fact supply information to Special Branch and clearly was involved at a low level in IRA affairs. Partly as a result, and partly from the initiative of the police at Luton, Bedfordshire, three men were sentenced to ten years' imprisonment at St Albans Crown Court in December for conspiracy to commit armed robbery. He was also responsible for the discovery of an arms cache containing shotguns, ammunition, explosive devices and incriminating documents. In January 1974 he was arrested at Birmingham with another man for conspiring to effect the escape of a prisoner from Winson Green prison. The second man was a member of the IRA and Lennon told the police that his own activity was motivated only by his desire to get information for money. The Director of Public Prosecution was told. There was no question of withdrawing the charge against him, not least because it would have put his life at risk. Lennon's companion was convicted but he was acquitted. On 9 April 1974, the day following his acquittal, he met a member of Special Branch in London, expressed willingness to continue his role as an informer but was obviously nervous about returning to London. He was not seen alive again.

Enquiries showed that on 10 April he had called at the offices of the NCCL and had there had a long conversation with a member of the staff who took lengthy notes from which to prepare a statement for Lennon's signature. He was in fact killed before he could sign it. This did not prevent the NCCL from publishing the 'statement' on 16 April giving the impression that it had been signed by Lennon. It is pertinent to mention that a police officer giving that misleading impression would have been dismissed from the force and such a statement would never have been presented to a court by a prosecution lawyer. The original notes would have been presented and the notetaker would have been examined on them. Unfortunately the NCCL were more concerned to use Lennon to attack the police than to afford him the protection he was seeking. They formulated allegations that the police had coerced Lennon into becoming an informer blithely disregarding that the police had no hold over Lennon with which to coerce him. He gave the NCCL the impression that he was wanted by the Royal Ulster Constabulary for an offence and that the Metropolitan Police had it in their power to have his sister 'locked up'. Both these allegations were not only untrue but would not bear credence on even cursory examination and consideration. They they should seem to be credible was necessary if the NCCL allegations were not to be dismissed out of hand. The NCCL also alleged that Lennon was an 'agent provocateur', that the police had manipulated the evidence to secure his acquittal and then failed to ensure his safety.

The only one of the allegations about which I felt there

was some substance was the last. Even though the acquittal was perfectly proper, resulting from eloquent submission by defence counsel, there was, I think, a danger that it might have *looked* suspicious, especially in view of the conviction of the other accused. It is always easy to be wise with hindsight but I cannot help but feel that in the circumstances, his limited value, his doubtful reliability, his vulnerability it would have been wiser to have arranged his departure to a healthier clime. But, of course, all informers run risks, none more so than the Irish and dealing with them continuously does tend to dull sensitivity. The same is true of the casual disregard by police of their own vulnerability. In dealing with the most dangerous criminals and situations they continually omit to take appropriate measures for their own protection probably because of the old, complacent assumption that 'it just doesn't happen here'. Lennon and Ross McWhirter sadly demonstrated the falsity of that assumption.

The really inexplicable aspect of the affair was not the attack on the police by the NCCL, which was predictable, but, assuming they believed Lennon's story, their total disregard of the need to ensure his safety. The action open to them was limitless. They could have taken him to the Home Office, to the editor of a newspaper specializing in their kind of interests, they could even have housed him themselves. Instead they abandoned him to the fate to which, they were later to assert, he was condemned by the police. Even viewed charitably and with due regard for their lack of experience and gullibility it does seem an extraordinary course to have followed. I think in fairness that neither the NCCL nor the police can look bank on the incident without regret. I still wish, however, that Roy Jenkins had made clear to the world my repeated request for a judicial enquiry into it even though I do not question his judgement in declining to follow that course.

About this time we were faced with a rather unusual problem. An IRA man, Michael Gaughan, had starved himself to death in prison on the Isle of Wight and the IRA were determined to make the most they could of it. I had a word with Douglas Osmond, the chief constable of Hampshire, on the telephone, but realized that it was going to be our problem. The intention was to bring the body to Kilburn for a funeral service before flying it home to Ireland. I pondered long and hard about what to do. It was open to me to stop the vehicle carrying the body as soon as it entered the Metropolitan Police district. Thereafter, it was a question of judgement, on which the police depend so much. I had no legal right to take possession of the body but that did not worry me very much. It would be quite possible to seize it, put it in a police van, take it to Heathrow and put it on a plane for Ireland. Admittedly, the relatives would protest and the Press would undoubtedly focus public attention on the issue. I privately thought this would not matter very much once the incident was over. On the other hand, to let events take their course, with a sordid parody of a ceremonial funeral, was sure to arouse the digust and revulsion of the great majority of people. And so it turned out. The funeral was so arranged as to offend almost everyone. It was like the black comedy which had enjoyed temporary popularity on the London stage. There was a strong reaction from the public, who were disgusted by the funeral and outraged that the law should permit it. All in all, we felt quite grateful to Mr Gaughan, who served a better purpose dead than alive. He did much to prepare public opinion for legislation later in the year to put an end to overt public activity in support of the IRA and for that deserves a grateful mention.

Finally, in November the Birmingham bombs awoke in both public and politician alike a profound contempt for the IRA and all that it stood for, and perhaps more significantly led to the immediate introduction of the Prevention of Terrorism (Emergency Provisions) Act, which put an end to overt fund raising and led to the departure of a number of Irishmen who had long abused civil liberty in order to undermine it. Of course the NCCL objected but that, if anything, tended to commend the new legislation to the public. Oddly enough however, it was not sought by the police. It was introduced by the Home Secretary because he felt a need to reassure the public of the willingness of the government to take firm measures in the face of Irish terrorism. The police were largely indifferent. The NCCL were quite right in assuming that we would not let any legal niceties prevent us from dealing with terrorism and that we were therefore not all that interested in what we thought was essentially a propaganda measure. In fact, the real beneficiaries were the one and a half million decent Irish people living and working in this country who were overnight relieved of the embarrassing spectacle of their intellectually subnormal compatriots collecting money openly for the IRA or indulging in childish melodramatics on their behalf. That was about the only real benefit afforded by the Act, but I have no doubt that Irish minority were very thankful for it. We had received something in the order of 8000 bomb threats during the year so we had a real interest in discouraging insensitivity to the potential threat of Irish terrorism. The new legislation was undoubtedly helpful in that it curbed the activities of the civil libertarians who are always so anxious to enhance the freedom to bomb, to maim and to kill.

Not a vintage year, but not a bad one.

# CHAPTER 14

# Balcombe Street

After the trials and tribulations of eight years in the Metropolitan Police, 1975 was undoubtedly a tonic. It began with a rather damp squib when a man in a British Airways plane at Heathrow produced what appeared to the crew to be a pistol and an explosive canister and demanded to be flown to Paris. The aircraft was in a fairly remote part of the airfield and both police and army were there in adequate numbers. Negotiations with the hijacker, through the medium of the crew, lasted nine hours but in some odd way never seemed to carry conviction. A number of us listening to the verbal exchanges had a hunch that we were not up against a determined fanatic but we were still not able to bring the incident to a rapid end. The forty-six passengers had been allowed to leave and the aircraft doors were closed with only the five members of the crew and the hijacker on board. Finally, it was decided to comply with the hijacker's request, at least in outward appearance. The aircraft took off ostensibly on its way to Paris but after circling for a time landed at Stansted. During the flight a plane full of police and soldiers had flown from Heathrow to Stansted with just sufficient time to arrange a reception committee. The man alighted from the aircraft and was quickly arrested. There was nothing very encouraging about this incident. It illustrated the difficulties of achieving surprise in attacking an aircraft with closed doors. It showed up the weaknesses of our communication system and, in particular, how easily it could be penetrated by unauthorized listeners. About the only good thing that could be said about it was that no one was hurt and that it gave us much food for thought.

A few days later we had to contend with a demonstration

on behalf of the Shrewsbury pickets, who had been sent to prison in the previous year following conviction for behaviour to which most people, including trade unionists, deeply objected. The Home Secretary, Roy Jenkins, displayed an admirable firmness in refusing to be intimidated by the less attractive adherents of the Labour movement.

By this time we had rid the force of about three hundred officers following complaints from members of the public. Twenty-three policemen had been sent to prison for varying terms, one hundred and forty-five had resigned before formal proceedings could be instituted or completed and about fifty were suspended from duty. Rather more than a thousand complaints were under investigation, most of them trivial, some of them malicious and a few of them serious. The point was, however, that police, public and even the criminal were conscious of the system and that confidence in it was well established. Indeed, perhaps its staunchest supporters were the members of the Joint Executive Committee of the Police Federation, representing all ranks of the Met from constable to chief inspector inclusive. There was a healthier smell in the air.

We were all surprised but delighted when in February a message arrived from the Palace that the Queen would like to visit the Bomb Squad. We had by that time had many explosions, unexploded bombs, letter bombs and incendiaries since the first car bombs were planted in August 1973 and painstaking and often courageous work by the surveillance team, bomb disposal officers, fingerprint experts, photographers, dog handlers and others had not enjoyed the success we had hoped for. Their combined efforts had, however, compiled a mass of evidence that was to prove invaluable. We showed the Queen a kind of giant snakes and ladders design on a wall on which appeared all the incidents which had taken place, with indications of the evidence which would tie one incident in with another. Eventually, by this means we were to clear up every major terrorist incident in London, except the murder of Stephen Tibble, who was callously shot down thirteen days later. But at that point in time we were feeling the frustrations implicit in G. K. Chesterton's comment that 'Society is at the mercy of a murderer without a motive', although in this case we were trying to find murderers with an irrational motive, which is just as difficult. We did not, and could not, know of the success just around the corner, that we were to achieve before the end of the year. Perhaps, mercifully, we did not know of the price to be paid for it. PC Tibble was shot dead whilst pursuing a man suspected of terrorist activities. Captain Roger Goad, one of our gallant band of explosives officers, was blown to pieces whilst bravely trying to defuse a bomb. Gordon Hamilton Fairley, the distinguished cancer specialist, was killed by a bomb later in the year and Ross McWhirter, a notable upholder of freedom for the individual, was shot down in cold blood on his own doorstep in the presence of his wife, whose fortitude and restraint, like that of Mrs Jane Ewart Biggs, whose husband, the Ambassador to Ireland, was murdered in the following year, aroused nationwide sympathy and admiration. Indeed, the events of the year left me with a depressing realization that if there is one characteristic which has consistently marked the activities of the IRA throughout the years, it is stupidity. And stupid people always present much greater problems than the intelligent because they are always so unpredictable.

The funeral of Stephen Tibble was a most moving occasion. His young widow and his family were engulfed in a tidal wave of police whose emotion was only too clearly plain. The ordeal of the family cannot have been made any easier by so many sympathizers. The public and police response to a fund set up for his widow was overwhelming. It would, however, be hypocritical to pretend that tragedies of this kind do not have their beneficial aspect. Tibble's heroism and sacrifice brought home to the public as nothing else could the extent to which they depend on the police for protection against extremism and brutality, the traditions of Irish politics. The same was true of Roger Goad, whose funeral at Basingstoke is unlikely to be forgotten by anyone inside or outside the church. He had diced with death once too often, but knew only too well what he was doing. I felt these two deaths personally and deeply and found giving the address at the funeral of each perhaps the worst of all the difficult tasks of my entire police career.Of Roger Goad I said:

According to Saint John in the 13th verse of the 15th Chapter of his version of the Gospel 'Greater love hath no man than this, that a man lay down his life for his friends'. Those immortal words prompt the thought that such love is even more remarkable in a man who lays down his life not for his friends but for his fellow men. For this is what Roger Goad did in the full and certain knowledge of what he was doing.

Can there be any greater contrast for man to contemplate than his quiet courage and self sacrifice with the behaviour of those who caused his death? The spawn of hatred, ignorance and prejudice, whose recourse to indiscriminate murder and destruction bears eloquent testimony to their inhumanity and unreason.

We are here today, police, army and civilian to pay tribute not only to Roger Goad, richly though he deserves our respect and admiration, but to pay tribute also to the ideals which he personified and which we, as a nation value above life itself, that man should live in a world which puts justice before force, logic before emotion, and humanity and compassion above all.

His cruel and wicked murderers might understandably evoke our hatred. but that would not be what Roger Goad would wish. For he was willing to give his life for the preservation of those standards we most value. Rather are they to be pitied for the mindless brutes they are, devoid of reason, devoid of humanity, deserving only of the contempt of their fellow man. They do, however, serve one useful purpose. They offer a stark contrast against which the nobility and unselfishness of this gallant man will be judged not just by his family, his friends and his colleagues but by the world itself.

Roger Goad's wife and children are called upon to pay

the heaviest price of all, the loss of a beloved husband and father, and we must do all we can to lessen their grief and their burden. We all share that loss; but paradoxically we are the richer for it. For there are few acts which by their nobility, their unselfishness and their example enrich us all. And this was one indeed.

Another Briton, facing on 12 October 1915 the certainty of a no less barbarous and unnecessary death, used words not dimmed by time which still voice the noblest aspiration of civilized man.

'I realize that patriotism is not enough I must have no hatred or bitterness towards anyone.'

That is an ideal not likely to be attained by all but it is an ideal to which all should aspire. Whatever our reaction as individuals, however, this pledge I offer to Roger Goad, his wife and his children that in dealing with the evil which cost him his life, whatever its source or numbers, we shall not weaken or relax our efforts whatever the cost, whatever the sacrifice. His memory will be hallowed so long as freedom and humanity mark the British way of life.

May he rest in peace; may his family be sustained by the splendour of his example and comforted by the sorrow and sympathy of his comrades and may we, the police of Great Britain, be inspired by his sacrifice.

Conscious of the growing wave of public support, partly because of our containment of demonstrations and our struggle against terrorism, and confident of our preparedness for closer examination of our internal affairs I rang up Harold Evans of the *Sunday Times* and asked him if he would like to put a reporter of his own choice into A10, the complaints branch, to satisfy himself that it worked as well as we were telling the world it did. He jumped at the chance, on one condition, that it was his idea! He sent along a hard-nosed, cynical, disbelieving Australian, Phillip Knightley, who clearly was going to question everything he was told. He spent a fortnight with us, asking the most trenchant, percipient and embarrassing questions but went away thoroughly convinced and on 5 April wrote an article 'The Straightening of Bent Coppers' which had more effect on Fleet Street and the public than anything else we had done. Strictly speaking, I suppose it was unlawful to let him look at files, listen to telephone calls and, in fact, do anything he wanted, subject only to an undertaking that he would not break any judicial rule or impair the privacy of any individual. He and his editor honoured that undertaking scrupulously and, whatever the legality of the exercise, for which I accepted full responsibility, its beneficial effect on both Press and public was incalculable. Never before had a police force in Great Britain given a journalist such unrestricted access to its most sensitive affairs. I can only say that, whatever the risk, its success exceeded our most optimistic hopes.

Whilst all this was going on our manpower was steadily improving for the first time for years and we were making dramatic inroads into deliberate crime against high value targets. More and more people were being charged with serious crime and the morale of the force and of the CID in particular was soaring.

I went to Toronto to exchange views with the Canadian chiefs of police and to tell them about our problems. There were two rather amusing incidents on this trip. One was that I explained to them carefully and at length the reasons why police in Britain should oppose the return of capital punishment, not knowing that they had almost unanimously voted for its retention the previous day. The other was that, assuming my relations with the Canadian Press were likely to be on the same basis of trust as those with the British Press, I remarked indiscreetly in conversation with one of its members that I thought it was high time that the train robbers were paroled. After all, far more dangerous and violent criminals were being convicted in London every day and getting much more lenient treatment. I should not have been surprised that the headline in the *Daily Telegraph* handed to me as I boarded the plane home was 'Commissioner says Parole the Train Robbers'. I must say I felt unrepentant, although I would not intentionally have dreamed of making a public remark likely to embarrass the Parole Board, which, in my view, does an extremely difficult job conscientiously and well.

Predictably, Roger Goad's funeral on 5 September was marred by further IRA bombs, which had the effect of reducing my holiday that year to a few days in Guernsey. Tails were well up, however, and there was an unmistakable feeling of the hunt closing in for the kill. At the suggestion of a junior member of the force we had carefully analysed the shootings and bombings of the last two years and had come to the conclusion that they followed a predictable pattern. A and C departments therefore decided to mount a combined operation, using about 700 volunteers, in the areas we thought most likely to be attacked. Their leaders were called into the Yard for briefing on the day the operation was to take place. One of them, true to the old corrupt relationship between police and Press which had largely been destroyed by the new Press policy, telephoned the *Evening News* and gave them forewarning, no doubt for money. The *Evening News* thereupon printed the whole story prominently on the front page, thus giving the bombers forewarning of our intentions and destroying the value of a very costly operation to protect the people of London. Conduct like this, of course, beggars description and tests severely the self-control of those affected by it. I did not, and still do not, think it was approved by the editor. I assumed it had been authorized by some halfwit who had not even stopped to think of the possible consequences. Still, I was determined to adhere to our new Press policy of tolerance rather than retaliation so I wrote to the proprietor, Vere Harmsworth, in what I thought was vintage Ernest Gowers, as follows:

24 November 1975

I feel I must bring to your attention an incident involving the *Evening News* the significance of which you may be unaware.

At about 1.30 p.m. last Friday a briefing took place at Scotland Yard designed to achieve a concentration of about 700 uniformed and detective officers that night in the areas in which experience suggested that the I.R.A. bombers might be active. Needless to say secrecy was essential to the success of such a large and costly operation. Later that afternoon the *Evening News* carried the story of the operation on its front page. The source from which it was obtained can only have been dishonourable or corrupt but that is not the main point I wish to make.

The use of news so obtained destroyed the value of the operation and can be said without doubt to have given invaluable help to the terrorists who are presently attacking central London. I should add that no enquiry was made either of the CID or Press Branch before the story appeared.

Behaviour of this kind seems to me to be in sharp contrast to the efforts of this Force to achieve a mutually helpful relationship with the Press outlined in the enclosed memorandum agreed with all editors in 1972.

I am, needless to say, greatly disturbed by this incident. That so reputable a newspaper as the *Evening News* should deliberately give aid to the self proclaimed enemies of the British people seems hard to believe but I am at a loss to know how else to interpret the incident.

I should be grateful for your comments in view of the anxiety for the future which it provokes.

Needless to say, I did not receive a reply. An embarrassed editor rang me a few days later making apologetic noises but he was so clearly not responsible that I treated him both courteously and kindly. It is nevertheless a classic example of journalistic irresponsibility which should not be overlooked.

Fortunately, our assessment of the intellectual capacity of the bombers was not mistaken and only a few days later they mounted the very operation against which the *Evening*

*News* had so considerately warned them. The story is now history. On 6 December the principal four terrorists drove past Scott's Restaurant in Mount Street, Mayfair, firing an automatic weapon. They clearly were unaware that they were in the middle of a small army of police all hoping for their arrival. The chase was on immediately and in the panic they abandoned their automatic weapons, which were quickly recovered. Once holed up in Balcombe Street by their own stupidity as much as anything else the now famous siege was on. We were confident that we had the team responsible for virtually all the London bombings but were not sure whether any had got away in the confusion. Most of all we were anxious to ensure that we had 'Z', the code letter we had allotted to one person whom we could identify evidentially with many incidents.

We were fortunate in having gained much valuable experience only a month or two earlier from the siege of the Spaghetti House restaurant in Knightsbridge, which I will recount later. We therefore slipped quickly into a drill which we had devised from the debriefing of that incident. The Home Office were asked to send a liaison officer, permission was obtained to move up the Special Air Service for use if required and an invaluable team of psychiatrists, headed by the admirable Dr Peter Scott of Bethlehem Maudsley Hospital, was quickly gathered together. Arrangements were made to cut off the public telephone system from the flat and later to disconnect the electricity. We knew the terrorists had a battery operated radio but its life was clearly limited and we did not want them to see themselves as heroes in a nationwide melodrama. Instead, a field telephone was lowered to them from the flat above, as was a portable lavatory. This was intended, in the event successfully, to convince them that we were in the flat when that was not always the case. Police marksmen were brought into position, hard-nosed dogs making most unfriendly noises were put in the flat beneath, the field of fire from the flat was clearly marked by tapes and we settled down to the inevitable war of attrition. It was to last for 5 days, 18 hours and 55 minutes before the humiliating surrender of the four terrorists in the eyes of the whole world.

Contrary to general belief, the operation was quite simple and straightforward once we were sure of the problem. Though we were deeply concerned about the safety of the hostages I did not consider for one moment that they were not expendable. I felt heartfelt sympathy for Mr and Mrs Matthews but felt that human life was of little importance when balanced against the principle that violence must not be allowed to succeed. Fortunately, in deciding that policy, there was no need to consult anyone, nor did I do so. The four terrorists were common criminals and the responsibility for dealing with them, unless I decided to use the SAS, was mine and mine alone. It was not so much a difficult decision as no decision at all. There was no question of giving the gunmen anything, other than the bare means to sustain life. I would not have varied that decision in any circumstances though, in fairness to those to whom I was accountable, no one even hinted that I should. But having made it, every effort was made to ensure that we should get the hostages out safely. In this the news media helped us. They asked, at our prompting, loaded questions such as 'What about the safety of the hostages?' which enabled me to reply, 'The best guarantee of their safety is the swift and ruthless retribution that will follow any harm that befalls them.' The main responsibility for the hour to hour control fell upon Wilford Gibson of A department and the redoubtable Ernie Bond of C department, probably one of the most efficient and dedicated detectives ever to serve the Metropolitan force. They performed splendidly. That is not to say that there were not anxious, sometimes agonizing, moments. Dr Peter Scott, essentially a very gentle, though firm and determined man, provided just the check that was needed at moments of mounting tension between terrorists and police.

During the siege we managed to obtain, by means into which I will not go, the vital fingerprints we wanted. We then knew with certainty that we had 'Z', who had been formally 'buried' in Eire long before the bombing started so that he could come over to England as a 'sleeper'. The end came partly through the commonsense of Gibson and the help of the news media. As the days went by the irritability, sullenness and tension of the gunmen was becoming more noticeable. We all felt a shoot out was likely and we arranged for the SAS to prepare a contingency plan. But we certainly did not relish the prospect of the 150 or so news and television cameras filming what might be a gory end to the siege. We knew only too well that Irish folklore would use the film to convert four seedy, cowardly degenerates into martyrs and that was the last thing we wanted. Gibson therefore suggested tying a length of cloth about 40 yards long and 40 feet deep across the end of the square to block the view of all the cameras. I had no illusions about the reaction of the cameramen but thought he was right, whatever the fuss. He went ahead, and, coincidentally, both the *Daily Express* and the BBC disclosed that the SAS were there. This was, of course, broadcast on radio for the encouragement of the terrorists. Thereafter they could hardly surrender fast enough. They went through the pretence of delay, demanding a meal as a show of bravado, but not for them the prospect of dying for Mother Ireland. They came out shaking like leaves exposed in their true colours for all the world to see.

The hostages, though badly shaken, were physically unharmed and were to recover from their appalling ordeal. I would not like my attitude towards them to be thought heartless. Far from it. They were rarely out of my mind. But we had agreed at the Yard that if any senior police officer was taken he was to be written off. A touch of grim humour was added when I was asked what we should do if they took a politician, or even a cabinet minister, to which I replied without hesitation, 'Ask them if they would like a few more.' Apart from catching the four terrorists the Balcombe Street operation paid enormous dividends. The men were not as silent as we thought they would be and we had a mass of invaluable evidence. Public co-operation was limitless and soon led to the discovery of bomb factories and further evidence. We were not alone in our success. The provincial police had scored some resounding triumphs, especially in Hampshire, the west Midlands and Surrey and at long last it was becoming clear that Great Britain was not a very safe sea for Irish terrorists to swim in. By the end of 1976 there had been 263 incidents in England and Wales involving 302 devices. In London alone there had been 182 explosive devices and 11 shootings. 58 people had been killed and many more injured but 148 persons had been arrested, 49 of them in London, where 68 per cent of all the terrorist incidents had been cleared up. And throughout all this we had not killed or wounded a single terrorist!

# CHAPTER 15

# *Spaghetti House*

The total of 29 bombings and other terrorist incidents during 1975 killing ten people and injuring another one hundred and sixty-nine, was not allowed to divert the main body of the CID from their primary task, the war against crime. In the event the year afforded considerable satisfaction in other fields far removed from terrorism. Though crime continued to increase statistically, success against the professional criminal reached new heights and even more encouraging the efforts of the CID as a whole indicated that their morale and enthusiasm were high. 103,252 people were arrested for committing crimes of one kind or another, 5 per cent more than in 1974, 16 per cent more than in 1973 and more than double the number in 1967. And this notwithstanding only small increases in desperately inadequate manpower. Robberies in which firearms were fired remained at a low level, 35, but weapons were used to intimidate in 621 other cases. The number of violent crimes cleared up increased by 8 per cent to 8600 of which 1577 were robberies or violent thefts. But, of course, the daily total of muggings, minor robberies, woundings and burglaries continued to increase. Whilst the more hardened and experienced criminals were being arrested in ever larger numbers it would be unrealistic to pretend that we had the means to contain or reduce crime generally. The raising of the school leaving age, for example, with its consequent increase in truancy, was followed by a significant increase in burglaries and auto-crime in Inner London.

Faced with all these problems, what was happening was that we were more trusted, in particular by criminals. We were therefore getting more and better information and making spectacular arrests in the field of big-time crime. The productivity of our inadequate detective force had just about doubled and was being put to much more intelligent, selective and enthusiastic use but we were facing a task in which we could never hope to achieve more than limited success. Nevertheless, in dealing with the worst forms of crime our tails were well up. Hi-jacking of high value lorryloads, of whisky, gin, television sets and so on had been reduced by two-thirds and was later to fall to one quarter of the 1972 total of about 400. But, of course, a vast amount of recorded crime is of little interest to the public, though it can be painful indeed to the victim.

The difference between the fictional impression of crime and its reality is not generally understood by the public who like their criminals suave, their heroines elegant and attractive and, generally, a happy ending. But it is seldom like that in real life. 62 per cent of those arrested for robbery or other violent crime were twenty years old or younger, almost half those arrested for burglary were under seventeen, as were 40 per cent of those arrested for autocrime, *viz* theft of or from vehicles. Criminologists, sociologists, civil servants and policemen have to consider the implications of such figures, but not the public. They prefer the spectacular. Apart from Balcombe Street, we were able to satisfy them twice in 1975, with the Spaghetti House case and the kidnapping of a Greek Cypriot girl, Aloi Kaloghirou, although in the second case perhaps they felt cheated by the revelation of the drama only after its conclusion.

The Spaghetti House case was, I think, the most difficult and potentially explosive of all the various problems with which I had to deal in my twenty years as a chief officer of police. It had all the necessary ingredients of a manufactured cause *célèbre* – black gunmen, Italian hostages and an ethnic Press which was frequently prejudicial and unfair. The Spaghetti House Ltd operates a chain of restaurants in central London specializing in Italian cuisine, and its managers used to meet at its Headquarters in Knightsbridge late each Saturday night to discuss business and to pay the collective day's takings into the night safe of a nearby bank. Nine staff members were there during the early hours of Sunday, 28 September, when three coloured men carrying firearms attempted to rob them of the takings, which amounted to nearly £13,000. One robber had a double-barrelled sawn-off shotgun, the other two had hand guns. They shepherded the nine Italians down a flight of stairs into the basement, but one of them, Signor Giovanni Mai, made a courageous and successful dash for freedom through the rear stairs, of which the gunmen were clearly unaware. He escaped from the premises, ran along Knightsbridge to the Berkeley Hotel and raised the alarm. In the meantime, the remaining eight Italians were ushered into the basement, which had no windows, only one door and which measured 13½ feet by 15 feet. There were four short staircases to the basement, two at the front and two at the rear, but the only access to the room which was strongly built, was the door, which was 6½ feet by 2½ feet. Police response had been immediate and in a matter of minutes the robbers and hostages had been located in the basement. Matters were to some extent simplified when the leader of the gunmen identified himself as Franklin Davies, a Nigerian, who had just served a sentence of ten years' imprisonment for armed robbery. The names of the hostages were quickly established.

From the outset it was rightly assumed that this was a simple armed robbery that had gone wrong and any attempts by Davies, the Nigerian, to represent it as a political act were received with the derision which they clearly deserved. The gunmen were invited to surrender and declined impolitely. The drill to which we had given so much thought during the preceding two years was then applied in full. The area was sealed off, but with minimum inconvenience to ordinary traffic, the Home Office were asked to supply liaison officers, in view of the possible need for troops and the involvement of foreign nationals, and their help was invoked to obtain psychiatrists who had made a study of this kind of problem, in particular of Dr Peter Scott, who, in the event, was to prove worth his weight in gold. The gunmen by this time had decided to represent themselves as members of the Black Liberation Front, demand the release of black defendants in current criminal proceedings, and the presence of the Home Secretary. They also asked for a radio, and after some consideration, it was decided to accede to the last request. It was thus possible to make clear to them, not only in shouted conversation, but through the news broadcasts, that they were going nowhere except to a cell, or, by implication, to a mortuary, if they preferred that. That afternoon, they released one of the hostages who appeared to be unwell. Happily, he quickly recovered. The siege then settled down in earnest.

The Home Office had, of course, informed the Italian ambassador and Consul General, both of whom came to Spaghetti House from time to time, the latter, Dr Mario Manca, proving of inestimable value in dealing with the hostages. We had decided to provide accommodation across the road for the relatives of the hostages and I thought it my duty to visit them twice daily to offer what consolation and encouragement I could. It was not easy. One or two clearly thought we should accede to the gunmen's demand for an aircraft and guarantee of safe conduct and found it difficult to accept my view that in no circumstance at all would we agree. To their very great credit, the overwhelming majority of the relatives, despite their anguish, were solidly behind us in our determination not to give way. Whilst all this was going on, C7 Branch had been reaping the reward of extensive research and experiment during the last two years and first provided us with a sound recording of all that was going on in the locked room and then a reasonably good television picture. I naturally do not propose to go into the details of how this was achieved.

By this time, if the gunmen and their hostages were besieged, so were the police. Press, radio and television infiltrated the surrounding flats and other premises and every kind of listening and watching device was employed to monitor the drama being played out in the small and suffocating basement. An accidental shot inside the base ment might have caused much anxiety were it not that our equipment enabled us to know, with certainty, that it had no sinister significance. As the days went by the three gunmen suffered increasing bouts of bad temper and their conversations with police were frequently irrational, insulting and threatening. During this period, Dr Manca reassured the hostages, who were understandably apprehensive, and at one point offered to take the place of a hostage who was said to be ill. Whilst full of admiration for him, I refused to allow the exchange, reasoning that an unwell hostage was likely to be a far greater embarrassment to the gunmen than a healthy Consul General.

In the meantime the CID had been working at full stretch on the background to the robbery. They established that it was a job inspired from the inside and arrested the Italian who had set it up. From him they found the identity of the man who was alleged to have supplied the guns and the gunmen. I say 'alleged' because at the subsequent trial he was acquitted. I shall, for that reason, refer to him as X. About 2.15 p.m. on 2 October, the fifth day of the siege, Detective Superintendent Hucklesby arrested X and put us in a position to end the siege by psychological warfare. Incidentally, in view of the publicity attracted by the *Daily Mail* and its editor in the Leyland slush fund story a few years later, it is perhaps appropriate to recount his reaction to a request by me arising from that arrest. I thought it important for the safety of the hostages to avoid any suggestion on the radio that the Italian we had arrested had given us any help. I thought the gunmen might have taken it out on the hostages. It seemed to me wiser to attempt to attribute any blame for their predicament to X, who was not Italian. Unfortunately, when X was arrested, a *Daily Mail* reporter happened to be present, as a result of his own pertinacious enquiries. It required no genius to see that if the radio broadcast the link between X and the Italian in a way which might anger the gunmen, already in a distraught and unreasonable state, the result might be disastrous. There was a very real difficulty. At that time there was no hijacking.

No coup d'état. No drunken celebrity denouncing the Royal Family. In fact, there was no news except Spaghetti House. David English, the editor of the *Daily Mail*, therefore unquestionably had a world scoop. I nevertheless rang him up and asked him to kill his reporter's story in the interest of the hostages. After he had recovered from the shock he said, in effect, 'You tell me the truth about the reasons for your request. If I think it is justified, I will agree to it. If I don't, I shall feel free to print anything you tell me.' I told him the whole story and the reasons for my anxiety and after a moment's pause he said, 'Right. The story's dead.' The interesting aftermath was that when the case was over we issued a formal statement of thanks from the Yard to the whole Press, but, so far as I know, neither the *Mail* nor the rest of the Press printed it. It was almost as if they felt that there was something wrong in suppression of news in the interest of saving human life. Whatever their misgivings, however, my gratitude was unqualified.

Happily, the *Daily Express* had given half its front page to a photograph of Davies and that night I got Ernie Bond to write across it in chinagraph pencil 'X got £500 for this'. We then slipped it under the door of the basement, and watched the two gunmen who were still awake scratching their heads and discussing it. Davies was asleep in a corner. They eventually tore up the newspaper and threw it in a bin. We therefore waited until Davies woke up and, having sent for another copy of the *Express*, repeated the performance. There was no possible doubt of its effect on Davies. The thought of being cooped up in that smelly, horrible basement with no hope of escape whilst X was making money out of their predicament must have proved too much. Just before 4 a.m. the gunmen decided to give up and as the siege entered its sixth day, they released the hostages and surrendered. It must have been a bitter pill for Davies, who shot himself in a half-hearted way before surrendering.

So ended the most dramatic and difficult siege since Sidney Street, without the police having fired a shot or harmed anyone. The hostages, weary, exhausted, dishevelled were whisked to hospital and the gunmen, as we said they would, went straight to a cell or hospital bed. Congratulations flowed in from all over the world and we were able to reproduce some in Police Orders for the encouragement of the force:

Metropolitan Police Orders    Tuesday 7 October 1975
1. Message from the Commissioner
Amongst the many letters and telegrams of congratulations and good wishes following the Spaghetti House incident I have received the following:

1. From the Private Secretary to Her Majesty the Queen.

'I heard you describe the Spaghetti House kidnapping as a classic case, and the Queen thought that the handling of it could aptly be described in that way too.

Her Majesty has told me to congratulate you, and all members of the Metropolitan Police who were involved, on taking such difficult decisions so calmly and well, and in bringing about such an eminently satisfactory result.'

2. From the Prime Minister.

'The Home Secretary has kept me fully informed during the past week of the progress of the incident in Knightsbridge and I have heard with admiration the news of the release of the hostages. We owe a considerable debt to the Metropolitan Police for the patience and restrain you have shown in carrying out your responsibilities. Please convey my warmest congratulations to all the men under your command for the way in which they have conducted themselves.'

3. From the Home Secretary.

'The release of the hostages held in the Knightsbridge incident and the arrests which have been made are a most satisfactory outcome to a very difficult problem. I know that you will examine carefully the lessons of the past week, but the success in dealing with the incident clearly indicates that the restrained and patient approach was very much the right one.

It was kind of you to say that the presence of Home Office officials in the circumstances you faced was of assistance. These officials in turn have spoken highly to me of the reception which you accorded them, which I appreciate.

The way in which the Metropolitan Police, in the full glare of publicity, have carried out their responsibilities has deservedly won great respect throughout the country. Please express to all those under your command my warm appreciation of a difficult job well done.'

4. From Admiral of the Fleet, The Earl Mountbatten of Burma, K.G.

'*Operation Spaghetti* admirably thought out. Brilliantly carried out. An example to the world. Many congratulations to you and all concerned.'

All have been suitably acknowledged.

I would like to convey to all members of the Force and civilian staff concerned in the incident my warmest thanks and admiration for their tireless patience, their courage, their good humour and their complete unity in seeking to achieve the end they finally brought about.

I have already thanked on behalf of the Force all those others, not least the news media and the Home Office, who gave such invaluable support.

The driver of the getaway car, who had fled the scene, was subsequently arrested and all, except X, were duly convicted and received long sentences.

The real lessons from Spaghetti House were that the uniformed branch and the CID really could work as one, each taking pride and pleasure in the achievements of the other and that, no less important, we could depend upon reasonable co-operation from Press, radio and television provided that we played fair with them, and by playing fair, I mean treating them as trustworthy and responsible and giving them all the information we could with as little delay as possible. In fact we were to be richly rewarded by the Press for our growing trust in them only a week or two later. On 6 November an eighteen-year-old Greek Cypriot girl was kidnapped from her home in North London and a demand was received by her relatives for a ransom of £60,000. We had long foreseen that we should sooner or later be faced with such a situation and John Wilson, the assistant commissioner (Crime), was therefore not without some precedent to guide him, the benefit of research at home and abroad. In a case of this kind, unlike a political kidnapping, the kidnappers desire no publicity and in particular, that no information should be given to the police. It is customary for their ransom demands to be accompanied by threats to kill the victim in the event of disclosure. Moreover, once the Press are aware that a kidnapping is in progress they cannot help but impede or prevent altogether the successful outcome of the enquiry. Reporters and photographers besiege the home and block the telephone. Communication and movement both become impossible. Secrecy, in the first instance, is essential, but not easy to achieve. The police have no D notice system. Instead we have in London a system agreed with the Press for sending to all editors a written *request* to abstain from publishing a story in the public interest. It is not unreasonable, in such circumstances, for the Press to be told of the reason for the request. Accordingly, Wilson made the request, which was honoured, but after two days realized that the Press could not be expected to hold their hands for ever without being given convincing reasons. He therefore arranged regular daily Press conferences at the Yard at which the Press were told in confidence of the progress of enquiries. In the meantime the hunt went on relentlessly, day and night. From Friday, 7 November, until the early hours of Sunday, 16 November, the Press, with the notable exception of a Workers' Revolutionary broadsheet purporting to be a newspaper, voluntarily complied with the request for secrecy and as a result the girl was recovered unharmed, the ransom money was recovered and the kidnappers were arrested. It was a truly remarkable case, remarkable not least for the heartsearching of the Press itself over their own conduct. However, despite their misgivings and forewarning of anxieties for the future there was no doubt in the minds of the police who took part in the case that the Press had played perhaps the most important part in making possible the safe recovery of the girl. My Christmas, at least, was made all the happier by a Christmas card, which read simply 'With love, Aloi'.

# CHAPTER 16

# An Unacceptable Act

To the casual onlooker with an interest in crime, police and public order, the end of 1975 must have seemed like the 'dawn of a new and happier era. Terrorism was being defeated rather than contained. Serious crime was affording the police frequent and well-publicized successes. The violence of Grosvenor Square and Red Lion Square seemed to have receded and, perhaps most important of all, there was for the first time for years, a discernible and significant improvement in the relationship between the Metropolitan force and the Press. In other words, everything seemed set fair. In fact, however, to the very few people in the know, the first step towards the lessening of that pleasant prospect had already been taken and the seeds of disagreement and disillusion had already been sown. Everything that happened to the Metropolitan Police in the operational, administrative and political sphere during 1976 ought therefore to be viewed against the growing likelihood of unwanted and unacceptable change and, from my personal point of view, the suspicion that my police career was rapidly coming to an enforced end. I think that I ought to explain all this in detail so that the curious may be satisfied of the reasons for this seeming paradox and in doing so I shall try to present as fairly as possible the conflicting views which brought about this situation.

Notwithstanding that police affairs generally seemed to be going so well there had always been one contentious area in which we had never been able to satisfy our critics, and, to be quite honest, had not always wanted to – the procedure for handling complaints against the police. In the post-war years in particular this had become a kind of permanent controversy, sometimes latent, sometimes furious, dependent on public reaction to incidents involving the police. The Shepherds Bush murders of three policemen, on the other hand, made criticism of the police unpopular, at least for a time. Both reactions were illogical, but illogicality and emotion, rather than evidence, have always dominated the approach to this problem.

Every few years a furious row would break out over some incident or other in which the police were accused of wrongdoing or excessive use of authority. It has gone on for so long that it has become as predictable as the four seasons. As long ago as 1928 a committee of enquiry had been established because the Metropolitan Police had the temerity to accuse a baronet, Sir Leo Money, of indecency with a Miss Irene Savidge. An incredulous magistrate dismissed the case awarding costs against the police, the incident arousing much indignation in Parliament. Not long afterwards Sir Leo made the mistake of repeating the performance in circumstances which made acquittal impossible. He chose a railway carriage, not the most flexible setting, from a defence point of view. The incident did not attract the same publicity as his début, because this time the police were not the target. This incident was not in itself particularly noteworthy. In fact it was of a kind with which public and police had become familiar over the years.

After the 1939–45 war, however, the reaction to police misconduct, real or alleged, was noticeably different. No longer did the police enjoy the implicit protection of the establishment. The social order had changed or was changing and their behaviour was certain of more searching and effective scrutiny than when their primary purpose was to support the rights of those with money and property. It was not so much that police behaviour deteriorated. It was that when they did misbehave they were less likely to get away with it. Moreover the extensive publicity given to proven misbehaviour lent a dubious credibility to complaints of wrongdoing without any foundation but generally not open to convincing public rebuttal. This is the bitter truth which all policemen must sooner or later come to accept; that the unpopularity of the police function, when allied to instances of proven wrongdoing by individual policemen, puts the reputation of the whole service at risk and lends unjustified credence to the revengeful, the malicious and to the politically motivated. And, it must be said, to those who look upon suspicion of the police as part of their duty. Snippets in both the *Guardian* and the *Sunday Times* suggested an anticipatory relish in the expectation that the report in December 1977 by Sir Henry Fisher into the Confait affair, the murder of a homosexual, would condemn police conduct of the case. In the event, the criticism of the police was of less importance than that directed to others involved in the affair. Their position was well summarized by my successor describing a constable sardonically regarding two or three pigeons flying around over his head in Trafalgar Square and saying, 'Go on, you might as well, everyone else does.'

There were, however, enough spectacular cases of police misbehaviour in the post-war years to convince even policemen themselves that changes were needed in the arrangements for looking into complaints. Prosecution of the chief constables of Brighton and Worcester, public anger at the police handling of the Trafalgar Square demonstrations against defence policy in 1961, the enormous publicity attracted by the enquiry into the conduct of Detective Sergeant Challenor who was alleged with others to have planted incriminating evidence on people protesting against a visit by Queen Frederika of Greece. These were some of the more memorable cases. There was, too, the beating up of prisoners at the Roberts-Arundel industrial dispute in Stockport, the famous if fatuous Scottish case of the Thurso boy who was cuffed by a constable and, of course, the incident in which Constable Eastmond of the Metropolitan Police clashed with Brian Rix, the actor, over his treatment of a motorist. The last incident led directly to the Royal Commission on the police of 1961–62 from which a great deal of good flowed. It made possible the reduction in the number of forces and abolished the differences between administrative control of county, city and borough forces. Hitherto the responsibility for appointment, promotion and discipline had been vested in the chief constable in county forces only. In cities and boroughs it was exercised by Watch Committees of the council of the local authority. Henceforth those powers were to be vested in chief constables only and the composition of the Standing Joint Committees, responsible for the administration of county policing, and Watch Committees in cities and boroughs, was standardized. Each was to consist of a number of elected councillors and magistrates in the proportion of two to one. The one problem not satisfactorily resolved by the Commission and the subsequent Police Act of 1964 was the handling of complaints against the police. This has been so acrimonious and contentious that it might be as well to explain the position in detail.

No fewer than 22 of the 111 conclusions of the Royal Commission related to complaints and these were embodied in the Police Act of 1964.

The Commission was adamant that the control of police discipline must remain in the hands of the chief officer and, in effect, asserted that the judicial function of trying disciplinary issues was not an appropriate one for elected representatives.

Simply put, the system resulting from the 1964 Act and consequential Regulations was that every complaint by a member of the public must be recorded, that investigation must be undertaken by an officer not associated with the 'accused' officer, that only the Director of Public Prosecutions should decide whether or not to prosecute in all criminal cases and, not least important, that the responsibility for instituting disciplinary proceedings should be exercised by the deputy chief officer, since the chief officer would ordinarily try the case. The system required the local police authorities, now to consist of magistrates and elected representatives, to satisfy themselves about the number of complaints and the manner in which they were dealt with, although it must in fairness be said that it did not make clear just how they were to go about it. It also required a close annual scrutiny of complaints by HM Inspectors of Constabulary and empowered the Home Secretary to demand the disclosure of any information he thought necessary. For the first time outside London the system was opened to Parliamentary Question. The Act also empowered police authorities to dismiss chief officers with the consent, or by the direction, of the Home Secretary. So much for those who argued that the police were judge and jury in their own cause. In fact, their degree of accountability exceeded that of any other public service.

There is no doubt that throughout the provinces the new system generally worked well. There were of course occasions on which its operation left something to be desired but it was at least possible to bring such failures into the open and they were mostly found to be due to human error, faulty judgement and only rarely to deliberate wrongdoing. Unfortunately, however, public confidence in the system was undermined by the inexplicable failure to apply its most important provision, the establishment of the deputy chief officer as the *de facto* disciplinary authority, to the one police force for which it was most necessary, the Metropolitan, which had long been involved in more routine wrongdoing than most of the other police forces in England and Wales put together.

The omission was particularly ironic in that the police authority for the Metropolis is the Home Secretary, who had thus not applied to his own force a reform which he had thought necessary for police forces generally. There was no question of the omission being deliberate. It arose from an unfortunate oversight, a failure to appreciate the immunity of the Metropolitan CID from the new system. In 1879, following a rather scandalous trial involving senior members of the then Metropolitan detective branch, a Home Office departmental committee, without a police member or the benefit of police advice, conferred on a newly appointed Director of Criminal Investigation, who was later redesignated assistant commissioner (Crime), the authority to investigate all allegations of crime, including those alleged to have been committed by policemen. The authority of the deputy commissioner to investigate complaints against the police could only therefore be exercised in respect of allegations not amounting to crime, *viz* neglect, incivility and so on. The practical effect of this omission was that all allegations of crime against Metropolitan detectives between 1879 and 1972 were investigated by the Metropolitan CID, who resisted stoutly the innovation of calling upon members of other forces or of the uniform branch to help them with particularly difficult cases. Had the Met CID not enjoyed this immunity it is unlikely that agitation for further reform would have carried much weight, but the cumulative effect, particularly when contrasted with the ever improving standard of probity in the provinces, was disastrous and caused bitter dissension within the Met itself. It was, therefore, the failure of the Home Office to discharge its duty in relation to the force for which the Home Secretary was responsible which provided the weightiest ammunition for the reformers.

General and justified uneasiness about the Metropolitan situation in particular had earlier led Robert Carr, during Edward Heath's administration, to set up a working party to look at the position again. This was by no means unwelcome. Within a few days of taking office as commissioner I had written to Maudling on behalf of the newly created policy committee of the Metropolitan force asking for the introduction of an independent element in the procedure for investigating and dealing with complaints against the police. My view, and that of my colleagues, was that this could best be done by way of *ex post facto* review, activated either by a dissatisfied complainant or by the officer in the case. Since very few complainants continue to express dissatisfaction this seemed to us likely to obviate a great deal of unnecessary work, expense and delay and yet likely to satisfy the public. It is, of course, important to remember that some complainants will never be satisfied and that the primary object of change should be to satisfy the public. The objectors to this proposal argued that it would involve double jeopardy.

This was untrue. Double jeopardy means literally being put in danger of punishment twice for the same offence. *Ex post facto* review implied no more than the ombudsman principle, which had worked very well under the Police Act, the public in every case being satisfied by disclosure of the facts.

A number of other suggestions were put forward for consideration. The most important of these was a paper prepared by the Police Federation, representing all ranks beneath superintendent. Its Joint Central Committee suggested a scheme which it knew at the outset to be unworkable and unacceptable, involving a disciplinary adviser with no power to discipline, trial boards including a lawyer and a layman, appeals to Crown Courts and so on. The purpose of the document was to undermine the police discipline system and the Metropolitan branch of the Federation, who strongly supported the clean-up of the force, opposed it but were in a minority and had no separate voice. The Federation banked on ministers not realizing they were being hoodwinked. Their paper, which they could not even explain satisfactorily themselves to the working group, was a powerfully disrupting factor which put an end to any hope of achieving an effective inexpensive and generally acceptable solution. Other proposals by the Superintendents' Association, by Justice, by the Community Relations Commission, by an academic and by the National Council for Civil Liberties were considered at length, without attracting support. The issue was really whether a form of *ex post facto* review, favoured by the Met and the Association of Chief Police Officers would be acceptable or not. In the event, no proposal was acceptable to anyone but its proponents and after presentation to Parliament in March 1974, the working group's report was quietly buried.

Roy Jenkins had returned to the Home Office in March 1974 accompanied by non-elected, non-Civil Service advisers. Other than keeping pace with events, there really was very little for him to tackle in the police world, apart from the maldistribution of police manpower, which was politically not a very attractive problem. It was largely to his personal credit that this was so. During his last period at the Home Office, before going to the Exchequer, he had improved police mobility and equipment, particularly wireless, and introduced majority verdicts. Even more significant, against intense opposition from police and local authorities he had arbitrarily reduced the number of forces in England and Wales from 123 to 47 and in a remarkably short time had been found unquestionably to have been right. He was, in fact, the architect of the present police structure which has all the advantages of a national force with none of the disadvantages and during that period had been probably the most successful and effective Home Secretary in living memory. It must have been heady stuff, success of that kind, when you consider the opposition he had to overcome. On his return, therefore, he must have been attracted by the prospect of solving yet another seemingly intractable problem that had baffled everyone else. He embarked upon the task in the same uncompromising way. Unfortunately, it does not seem to have occurred to him that police organization is an administrative problem not involving any weighty constitutional principle. The investigation of complaints, on the other hand, touches on very serious principles indeed. The operational freedom of the police from political or bureaucratic interference is essential to their acceptability and to the preservation of democracy. The police must not even seem, in dealing with industrial disputes or political demonstrations, to reflect the wishes of the government of the day. Their manifest impartiality is their most priceless asset. The reverse of this principle was to be seen only too sadly in Ulster before 1969 and obtains in American cities today.

Jenkins, like his predecessor in 1879, did not arrange for practical research in the Met, for which he was police authority. He decided to announce a new scheme for dealing with complaints and produced it like a rabbit from a hat on the last day before the dissolution of Parliament. A day or so before, he sent for me at 4 p.m., told me he had a meeting at 4.30 p.m. and then read his proposed statement to the

House. I told him it was too complex to absorb in so short a time but asked two questions. They were answered by Lord Harris, his Minister of State, who left me no wiser. It was clearly to be an imposed solution, without research or prior consultation. On 30 July the statement was read to the House and was well received both by members and the Press. But did they even dimly grasp its meaning? It read:

MR ROY JENKINS

It is my view that an effective independent element, commanding public confidence, must be brought into operation while a complaint is being dealt with – both before the decision is taken whether to bring disciplinary action and, in sufficiently serious cases, in the hearing of any disciplinary charge; it would not be sufficient merely to have some kind of inquest after the event, with no power, even retrospectively, to alter the outcome of the case. It is equally important to avoid bringing to bear a disproportionate weight of skilled resources on matters of a minor nature; the new arrangements should provide for early identification, and the expeditious handling by the police, of intrinsically minor complaints.

None of the schemes examined by the Working Group seem to me entirely satisfactory, but they contain features which can, I believe, be built up into an effective and practicable scheme. The following is an outline of the scheme which I propose. These proposals will form the basis for detailed consultations which I shall now be having with the police service and police authorities, with a view to having the scheme fully worked out later this year. Legislation will be required to give effect to it.

The substance of his proposals was that there was to be an independent statutory commission with members drawn from a national or regional panel and including police members only for the purpose of trying cases. All complaints would continue to be investigated by police and, if alleging crime, would continue to be forwarded to the Director of

Public Prosecutions. In all other cases, and those in which the Director took no action, the papers were to go to the Commission who would decide whether any further investigation was required, whether disciplinary proceedings should be brought or whether no further action was necessary. It was to be open to the complainant to ask for a tribunal hearing or for the deputy chief officer to arrange one. It was also to be open to the Commission to direct hearing by tribunal.

There were obvious defects in the proposal. Why, for example, restrict the power of the deputy chief officer to institute disciplinary proceedings without further ado? There might well be some point in his being required to forward all cases in which he thought no action was necessary but why introduce an unnecessary delay and possibly a less competent adjudicator in cases which he thought should be pursued? At this time the average ongoing daily number of complaints under investigation was about 1350 in the MPD alone.

Another no less important aspect was the intention to hand over the ultimate responsibility for police discipline to political nominees. This was surely even more open to objection than the proposal, unanimously vetoed by the Royal Commission, that it should be discharged by elected representatives.

The practical implication of the proposals was that some 10,000 to 15,000 files would be forwarded to political nominees notwithstanding that less than 5 per cent of them would relate to a dissatisfied complainant, some would cause delay in proceedings already obviously necessary and, worst of all, the adjudicators would be less competent than deputy chief officers to decide the issues and as political nominees might not in any case be seen to be impartial.

The real irony lay in that since the clean-up of the Met began there had never been less meaningful agitation for change. The *Sunday Times* A10 article had done enormous good. The steady departure of bent policemen, the increasing effectiveness of the CID, the growing harmony with provincial forces, all these indicated that there was no real need for change, and although the complexity and problems of the Metropolitan complaints branch were available to the Home Office just across the road, no one came to seek information or to enquire the implication of the proposals.

They were so obviously devoid of merit that I suspected that they had not been drafted by a civil servant. I suspect that they were not the work of Jenkins either. I thought them the product of one of the non-Civil Service non-elected advisers with which most ministries these days are infested. And there is no doubt that one of Roy Jenkins's more admirable qualities, loyalty to his subordinates, might prevent him from disclaiming authorship.

Having recovered from my initial shock and disbelief, I telephoned Jimmy Waddell to enquire whether the statement was meant seriously. He told me it was. I thereupon asked him to tell the Home Secretary politely, but firmly, that I would do everything possible to oppose it both publicly and privately. Just to make doubly sure, after the election I wrote to Alec Gordon Brown, the assistant secretary handling the matter, in the following terms:

19 August 1974

On 30th July you sent me a copy of the Home Office proposals for reform of the complaints procedure. I had these copied and forwarded to a number of senior officers for study and comment. I appreciate that you will be arranging discussions to begin in September but I shall be away on leave then and I thought it might be helpful to make it clear from the comments I have received that it will be necessary in the interests of both public and police to oppose the proposals energetically. Indeed, I hope to persuade the Home Secretary that far from having the intended effect the implementation of these proposals would be likely to undermine the confidence between police and public, to encourage the most dangerous kind of police malpractice and that they would be unlikely to offer adequate compensatory benefit. They would be likely also to harm immeasurably the efficacy of control of the police service, on which so much depends. Quite apart from these objections of principle, the machinery proposed would in my view be too cumbersome to be workable, at any rate in the Metropolitan Police.

I am, of course, speaking for the Metropolitan Police alone, and shall be prepared to give reasons for my views. Their formulation will, however, take some time and I thought I should give you the earliest possible forewarning of my reaction.

This letter was followed by an invitation to lunch privately with Roy Jenkins at a hotel in St James's. I must at this point make it clear that throughout the unhappy months that were to follow I was always treated with impeccable courtesy by the Home Secretary. If there was any bluntness to the point of rudeness it was on my side and his reaction was what you would expect of him, polite, considerate and placatory. But then, it was not his Service that was being undermined. I told him without frills during our first discussion that if he pursued his original statement and in particular, if he deprived the deputy chief officer of the power to institute discipline proceedings, he would go down in history as having done the British police more harm than any man in this century. He asked me if I would give him my reasons for saying this and I said I would do this in writing. In consultation with my colleagues, including the Metropolitan Police solicitor, I then put the following points to him for consideration:-

1. The Metropolitan force received 5578 complaints in 1973. The provincial forces received 10,589. Only in a minute proportion of cases was the complainant dissatisfied with the investigation or the result.
2. There was no evidence of dissatisfaction with the existing system.
3. The size of the task of investigating complaints was enormous. Its complexity was such that anyone without

lengthy experience of police administration could not hope to discharge it effectively.

4. There was no evidence, logic or justification to restrict the right of the deputy chief officer to institute disciplinary proceedings. Though it was acceptable to refer to the Commission every case in which he decided not to do so.

5. There is no evidence to justify removal from the chief officer of the responsibility for deciding guilt and awarding punishment in disregard of the unanimous recommendation of the Royal Commission.

I then went on to explain that in practice the most difficult cases are those in which the Director of Public Prosecutions take no action and those in which prosecution ends in acquittal. Some of those cases are lengthy, complex and exceedingly difficult to assess, occasionally involving disregard of orders and regulations allowing the inference of blackmail, corruption and other wrongdoing not capable of proof in a criminal court. This is without question the most sensitive and vulnerable part of the whole of the machinery for dealing with police wrongdoing because the assessment of each case, and the decision of the deputy chief officer, is made against the known background of an acquittal or a decision by the Director of Public Prosecutions not to prosecute.

I explained with care the inadequacy of the ordinary criminal law for the purpose of maintaining an honest police force and that half the 50 officers prosecuted up to that time had been acquitted. Of the 25 acquitted, 11 resigned to forestall disciplinary proceedings, 3 were disciplined (1 required to resign, 1 reduced in rank, 1 reprimanded) and 10 were reinstated without disciplinary proceedings. 6 of these 10 and the officer reduced in rank were transferred from CID to uniform duties. One case awaited disposal.

During the same period a much larger number of officers, 201, resigned voluntarily, some of them in order to forestall disciplinary proceedings. 45 were suspended pending criminal or disciplinary proceedings. A total of 296 officers had, therefore, been the subject of serious complaint in 29 months, of whom 251 had been dealt with under the discipline code, 25 after conviction for crime, 45 remaining suspended. I argued that the strongest inducement for the errant police-man to resign voluntarily is not the doubtful likelihood of conviction by a jury but the certainty that senior officers responsible for instituting disciplinary proceedings and deciding the outcome are exceptionally qualified to recognize wrongdoing not amounting to crime and to deal with it effectively. And that any adulteration of that process by the inclusion of laymen in decision making or trial, no matter how well qualified technically, is not only unnecessary from the point of view of satisfying the public but could be positively harmful.

I pointed out that the proposal would involve referral to the Commission of –

  *a* all cases in which the Director of Public Prosecutions decided not to prosecute.
  *b* all cases ending in acquittal.
  *c* an additional 2000 or 3000 cases in which criminal proceedings had not been contemplated.

The Commission could not dispose of any of the additional 2000 or 3000 cases before the completion of meticulous enquiry into each. It is the cavalier disposal of trivial complaints, not the unsatisfactory outcome of serious com-plaints, on which public dissatisfaction with the present system is founded. The establishment of the Commission would thus not lessen the workload or shorten investigation. It would simply add a further stage unnecessary in almost every case.

I then went on to explain that public dissatisfaction with the present system is very difficult to define. Dissatisfaction with the outcome of cases involving criminal or disciplinary proceedings is so rare as to be exceptional. Most dissatis-faction seems to relate to police policies or operations which in themselves, though sometimes rightly criticized, would not involve formal proceedings against individuals. Public dissatisfaction mostly consists of theoretical objections to the principles governing the present system. Dissatisfaction of that kind is much harder to remove than is that felt by an individual in a particular case.

It was clear that implementation of the proposal would require a large and continually increasing staff mostly engaged on wholly unnecessary work. The Home Secretary himself had been at pains to emphasize that he did not contemplate the Commission taking positive action in more than a handful of the thousands of cases forwarded to it each year. I expressed doubts about the availability and qualifications of staff for an organization clearly devoid of career prospects. If it was seen to be part of the career structure of the Civil Service it would command no more confidence than the Home Office already enjoyed. The members of the Commission (or Police Complaints Board, its eventual designation) laboured under two unavoidable disadvantages. If they were establishment figures, competent for the job, they would not satisfy the radicals who wanted change. If they were non-establishment figures and excluded criminal lawyers and former policemen, which I think not so much proper as essential, they would not, in assessing police misconduct, to put it crudely if colourfully, know their backside from their elbow.

I summarized my objections to the new proposal as follows:

a It will weaken the protection of the public by adulterating the procedure for deciding issues and trying cases.
b It will remove the control of discipline from the chief officer with a consequent lessening of his authority.
c It will create a large new bureaucratic machine with staff of untried quality to deal with matters for which police experience is essential.
d It will add unnecessarily and weightily to an already too slow and cumbersome procedure.
e It will not increase the likelihood of public confidence

in the system to an extent greater than that enjoyed by the Home Office, Provincial Police Authorities and Chief Officers of Police.

*f* It offers no measurable compensatory benefits for the very considerable disadvantages it ensures.

Having been bluntly critical, I then tried to be helpful by suggesting a modification that I thought had obvious merit. It read:

> The new proposal could be adapted so as to meet with general approval and to promote the public interest, bearing in mind that it is the appearance, rather than the reality, of impartiality and thoroughness, which the present system lacks. That disadvantage might be overcome if the new Commission was excluded from playing any part in deciding whether or not to institute disciplinary proceedings or in trying disciplinary cases but was empowered at the behest of a dissatisfied complainant to examine every case in which neither criminal nor disciplinary proceedings had been taken. This would make it possible speedily to review the comparatively few cases, less than 100, in which the complainant was dissatisfied whilst avoiding the creation of costly, cumbersome and ineffective additional procedures for the other 3000 or 4000 cases in which no one expresses continued dissatisfaction. Such a scheme ought to be sufficient to satisfy any reasonable critic of the present system and would go well beyond the accountability of public servants generally.

I omitted one telling argument from this document from a wish not to seem needlessly offensive. It was the argument that with a Home Secretary of the extreme right or extreme left, how could a commissioner send his men to a Red Lion Square knowing that the Home Secretary's creatures on the Board would have the power to order discipline proceedings and find guilt by a majority? Of course, there was no question of Jenkins behaving in that way but could one feel the same confidence in some of his colleagues? Why, in any case, create machinery that could be abused by others?

There was one incident in my discussion of the document with the Home Secretary worth relating because it demonstrates how impossible it is to dislike him even though locked in disagreement. Having read my submission he looked clearly ill at ease. The point about the deputy chief officer was clearly indisputable and showed what seemed to me an error of judgement and lack of practical knowledge in compiling the original statement to Parliament. Sensing his appreciation of this I said, 'Home Secretary, you have published your views. The local authority associations, the chief officers, the superintendents and the Police Federation have all published theirs. I am the only person so far not to do so and I have more wrongdoing to deal with than all the rest put together. I think perhaps I should now publish that document on the table.' To which he replied, without hesitation or batting an eyelid, 'I don't deny that publication of that document at this moment might cause me grave embarrassment but I would not think it right for that reason to restrict your right to publish.' I nearly laughed aloud in admiration. He knew perfectly well that if he had forbidden me to publish it would have been issued that very evening from Scotland Yard Press Office. But firstly he was too big a man, and secondly too shrewd an operator to behave in that way. He rightly banked on my unwillingness to embarrass him by disclosure of the error. His reaction, of course, made it quite impossible for me to make the document public until it was too late but I bear him no grudge for that because I think his reaction was entirely sincere. I allowed one or two selected journalists to see it privately with the knowledge of the Home Office but on condition that they did not reproduce it. I am bound to admit that this had no beneficial effect.

Having given further thought to the matter he made a revised statement to the House of Commons on 15 July

1975, which contained, without explanation, the following significant departure from the original:

> In any given case, a Deputy Chief Constable will consider, before anything goes to the proposed independent commission, whether to institute disciplinary proceedings following a complaint. Only if he takes the view that disciplinary proceedings should not be instituted will the case be referred for examination by the commission, which will consider that view, and will have power in the last resort formally to require that disciplinary proceedings be brought.

The change in this paragraph was of incalculable importance but raised no comment from the House, a number of whose members may not have understood it. It afforded the clearest possible indication that whoever drew up the original statement had little or no idea of its practical implications. In retrospect, in some ways I rather regretted insisting on the change, since the task of formulating every charge, or deciding on the formulation of every charge, would inevitably have resulted in chaos within a few days of the establishment of the Board.

In the event, Parliament refused to agree that the Home Secretary should appoint the new Board, since he was the police authority for the Metropolis. Instead, it conferred that power on the Prime Minister. It is perhaps just as well that the eventual resignation honours list was then unknown.

The scheme caused widespread dismay throughout the whole police service. Neither the Press nor Parliament appeared to have made any attempt to understand it because it *seemed* unexceptionable. Only those intimately concerned with police discipline could see the objections, whether of principle or practice. It all made no difference. Least of all did people understand that what I feared was not increased police accountability but the undermining of police discipline and constitutional independence. I realized quickly and sadly that neither of these two causes was likely to appeal to any of the political parties of today. Each would clearly prefer a police force subservient to their wishes and control as in the United States. Something precious and unique to our way of life was to be destroyed without any attempt at rational justification. The Bill predictably attracted little interest and small attendances in Parliament. It was easily pushed through.

But this time it was a Pyrrhic victory. The new Act went too far for some and not far enough for others. All those urging reform, whom the Act was intended to placate, expressed dissatisfaction with it and the police, for a variety of reasons, not all of them logical, regarded it as downright betrayal. Even we were divided. The Federation kept insisting that a copy of the complaint should in every case be given to the 'accused' officer. This is clearly not in the public interest and in some cases might actually obstruct the cause of justice and therefore be unlawful. I opposed this from the outset and argued that chief officers should continue to exercise discretion in this matter, but the Federation continued, in my view quite wrongly, to use this as a stick to beat the Home Secretary with.

The Bill received the Royal Assent in mid-1976 and this, of course, meant the end of my police career. I did not expect the years of bitter struggle as deputy commissioner or the later years of painful and sensitive surgery to end in this way but I did not want, now that Jenkins had loosened the patient's stitches, to preside over the inevitable relapse. All 43 chief police officers had opposed the change, the only time I have known them to be unanimous about anything controversial in my twenty years as a chief officer. The commissioner, however, was affected more than any of them, and not merely by the history and extent of police wrongdoing in London. He is the only chief officer whose administrative orders are subject to the approval of the Home Secretary. Now that discipline is to be administered by political nominees he inevitably becomes an administrator rather than a leader, his status and independence being sadly diminished. I do not mean this to imply a sense of personal belittlement. Rather do I think of it as a lessening of democracy and a potential increase of political influence in a field from which it should be resolutely excluded.

Though the months had been sad and distressing there was no ill will or discourtesy between the Home Office and me. In order to be as helpful as possible I had made it clear privately that I would resign rather than administer an Act I regarded as repugnant. The way in which this was conveyed to the Commons and the Lords was typical of the manner in which the Bill had been forced through. When asked point blank whether I would retire as a result of the new Act, spokesmen in both Houses replied that I would reach my normal retirement age before it could be brought into force. Both spokesmen knew that the commissioner has no retiring age. He is *entitled* to retire at 60 should he so wish, but I think I am the first to exercise that right. Neither spokesman told an actual lie, of course. They were just careful not to tell the whole truth. I do not however complain of this. It is sometimes better in the public interest not to reveal the whole truth. The success of our pornography corruption enquiry, for example, depended to some extent on lulling wrongdoers into a misplaced feeling of security by carefully worded but deliberately incomplete statements. And I had no desire at all for melodrama. But in an odd way, the answers, though not unfair, were a fitting epitaph on the whole affair.

I was to comment on retirement that the Act lent a new dimension to absurdity and demonstrated the lengths to which politicians will go to placate the implacable. I should have added 'and, in this case, unsuccessfully'.

The crowning irony is that Parliament, ministers and police all want the same thing, an independent element in the handling of those complaints against police in which the complainant remains dissatisfied, a very small proportion of the whole. Instead, from 1 June 1977, the files relating to some 19,000 or more complaints a year (the 1976 total) will make their way to the Complaints Board from all over England and Wales to a small group of people, appointed by political patronage, some of whom are partially qualified for the task by experience but as establishment figures carry no weight with those who urged reform, and the remainder, by reason of their virtuous and sheltered lives, unlikely to be fitted to deal with police wrongdoing. They have anxiously protested from the outset that they propose to intervene in only a tiny number of cases and are supposed to still a clamour for effective and impartial scrutiny of the whole complaints procedure. According to the *Daily Telegraph* of 2 June, the chairman, Lord Plowden, is said to have given an assurance that no use would be made in disciplinary proceedings of evidence considered by the Director of Public Prosecutions. I can only hope devoutly that he has been misquoted. Such evidence was essential to the clean-up of the Yard between 1972 and 1977 and if it is to be excluded in disciplinary proceedings the Board will throw a protective cloak over serious police wrongdoing more effective and damaging than ever before. Moreover, a test case in the Queen's Bench Division on 17 February 1977 (The Queen versus Commissioner *ex parte* Lindsay Cameron Todd) established the admissibility of such evidence in disciplinary cases. A man who is acquitted of blackmailing a prisoner has no defence against a charge of meeting a prisoner on bail without the consent of a senior officer. The latter is not a criminal offence, but the evidence for the discipline case is the same.

For about 95 per cent of the complaints files, some of which will be voluminous, the procedure will be pointless, since the complainant will not be dissatisfied before it begins, but I suppose if the process provides sufficient quangos for those lucky enough to attract the patronage of the Prime Minister, it can be said to have one beneficial aspect. It is the other 5 per cent of cases that are likely to be of interest, and they will not always relate to dissatisfied complainants. Cases in which the Director has decided not to prosecute, prosecutions ending in acquittals, cases in which an intimate knowledge of police orders, procedure and methods is essential to their determination.

Having done nothing at all worthwhile in respect of, say, 18,500 complaints a year, what is the new Board likely to do in relation to the other 500, many of which pose problems even for the thoroughly experienced, skilled and cynical police administrator?

Let me pose one or two hypothetical cases to illustrate my point. A policeman arrests a coloured man for a crime. Instead of charging him, he blackmails him but makes the mistake of demanding too much. The man complains to A10 who supply him with the money and attend the 'meet'. The policeman is caught redhanded. He goes before a jury with no defence. He is acquitted. One of the jury says to an A10 officer, 'You don't think we would convict a policeman on the evidence of that black bastard?' What does the Board do? If, in view of the importance of good race relations and the gravity of the offence it decides to appoint a tribunal, can it really expect two inexperienced laymen to convict on evidence rejected by a jury? If it decides to leave it to the police, why have a Board? Before 1 June 1977, the policeman didn't wait to find out. He got out whilst the going was good. Not, I think, any longer.

Cases like the one I mentioned are more common than might be supposed. Blackmailing people on bail, stealing valuable property from criminals who are not charged (in two such cases the Met, on the advice of counsel, paid the losers in full despite the acquittal of the policemen involved!), violence against individuals in which the evidence does not allow prosecution but a knowledgeable discipline board sacks the offender without hesitation and is supported by the Home Secretary on appeal. It is in this difficult and delicate area that the honesty and reputation of a police force is determined, not in the amount of noise that a dissatisfied complainant can generate. In some cases he may not make a noise because of the fear of a libel action.

In the *Guardian* of 2 June 1977, two officials of the Board are said to have mentioned the Red Lion Square riot, the Windsor Pop Festival and the Confait case as being suitable for the Board. I should have thought political nominees are the last people to be entrusted with adjudication of a politically motivated riot. The Confait case had already been considered by the Court of Appeal. Is the Board, no matter how high in the estimation of the Prime Minister, really likely to be competent to examine it? Whilst the Windsor Festival might give the Board something useful to do, what in fact would it do? It would be interesting to know. Or is its purpose really just a sham, a safety valve to allow the dispersal of hot air and to gain the Labour Party a few votes? And if so, is it not more likely to do more harm than good, especially in view of the fact that it cannot claim a single friend, apart from its sponsors and those whose pensions, other earnings or supplementary benefits it will enhance? And, of course, according to the Prime Minister, Parliament itself, for what that is worth.

Publication of the first annual report of the Police Complaints Board in May 1978 confirmed only too sadly the predictions of chief officers. Whilst the Board was happily rubber-stamping the beginnings of the mass of non-criminal trivia with which it would have to deal, the number of men in the Met suspended for allegedly serious wrongdoing rose by the end of 1977 by almost a quarter to an all time record.

# CHAPTER 17

# Civil Liberty and Public Order

1976 got off to a feeling of anticlimax. It was as if the Christmas and New Year break had put an abrupt end to the intrusion of gunmen and terrorism into the rather wearisome but demanding routine of administration, conferences and the social round. This is much harder than might be supposed. I am not one of those people who feel competent to speak extempore at lunches and dinners and like Mark Twain it takes me some time to prepare a reasonably good impromptu speech. One of the snags about being Commissioner, too, is that you have to be careful what you say in public, even in jest or attempted jest. I succumbed to the temptation to do a Desert Island Discs programme early in the year and was foolish enough to describe my eldest sister's rendering of a sonata by Anna Magdalena Bach as having all the delicacy of touch of a Battersea bricklayer. Sure enough this provoked a plaintive letter of protest from a Battersea bricklayer! It also brought a surprising number of pleasant letters from a wide variety of people, some strangers, some I had known only as a child, some just interested in what seemed to make me tick. Roy Plomley himself is a most agreeable host and doing the programme is fun, particularly trying to identify and search for the records of music that you can only hum, whistle, or otherwise convey to the amiable researcher. It is surprisingly difficult to choose eight records. Finally, I decided to split my life as nearly as I could into eight parts and choose one reflecting each, winding up, I hope slightly prematurely, with 'Sunset' by the band of the Royal Marines.

During these few weeks the long enquiry by Gilbert Kelland and his team of officers into allegations of corruption in Soho had gradually been approaching conclusion and the Director of Public Prosecutions had authorized applications for warrants for the arrest of two former commanders, a chief superintendent and nine other officers. Most of the twelve had already left the force and the others had been suspended. I couldn't help reflecting wryly that if the same machinery existed to suspend politicians, members of the legal and other professions and public servants generally on reasonable suspicion of wrongdoing there would have been quite a few notable gaps in public life during my term of office, but only the police have, and exercise, this ruthless procedure for putting on ice any of their members whose probity or integrity is in doubt. It can be hard to the point of unfairness. Of the average number of 40 and 50 policemen continually suspended during my time some had to wait as long as three years before being dealt with. Delays of this kind were not caused by dilatoriness on our part. Some enquiries were long and complex. The criminal process in London, too, can be very long drawn out, particularly for those on bail.

The arrests were, of course, sensational and inevitably attracted enormous publicity. It was little use saying that they all related to conduct which had ended several years earlier, that drastic administrative change had made repetition unlikely, that for some time Soho had been a great deal cleaner than at any time in this century. Inevitably the high rank of those arrested, the gravity of the charges and the public enjoyment of the humiliation of those once in authority all combined to give the impression that the case was a reflection of the current state of affairs, which was simply not true. Of course, time allows even incidents such as this to be seen in perspective and both Press and public eventually form a calmer and more balanced judgement. But for the innocent who suffer in the meantime, in this case the great majority of the Metropolitan force, it is easy to see the temptation to conceal, rather than expose, police wrongdoing in the supposed interest of the reputation of the force. It takes strong nerves and good judgement to see the need to put principle and probity first, knowing the price inevitably to be paid. It is only later, when the realization dawns that generations of young policemen to come will not be subjected to the same kind of corrupt influences, that there comes the satisfaction at having pursued the right course. Kelland and his men and, perhaps, more than anyone else, Jim Starritt, deserve an honoured place in Metropolitan Police history for putting an end to malpractice which had done the force incalculable harm for many years. For the time being, however, the *sub judice* aspect of the case restricted Press comment after the arrests and one or two IRA incidents quickly distracted public attention. In one of them a terrorist managed to score an 'own goal', as we say in the police, losing a leg, an arm and his matrimonial prospects by handling a bomb carelessly whilst it was in his mackintosh pocket. Eventually even the police could feel nothing but pity for him when he was brought to trial. Whether the surgical and nursing skill that preserved his life was in fact merciful I suppose only he can say. It certainly seemed like a miracle to those of us knowing of his injuries.

About this time also I had given way to the blandishments of Henry Hunt, Assistant Commissioner (Personnel and Training), who had long wanted to introduce girls into our corps. I was not easily persuaded because recruitment of women police was going well. They are an expensive investment, because on average, they serve under four years before leaving, usually on marriage, and I was a bit worried at the prospect of 120 nubile young women at Hendon where the cadet school houses 500 young men, healthy, energetic and full of go. With a touch of the Valentines I enquired acidly if Henry had provided for a professional abortionist to be assigned a police house at Hendon, or was it that recruiting was so bad that we now had to breed our own, as we had already attempted to do with dogs and horses? Henry bore all this with his usual cheerful good humour and was, of course, proved to be right. We had 40 applications for every place and were able to pick and choose. The amusing and encouraging effect, which we did not expect, was the notice-able improvement in the behaviour and manners of the boys. Incidentally, the girls consistently took the major share of academic prizes. The success of this innovation contributed to a spectacularly impressive Passing-Out parade in August.

It was during this year that I decided to tell the public the ground rules governing the relationship between the police and the army in England and Wales. I had been asked to talk to the Convocation of Leicester University and thought this would be a good opportunity to clear the air. There had been much talk of private armies and dark hints from political extremists about military involvement in civil affairs. The issue is one of great public interest and if no one in authority is prepared to come clean about it can be distorted to suit the cause of any radical activist. This time I was careful to get the agreement of the Home Office, who were very helpful, and, through them, the Ministry of Defence. The lecture described the present situation in detail and effectively put an end to the speculative nonsense which had caused public unease in the preceding twelve months. The real truth is so blindingly obvious that no one sees it. There are neither the power nor the resources to control Great Britain by force. The police and army are numerically inadequate and neither would contemplate the use of arbi-trary force against their fellow countrymen with the ruth-lessness necessary to such a policy. Like it or not, this country really does represent government by consent, even though at times this looks very much like no government at all. But this does not mean that the police and the army, or a combination of both, are unable or unwilling to meet unlawful violence with sufficient force to contain or suppress it. There is no threat to democracy in that. The limitation of resources, the traditions of both army and the police and the accountability of both will ensure that, for better or for worse, there is unlikely to be any change in that situation. Public opinion, however ill informed, prejudiced or partisan, expressed through the ballot box will continue to shape our way of life for so long as we remain free from foreign domination. This does not mean that democracy is safe. It means that if it is to be subverted it will be by gradual erosion of freedom by the government itself, a process increasingly discernible in the last few years.

My lecturing activities were not confined to Britain. In April I talked to a conference of American police chiefs in Washington and to the National Press Club there. I explained that the police in England and Wales were a little tired of being used as a stick to beat their American counterparts over the head. My theme was basically that the police are inevitably the most accurate reflection of the society they serve, to whom their faults or virtues are directly attributable. I was to explain my views in more detail during a lecture tour of North America after my retirement.

I returned a month or two later to give a talk on 'Kid-napping, Terrorism and the Media' to the International Press Institute at Philadelphia and got the biggest unintended laugh of my whole career. I was explaining, with Sir Denis Hamilton in the chair, that one of our most cherished policies in London was never to withhold news or information as a retaliatory measure for a grievance, real or imagined, against a journalist or newspaper and was taken aback when the large audience erupted into spontaneous laughter. It was only afterwards I learned that only a few days earlier distribution of the *Philadelphia Inquirer* had been stopped completely for 24 hours by several hundred large gentlemen in plain clothes who would not let anyone in or out. Apparently, complaints to the Mayor, a former police chief, and to the police got nowhere. It was perhaps pure coincidence that the newspaper had been sharply critical of the Philadelphia police. I was not surprised that I did not receive an invitation pressing or otherwise, to call upon the local chief. In fact, I was rather relieved to depart in case anyone should have thought I was interfering in local politics.

By this time Harold Wilson had resigned, the front cover of *Private Eye* affording perhaps the most fitting epitaph on his administration. It depicted the skipper of a dilapidated tramp steamer up to the bridge in water and clearly aground, handing over to his successor. I thought it a fairly apt summary, though I must readily admit that I make no claim to political skill or judgement. Indeed, I have not voted in an election since the war, preferring causes to parties. I did, however, vote in the referendum for the Common Market. But even that was with heart rather than head. My wife and I had agreed that the issue was so important that we ought to watch the long television debate before making up our minds. We did so and at the end I rose wearily to my feet and said, 'My God! If that's the lot who want us to come out let's get up early and go to vote to stay in.' I imagine thousands of others reacted in the same way. In fact I suspect that many elections are settled by the floating voter, voting not for, but against.

A rather more disturbing event was the disorder at the Notting Hill Carnival in late August. It was like nothing so much as a return to the sordid celebrations attending the hangings at Tyburn Tree. Blatant disregard of liquor and other laws, hooliganism, drunkenness, vandalism and most of all, pocket picking and robbery all occurred on a large scale and provoked the usual controversy. The police presence was said to be excessive and provocative, though I find the reasoning behind that suggestion rather hard to follow. We were in fact using far fewer men than at a Cup Final. Certainly, the scores of black people who were shamelessly robbed by young blacks in broad daylight did not share that view. The arguments followed thick and fast. Fortunately, some journalists had been in danger from thieves and robbers who thought themselves in danger of identification, so Press reporting was not so hostile to the police as is customary on these occasions. The real trouble is that no one is prepared to tell the simple truth when wrongdoing involves coloured people. Literally scores of young blacks had gone to the festival for no other purpose than to steal, rob or have a punch-up with the police. But it is not by any means popular to say so and there is never any shortage of politically motivated journalists and politicians to spin a web of lies and self-delusion before the sun has gone down. The real pity is that unless this trend can be stopped it is the ordinary decent black family who want to play their part in the community who will suffer. Those who urge a kind of Black Saturnalia in the interests of good race relations either need their heads examining or have sinister motives. There could be no more certain way to ensure polarization and possible disaster. Decent black citizens, and they are the overwhelming majority, do not want exceptional treatment. They want to be treated just like whites. And to suggest that they cannot enjoy themselves without licence to steal, commit acts of vandalism and to rob is insulting to them. One thing is certain. The problem will not go away. Running away from it by deferring to the wrongdoer is certainly not going to help. Not least instructive was the hopeless inadequacy of the ordinary criminal process for dealing with this kind of situation.

The cost of the carnival was some hundreds of robberies, looting of shops and other premises, many vehicles damaged, and 400 police and 200 civilians injured. Eighteen people were accused of a variety of offences in a trial before a jury consisting of seven whites and five blacks. It began on 26 April and lasted until August. At the end two youths of 18 and 19 were sent to prison for three years each, five were sent to Borstal and two were fined. Only two had been convicted on charges directly related to the carnival, of whom one had pleaded guilty. The jury, after a 14-day trial, had been out for a record 170 hours. They had delivered 51 verdicts, only eight of them guilty and were unable to agree on a further 28 verdicts. The cost of the trial was estimated at £¼m. The undecided charges were abandoned. It was a repetition, though more costly, of the farce played out in the summary courts after the brutal hooliganism of Red Lion Square on 15 June 1974. Of a total of 82 people charged with offences, 29 were acquitted, 12 were convicted but suffered no penalty, 36 were fined and 3 were given suspended sentences. Bearing in mind the deliberate nature of the violence the proceedings were a fitting comment on the remoteness of the stipendiary magistracy of central London from the realities of life.

In these kinds of cases the prosecution suffers every kind of handicap. The difficulty in gathering evidence, the delay in proceedings, the fact that only a small number of a mass of offenders can be caught and charged, the scope for defence lawyers to accuse the police of racial or political prejudice, even before a competent judge, as in the Notting Hill trial, the case is almost hopeless from the start. The inevitable failure then opens the way to a spate of retaliatory allegations against the police. The simple but unpalatable truth is that our system of justice is not fitted to deal with political or racial violence on a large scale and that no one knows what to do about it. The lawyers are quite happy with the situation because they make a great deal of money out of it. The Press sell many newspapers exploiting charge and counter charge. The police wind up bewildered and resentful. They are faced from time to time with a deliberate breakdown of law and order and can do little about it unless they are prepared to take the law into their own hands which might win the immediate battle but involve them in a war they must inevitably lose.

Very few people remember, or are aware of the classic judgement of the Court of Appeal in what is known as the Garden House case. The most important part, which should be compulsory reading for every magistrate and journalist, is as follows:

The next point to be mentioned is what might be called the 'Why pick on me?' argument. It has been suggested that there is something wrong in giving an appropriate sentence to one convicted of an offence because there are considerable numbers of others who were at the same time committing the same offence, some of whom indeed, if identified and arrested and established as having taken a more serious part, could have received heavier sentences. This is a plea which is almost invariably put forward where the offence is one of those classed as disturbances of the public peace – such as riots, unlawful assemblies and affrays. It indicates a failure to appreciate that on these confused and tumultuous occasions each individual who takes an active part by deed or encouragement is guilty of a really grave offence by being one of the number engaged in a crime against the peace. It is, moreover, impracticable for a small number of police when about to be overwhelmed by a crowd to make a large number of arrests ... If this plea were acceded to, it would reinforce that feeling which may undoubtedly exist that if an offender is but one of a number he is unlikely to be picked on, or even if he is so picked upon, can escape proper punishment because others were not arrested at the same time. Those who choose to take part in such unlawful occasions must do so at their peril ... In the view of this Court, it is a wholly wrong approach to take the acts of any individual participator in isolation. They were not committed in isolation and, as already indicated, it is that very fact that constitutes the gravity of the offence.

I do not pretend to know the answer to this problem. I doubt whether there is an answer in judicial terms. Not all problems are soluble. I suspect this is one that can perhaps never be more than alleviated and that by massive television and Press coverage. No doubt Trevor Huddleston's *Naught for Your Comfort* was meant to apply to South Africa. It has some relevance here. The most worrying aspect of the situation is not the wounded pride or the physical injury of the police. It is the distasteful possibility that the failure of the law may play into the hands of the extremists of the right, who may gather political support from public dissatisfaction with recurring incidents of this kind. Nor is the problem confined to London. A report 'Shades of Grey' by the Cranfield Institute of Technology, Bedford, asserted in late 1977 that a gang of 200 West Indians in Handsworth, Birmingham, committed more than 400 crimes a month and present a serious and growing problem.

However, against the background of discussion about Notting Hill, the Police Bill had been making its way through the Committee stage, shedding supporters and credibility along the way, and on 6 June the *Sunday Times* revealed at length and accurately the depth of police opposition and the likelihood of the resignation of senior officers unable conscientiously to administer it. The Association of Chief Police Officers had called upon each member by telex to express in unequivocal terms their opposition or support and without exception declared their opposition. But not being coalminers or power workers their views were not likely to receive much consideration and, indeed, they received none at all. As a final gesture we had offered to accept the concept of a tribunal provided that the two lay members acted as observers without power to determine guilt. That was not acceptable. The result was well summed up by *The Times* in the following leader on 7 August:

An Ironical Departure

Among the sheaf of Bills that received the Royal Assent yesterday was the Police Bill, which sets out to end the unsatisfactory state of affairs where complaints against the police are often investigated solely by the police themselves. No Bill that so clearly reflected imperfect public confidence in the integrity of the service would have much chance of being favourably received by senior police officers. In fact it aroused even more opposition among them than might have been expected. Sir Robert Mark, the Metropolitan Police Commissioner, has been particularly open in his hostility and indicated some time ago that if the Bill were passed unmodified he might retire, partly so as to avoid having to operate the procedures of which he has been so critical. It appears that he does intend to leave the force as soon as he reaches the minimum retiring age in March, just before the new procedures come into effect.

In the normal way any policeman who, by implication,

asked the Government to choose between him and an important public Bill would be making himself ridiculous. But Sir Robert's standing and achievements are exceptional, and his reservations deserve to be given weight. He was appointed at a time when there was great public disquiet about corruption in the Metropolitan Police, and by all accounts he has acted vigorously and effectively to eliminate it. Some 400 officers are said to have left the force, either voluntarily or under compulsion, as a result of his efforts.

His many public statements – about the jury system or the accused's right of silence, for instance – are often forthright expressions of the feeling that the police are already too much obstructed in the pursuit of crime. He lobbies frankly as a policeman, but as one who cannot possibly be charged with having an improper interest in veiling police affairs in convenient obscurity. There is a glaring irony in the spectacle of a law designed to improve police discipline driving from his post the officer who has probably accomplished more in that line than anyone else in recent years.

There is no great controversy over the need in principle to introduce an independent element into the handling of complaints. Without one, justice can never fully be seen to be done. The difficulty has been to arrive at a formula which would ensure an effective outside scrutiny without either undermining the responsibility of chief officers for the discipline of their forces or exposing accused officers to more than one judicial process on a single matter. The new Act creates a board (to be appointed by the prime minister) able to examine disciplinary records and set up tribunals to hear cases where the officer concerned has not admitted the charges made against him and where the case has not been referred to the Director of Public Prosecutions. The tribunals would consist of two members of the board and the chief officer of the force in question.

This should ensure that any case where an attempt has been made to hush up a serious misdemeanour will find its way to a tribunal. It is an elaborate system, and it is not clear where enough independent and sharp-eyed laymen will be found to man the board – but these objections would apply to any plan that had a hope of being effective. Sir Robert's main reservation is that it would allow a chief officer to be overruled by his two lay companions – gullible political nominees, in his eyes. At an earlier stage he proposed that lay scrutineers should examine cases after they had ended, and comment on their handling, rather as an Ombudsman might. This would have been unsatisfactory. Unless the assessors confined themselves to checking that the mere formal process of investigation had been gone through – which would be ineffective in cases similar to some that have occurred – an officer might find himself in the ambiguous position of being cleared by the police and censured by the scrutineers.

More recently, Sir Robert and other senior officers have suggested that the two laymen should sit on the tribunal, but only as assessors whom the chief officer would have to consult before making his own decision on guilt and punishment. In theory this might still expose an accused officer to a kind of double jeopardy, if there was disagreement in the tribunal and public controversy. In practice the chief officer would make his decision knowing what the assessors thought and knowing that they could make their reservations public. He would not be tempted to turn a blind eye to protect the reputation and morale of his force. This would have satisfied the main public requirement for a lay scrutiny that could make its presence felt. It is a matter for regret that Parliament has insisted on a scheme damaging to the morale and confidence of so many senior officers when an acceptable compromise was available.

Unfortunately the situation was complicated for me by the awareness that there were other very good reasons for contemplating retirement at the age of 60, and notwithstanding that I would still have gone had they not existed, I thought it would be dishonest not to disclose them. I therefore prepared with some care a speech to the Annual General Meeting of the Metropolitan Branch of the Police Federation in November. A little of it is perhaps worth repetition.

I think . . . that I should leave you in no doubt about the reasons for my decision to retire because, unlike the national Press, you know very well that there is no predetermined age of retirement for Commissioners. Indeed, so far as I can find, I shall be the first to exercise his entitlement to retire at 60. I made that decision without rancour or ill will albeit with some regret.

There are two compelling and two persuasive reasons why I think it best to go. Of the Police Act 1976 I will say no more than that, though I do not doubt the good intentions of its sponsors, I feel conscientiously unable to surrender the ultimate responsibility for police discipline to political nominees. It is a retrograde step opposed unanimously by the last Royal Commission on the Police and I can only hope and pray that the unnecessary, cumbersome, expensive and potentially sinister machinery created by it will not be abused. The Act is at least unique in two respects in that apart from its sponsors it cannot boast a single friend, and it is the only measure during my service about which all the chief officers unanimously agree!

I should be less than honest if I did not make it clear that the second compelling reason is that continued service after 60 would be financially punitive and might deny me the opportunity to provide for my family as I would wish to do.

Thirdly I should explain that I have, with your help, completed all the changes I had in mind when I took office. I suspect that my inventive capacity is running out and that it is time to make way for someone else.

Perhaps most satisfying of all my conflicting feelings is the confident assurance that my successor will receive at every level the warm welcome and whole-hearted co-operation that he deserves and needs.

It is perhaps the best of all evidence of the present state of the force.

Lastly, I am quite sincere when I tell you that I believe no one should exercise the authority and influence attaching to the office of Commissioner for too long. When Lord Acton talked about the corruption of power, I think he was referring to the danger of complacency, the diminishing willingness to pay adequate attention to opposing points of view and the inevitable tendency to dwell on past events rather than to seek new challenges.

For all these reasons I think it right to bid you farewell in the flesh whilst remaining with you in the spirit.

I should have known from long and cynical experience that the Press would ignore all the speech but the frank disclosure of the monetary disadvantage of continued service! The fact that my pension would be indexed led one newspaper to speculate that if inflation continued at its present rate I should be receiving more than £300,000 per annum by the end of the century.

The real truth was less newsworthy. My salary had long been frozen at £18,675 per annum, reduced by just over half by way of income tax, pension and national insurance contributions. My notional salary, fixed by the Top Salaries Review Board, was £21,000 and it was on this that my pension would be based. A police pension after thirty years' service amounts to two-thirds of the last year's pay. If I continued after my sixtieth birthday, I would therefore have been working for one-third of £18,675, less tax on the whole and pension contributions of roughly £1300 per annum, subject to tax relief, for a pension to which I was already entitled. In addition, if I wished to raise a capital sum by commuting one quarter of my pension the amount of £35,000 tax free would lessen by £1000 for every further year's service. Commutation would not affect my wife's entitlement to half my full pension on my death, but if I were to die whilst serving she would lose the whole £35,000 without any compensating increase in pension. I was advised that the commutation sum could be secured by a single annual insurance premium of £300 but was not sure that I would pass the necessary medical exam. I was never any good at mathematics but even I could see that the financial disadvantage of continued service was overwhelming. I had, too, a need for capital from which to make an allowance to my daughter whose marriage had broken down and who had two small children. Remembering my own father's attitude I wanted to give her support when she needed it but simply had not the means to do so adequately. My total assets at that time, after 39 years' police service, twenty of them as a chief officer, were about £8000 in capital and insurance and a very nice house with a substantial mortgage. Financial considerations were therefore very important and it would have been dishonest and hypocritical to pretend otherwise or not to say so. But they were not insuperable. My wife and I do not live extravagantly and my son, a successful and highly paid economist living abroad, was no less anxious to help his sister, who incidentally was demonstrating the willingness and ability to help herself. Money was not therefore an overriding factor. I had thought long and hard about it and had decided that even in the unlikely event of the Home Office offering to minimize the financial disadvantages of continued service I simply could not stomach the Police Act and would therefore have to go.

In order to dispel the rosy illusions created by the Press I readily disclose that my pension, after tax, amounted to just under £7000 for which I had paid heavily over the years. The taxpayers of Britain can now perhaps relax. Ironically enough, within weeks of retirement, my son-in-law's sad and premature death resolved, due to his foresight and concern for his children, my daughter's financial difficulties and I had more offers of employment than I could cope with. But both these eventualities were genuinely unforeseen when I addressed the Federation.

Roy Jenkins resigned on 10 September to become President designate of the EEC. I suspect he was glad to go. His stature, both intellectual and otherwise, must have made him an unpopular member of the mediocre crew in which he had served, but they were certainly the poorer for his loss. I bore, and bear him, no ill will over the Police Act. Disagreement without personal ill will or rancour ought to be the first requirement of public servants of every kind, and the loss of a battle does not always mean the loss of a war, especially if the loser retains a sense of balance and perspective. I am as confident of the eventual repeal or variation of the Police Act as I am of the eventual adoption of the Eleventh Report of the Criminal Law Revision Committee, and I do not think that this mistake, like that of 1879, will continue uncorrected for ninety-seven years.

# CHAPTER 18

# *Farewell to the Force*

In my view the Home Office deserve great credit for the development of police efficiency, organization and administration in the last fifteen years and I can readily understand how galling it must have been that this should have been obscured by the continued, though frequently unsought, publicity attracted by the Met. Far from receiving exhortations to stay, therefore, I was not at all surprised when Robert Armstrong asked if I would let the Home Secretary have confirmation in writing of my intention to resign. This I did on 27 October and in doing so I made it clear to Robert that I did not want, during my final months, to play any part in choosing the senior colleagues with whom my successor would have to work. I had always made, or recommended senior promotions only after consultation with the police members of the Policy Committee and I suggested to Robert that he might like to use the Deputy Commissioner as a medium for obtaining their opinions about Metropolitan candidates. For officers outside the Met, of course, he already had his own sources. I therefore took no part in recommending a successor to the Home Office or in consequential senior appointments. From the moment of resignation I was, in effect, a caretaker keeping an eye on things until the arrival of my successor. I was, however, determined that he would not receive the kind of welcome I got ten years earlier and when the choice was announced I got the Home Office to agree that he should come to London for a week as our guest to introduce him to his new colleagues and to make him feel welcome and at home.

In some ways this was the most carefree period of my ten years in London. I am not given to crying over spilt milk or to bearing malice. My inclination is always to look to the future rather than the past. My wife and I had spent our three weeks' summer holiday at home to see if we could bear each other all the time, and although the experiment was interrupted by Notting Hill, it worked very well.

There were, happily, a few cheerful incidents to brighten my last few months. I was invited to join the Board of the Phoenix Assurance Company Limited as soon as my retirement was announced. This gave me particular pleasure because the Chief General Manager, Bill Harris, had played Oliver to my Jill in the second act of A. A. Milne's *Make Belief* at Hulme over forty years earlier and I have a photograph of myself in gymslip and wig to prove it! Major-General Sir Philip Ward afforded me a privilege touched with sentiment. He had left London District on appointment as Commandant of the Royal Military Academy, Sandhurst, and he invited me to review the Remembrance Day parade. My wife and I had attended Sovereign's Parade earlier that year, the first time she had been there since 1943 when I slow-marched up the steps of the Old Building to the strains of Auld Lang Syne. Princess Anne was kind enough to come to our Annual Concert at the Festival Hall in December. It is really a force family party with just one outside artiste, in this case Harry Secombe. It was a crowded, happy evening.

Not least pleasant were invitations to accept the Honorary Freedom of the City of Westminster and the Honorary Degree of Doctor of Letters of Loughborough University. Conferment of the Freedom of Westminster is rare, Winston Churchill being one of the only five recipients. In my case, the Labour minority refrained from voting, which amused me because I thought it a very appropriate farewell to local government. It reminded me of the old joke about the clerk of a council committee writing to its chairman who had just undergone a serious operation and saying:

'I am instructed by the Committee to express their sincere good wishes for your rapid and complete recovery by a majority of eleven to seven, there being four abstentions.'

Since the Freedom was clearly meant for the force rather than me and the force deserved it, and more, I had no reservations about acceptance and the occasion itself was marked by the dignity and the generosity for which the City of Westminster is deservedly famous.

Loughborough I thought very kind. I was already an honorary graduate of Leicester and was touched to be remembered so kindly after so many years, and particularly by a university of the future.

In my last weeks the trial of the four Balcombe Street terrorists came to its expected end and allowed the Press for the first time to comment freely on the case. They were generous, to say the least.

The tally against terrorism since August 1973, when the first IRA bombs went off, was as follows.

277 incidents concerning bombs
(179 in MPD)
15 shooting incidents
(12 in MPD)
58 people killed as a result of these incidents
(21 in MPD)
1039 injured as a result of these incidents
(685 in MPD)
33 weapons have been recovered
(22 in MPD)
2936 rounds of ammunition have been recovered
(1737 in MPD)
2245 lbs of explosives have been recovered
(737 lbs in MPD)
908 detonators have been recovered
(474 in MPD)
130 people have been arrested in connection with bomb/shooting incidents
(45 in MPD)

I doubt very much whether any country or capital city in

the world can match that record in dealing with this conscienceless activity.

I was determined not to have any sentimental hooha before my departure but I gave myself the pleasure of taking the last Cadets Passing-Out parade of my time. This is what I said to the young men and women about to begin their service with the Metropolitan force:

### POLICE ACT 1964 SCHEDULE 2

'I do solemnly and sincerely declare and affirm that I will well and truly serve Our Sovereign Lady the Queen in the office of constable, without favour or affection, malice or ill will; and that I will to the best of my power cause the peace to be kept and preserved, and prevent all offences against the persons and properties of Her Majesty's subjects; and that while I continue to hold the said office I will to the best of my skill and knowledge discharge all the duties thereof faithfully according to law.'

All those of you leaving this School to join the Force will be required to make that declaration and I want you to be in no doubt that it is no mere form of words devoid of real significance. It puts you in a class apart. It means that with the members of Her Majesty's forces you undertake never in any circumstances to allow your own private interests to divert or deter you from your fundamental task and purpose, the service of your Queen and her people – and by people, I mean all her people without exception, even those with whom you come into conflict.

In honouring that undertaking you not only enhance a proud and flowering tradition, you join the noblest company in the land.

Of course you need the necessary rewards to enable you to exist in our material society and even more do you require the assurance that your numbers will be adequate for your tasks. No less is it necessary that the system of justice which depends primarily on you should be both reasonably effective and fair to all concerned. But during the crises inevitably by weak or misguided legislation, inadequate research and the subordination of reality to political expediency, it is for you, and you alone, to bear the strains until reason prevails.

I am in my 40th year as a policeman. I joined because I wanted not just a job, but a worthwhile job. Rather to my surprise, after surviving the early vicissitudes which all of you will face, I discovered that I had found a vocation, a vocation of every increasing insignificance and value to society as our problems as a nation increase.

To speak to the police service as a power in the land, as if in some curious way we fulfilled the same purpose as the police of Nazi Germany or of the so-called democracies of Eastern Europe is just not true no matter by whom it is said. We can more properly be described as the servants of the people and perhaps the most beneficial influence in our whole social structure.

The question of guilt and punishment will not be for you to determine. You have, and will have, no power at all in respect of which you are not fully accountable. Your only power will be the power to inconvenience, to require people to appear before the Courts. And because of our curious adversary system, you will frequently be more at risk whenever you invoke it than those you inconvenience. Do not allow that to deter you from your duty. You will not lack support. But do not also have any illusions about the task to which you are dedicating yourselves by embracing a police career. You must stand between the thief, the robber and his victim, you must contain those, supported by unscrupulous extremists, who would achieve political or industrial objectives by violence. You must tolerate attacks by lawyers and politicians often unfair and unsupported by evidence. You must, if necessary, risk your lives to contain or suppress violence. But you must never use more violence against wrongdoers than is strictly necessary to prevent the attainment of their ends.

It is inevitable in a free society that violence, lies and propaganda should play a significant part in public affairs. Shrewsbury, Saltley, Scunthorpe and Red Lion Square offer ample evidence of that. But it is by your fortitude and calmness in overcoming difficulties of that kind, just as by the steadiness of a regiment under fire, that you will be judged by your fellow countrymen. You must always deny the violent their objectives whilst avoiding yourselves any behaviour which would alienate the public, whose support is essential to you.

Whether of religious persuasion or not you will be called upon to demonstrate in practice the precepts of Christianity, courage, tolerance, humility and compassion to an extent not ordinarily required of your fellow countrymen. But in doing so you will achieve a high degree of immunity from those who for a variety of dubious motives would undermine your reputation.

Never have you been more needed than today if our way of life is to prevail, if change is to be by ballot box rather than by force or lawlessness. You join a Service whose standards and ideals continually rise and you are fortunate in that your period of preparation has been spent in surroundings such as these and subject to the influences of men and women dedicated to your happiness and well-being. It is right that occasionally you should be reminded of those whose foresight made all this possible, of Sir Joseph Simpson and Tom Mahir who conceived and developed the Metropolitan Police Cadet Corps, of your present Commandant and his predecessors and his staff but perhaps most of all of Colonel Andrew Croft who devoted the wisdom of long experience to laying the foundations and principles which have served the Corps so well in the last decade. I am sure that no material reward could give him so much satisfaction as the contemplation of his child grown to manhood – the Metropolitan Police Cadet Corps of today. Some of you may think I should have added womanhood – but ever since Roy Jenkins' Sexual Discrimination Act I have felt nervous about discriminating between the two – a nervousness, I am told, not always shared by cadets.

Do not be intimidated or perturbed by anything I have said. You are not facing Everest or the Polar Ice Cap. You are about to embark on a hard, demanding road which will tax your strength, both moral and physical, but which offers you rewards and satisfaction not to be gained by those inspired by lesser motives. And there is plenty of enjoyment along the way, comradeship, humour and the satisfaction of serving your fellow men. Don't try to clean up London single-handed in your first month. It may take a little longer. But be of good heart. Though our problems are great and our resources not yet adequate never has our reputation as a force been higher.

Simply do your best, knowing that though you cannot always succeed you can always maintain your integrity and that of the Force. It is the most precious commodity we jointly possess. Don't be frightened of making mistakes. The policemen who never made a mistake probably never made a decision. But if you make a mistake or do wrong, tell the truth about it. You will find the Force surprisingly human about that kind of thing.

Your turn out and bearing on parade today not only reflect great credit on you and your instructors, they are a reassuring sign that you have learned the virtues of discipline and self control, essential to a police career. I wish success and happiness to every one of you. It is yours for the taking.

Finally, to your parents I would like to say that you can entrust your sons and daughters to us with confidence. We really care about each and every one. The future of the Force and Service is in their hands and we will do our best to ensure their fitness for that task. Be of no doubt that they enter a proud inheritance.

The evening finished with 'Sunset' by way of farewell from the band, in which I had always taken justifiable pride.

And so to bed. I restricted my farewell party almost entirely to those who had helped me along the way, cleaners, waitresses, the groom, drivers, secretaries, junior, intermediate and senior officers, the chief commandant of the Special Constabulary and the Home Secretary and his two senior advisers, with whom I had enjoyed the most friendly and trusting relationship.

# CHAPTER 19

# The Police Function

I had vaguely imagined that retirement would prove a tear-jerking business. Leaving a service in which I had spent the whole of my adult life and to which I felt a devotion difficult to express in words. Saying goodbye to old friends and colleagues. Being on the outside of incidents in which I had for so long been at the centre. In fact it was not like that at all. Simple pressure of events left me no time for sentimental meandering. At one fell swoop I had lost my car and driver, two secretaries and my part share in a groom. I was receiving roughly fifteen letters a day, rediscovering the art of typing with two fingers, preparing for a trip to the Arabian Gulf, beginning a book and contemplating a five-week lecture tour of the United States. I rode on a train for only the second time in ten years in London, discovered the appalling cost of postage stamps and got used to the taxicab as a means of getting about. I simply didn't have the chance to dwell on the transition, and it was quite a long time before the change in my circumstances came home to me.

I was rather surprised to feel no sense of loss of status or rank. The Commissioner had always been regarded, at least by the police, as a unique figure but as a rather cynical northerner I had felt this to be overrated even when I was doing the job. I had always encouraged informality amongst junior as well as senior colleagues, their good manners, rather than mine, determining the lengths to which I could go. I found the continuing flow of letters and invitations kind but rather wearisome, as well as expensive to answer, but I suppose the continuous pressure softened the effect of parting. As the weeks went by and my sense of detachment grew I found it possible to look back at the changes of the last forty years and to see things more objectively because I was no longer involved and was not fighting for a particular cause.

I began to think about the changing pattern of the police service, its unnatural reticence in matters of public interest, the general poverty or lack of leadership over the years, and I began to question the order of priorities which had dominated the police outlook for so long. I had moreover arrived at the cynical conclusion that no political party really wants an effective, honest police force unswervingly dedicated to impartiality in all matters. Not, of course, that any party would admit this. And most politicians would hasten to pay lip service to the general principle. But at moments of crisis, each wants the police to see their point of view as the right one and resistance in the public interest requires moral courage and had not always been forthcoming. In the latter years, for example, the only difference between the extremes of the right and left has been the historical association of the former with racial discrimination. In all other respects both are equally odious to believers in moderation and democracy, but public and political reaction does not always recognize this. A National Front march or demonstration is sure to evoke strong protest, while those who control the murderous puppets who guard the Berlin Wall with dogs and machine guns are referred to as 'democrats'. Indeed, gullible political visitors fêted behind the Iron Curtain have been known to speak with enthusiasm of the eastern brand of social democracy, blithely disregarding the brutal and summary fate of those who wish to leave it! Polarization and emotion will not, of course, change this. But information and communication could, and it is for that reason that the police as much as any other section of society should expose rather than conceal their problems so that public opinion can assess them and if necessary bring about change. The police in this country could play an influential part in promoting racial harmony, discrediting political extremists and easing the social tensions prompted sometimes by propaganda and at others by misunderstanding or lack of information. Their potential for good goes far beyond mere prevention and detection of crime but longstanding tradition, limited intellectual capacity and sometimes even the fear of offending vested interests, in particular those of politicians and lawyers, have fostered an unnatural reticence which is not in the public interest.

Take crime, for example. Always good for a headline or for the politician whipping up emotional support. It monopolizes much of the television screen, the movie, the world of what laughingly passes for literature. It is an endless source of argument and debate. Of course to the victim of crime the word has real and often distressing meaning. But seen objectively against the background and problems of 50 million people it is not even amongst the more serious of our difficulties. Of the 2,100,000 crimes recorded in 1976 only 5 per cent could be classified as violent and of these a very high proportion were cleared up. There were only 565 homicides in England and Wales, including deaths from terrorism, and 548 of these led to arrests. That is less than two-thirds of the number of homicides each year in the single city of Detroit and hardly to be compared with the 18,780 homicides in the United States with a population only four and a half times greater than ours. Our 1094 reported incidents of rape, led an American friend of mine, comparing it with the US total of 56,730, to comment that we clearly weren't very good at it! Roughly 1,800,000 of our crimes consist of burglaries, thefts and stealing of, or from, cars, the great majority almost certainly by juveniles and young people, most of whom happily do not persist with a life of crime. Successive governments have been unwilling to increase the preventive capacity of the police by more men or wider powers and have tended rather to try to offset the effect of crime by payment of compensation for criminal injury, free medical treatment, by encouraging private crime prevention and the spread of insurance. No one really wants too large or too powerful a police force, not even the police themselves but there is no doubt that the present distribution of police manpower is so inappropriate that it offers little disincentive to violence in political demonstrations, industrial disputes or deterrence to the mindless vandalism and hooliganism which are such an everyday feature of our lives. Divided responsibility for police affairs, poor leadership, prejudice on the part of the police representative bodies and inexcusable lack of research have all contributed to what is now an unfortunate situation. Lord Denning is said to have been rebuked for remarking in 1977 that 'the mobs were out'. Whether that was so or not I do not know. I am sure that in any case he would be unmoved, because events in that year fully justified his comment. Physical force, not the Courts, was necessary to retain the appearance of the Rule of Law in some parts of London.

The forty years of my service have seen immense changes, some obvious, some subtle. To follow this it is necessary to have some understanding of the principles governing the policing of England and Wales, which differ from those anywhere else in the world. Few people understand that apart from a brief period under Cromwell the British government has never had any organized force at its disposal for the enforcement of the criminal law. This has always been assumed to be the responsibility of the people themselves through each local community. It was not until 1829 that the first professional police began duty in the Metropolis. Even then, the first two Commissioners were made Justices of the Peace partly to lessen opposition to the new force from the existing magistracy as well as people generally. The success of the new force ensured the spread of the system but only gradually. It was not made obligatory until 1856 and the establishment of police forces was made the responsibility of local government. Not only did this produce many forces of diverse standards and conditions of service, there were significant differences in their control. It was in those days untrue to assert that the police were free from political influence in their operational role. In the absence of a system of district attorneys political influence could, and often did, play a very important part in police affairs. The chief constable was only too often subservient to the wishes of the chairman of his police authority, the watch committee in a borough or the standing joint committee of elected representatives and magistrates in a country. No less significance was the variation in pay and conditions of service permitted by this system. Although the government eventually agreed to pay half the cost of police expenditure it was reluctant to interfere with local autonomy in police matters and there were wide differences in the conditions of the two or three hundred forces. Nor was there any machinery for encouraging a move to uniformity. The police were not allowed to belong to a trade union or political party and withdrawal of labour was for them a criminal offence. The most influential figure in the police world, too, the Metropolitan Police Commissioner, was a political appointee who felt himself bound to some extent by the traditions of the Civil Service and the armed forces and thus debarred from public utterances on behalf of his men.

This curious hotchpotch was to be cleaned up and regularized by two events of enormous importance in police history. The first was the Police Act of 1919 which followed Lord Desborough's enquiry into police conditions of service. The second was the Police Act of 1964, which followed the 1960/61 Royal Commission on the Police.

The first established, the Police Federation, which includes all ranks from constable to chief inspector, to negotiate with chief officers, local police authorities and central government on behalf of their members. It also empowered the government to control police pay. The second swept away the differences of control and administration between country, combined and borough forces and created the present threefold partnership of central government, local government and magistracy and the police themselves, all represented on a Police Council for Great Britain chaired by the Home Secretary. Though still denied the right to join a trade union or political party the influence of the Police Federation was increased enormously by the changes. The 1964 Act, on the other hand, diminished the influence of local government. This move to standardization opened the door for Roy

Jenkins's sweeping and courageous changes in the police administrative structure, reducing the number of forces from 123 to 47, later to 43 with immeasurable improvements in organization, equipment, procedures, accountability and in common or shares services. It is this period which saw the beginning of change from a fragmented, essentially artisan service, often dominated by local politics or the central government to a well-organized professional body much better equipped to resist outside pressures and to speak for itself. The 43 forces exercise exclusive autonomy in their own areas for the enforcement of the criminal law, subject to the reservation by Statute of certain powers to the Director of Public Prosecutions, and though administratively and financially subject to the influence of central and local government, they have never before been so free from interference in their operational role. Unlike the army, which represents the ultimate sanction of force under the command of the government, the police still represent the people and are dedicated to the doctrine of minimum force, or the use of only such force as will meet with the approval of the Courts and public opinion.

The most serious problem today is the containment or absorption of social unrest arising from a number of factors, unemployment, political and industrial strife, racial problems, vandalism and hooliganism. Since they have only a limited degree of mobility their maldistribution aggravates their difficulties, especially in view of the lack of worthwhile reserves from other sources. The special constabulary is small in number and is not, in any case, suitable for employment in 'confrontation' situations. The army traditionally is restricted to support in a logistical role only, or to the very rare incidents in which a close quarter battle with armed terrorists seems likely. Even the magistracy seem to find it difficult to see themselves as having an essential part to play in facilitating the continuance of the present methods of policing by inflicting salutary punishments on those resorting to violence for any purpose. The police are therefore very much on their own in attempting to preserve order in an increasingly turbulent society in which socialist philosophy has changed from raising the standards of the poor and deprived to reducing the standards of the wealthy, the skilled and the deserving to the lowest common denominator. The situation is all the more difficult in that the police are not seen by government as being entitled to any special consideration despite the increasing difficulty of their role. The so-called social contract when applied by a minority government means in practice that between the TUC and the government no one knows which is the ventriloquist and which is the dummy. But one thing is quite certain, only those sectional interests with powerful muscles can break it with impunity and the police not being amongst them inevitably suffer.

The commonsense solution is for the government to introduce three rates of police pay (1) for the Metropolitan force (2) for provincial Metropolitan forces, for example Liverpool, Manchester, Birmingham and (3) a basic rate of pay for all other forces. The Police Council would, of course, have to be consulted, but the Home Secretary has the power to make the change. A flow of manpower from the counties to the Metropolitan areas would no doubt cause an outcry. But I doubt whether Northumberland, Cambridge and Devon would be given over to looting and rapine. Certainly the hard-pressed, undermanned forces of the great cities would for the first time in thirty years be able to abandon fire brigade policing and begin to discharge their basic task of prevention.

But of course whether the government really wants this is quite another matter. A government maintained in office only by the support of its extremist and authoritarian left is hardly likely to welcome an improvement in police organization, more likely to suppress extremism on the streets. Little or no governmental criticism was heard of the disgraceful behaviour of left-wing extremists at Red Lion Square, at Grunwick or at some of the more spectacular industrial disputes in the provinces. A few crocodile tears for the police was their only response. On the other hand a better informed public may compel the change. A general election in the immediate aftermath of Grunwick might have led to a bigger defeat for the government than that suffered by the Conservatives in 1945. No one knows this better than the government with the result that their more traditionally passionate demagogues are actually heard denouncing violence and cooing like dove – demagogues who a year or two earlier would actually have been provoking and encouraging the violence. They know only too well the influence of the pendulum principle in British politics, the aversion to excess of force of the floating voter who decides elections. In the meantime, however, the role of the police will inevitably become increasingly difficult, though through sheer necessity their technical efficiency is likely to improve even beyond its present high standard.

The biggest disadvantage under which the police labour is the unnatural and harmful reticence of their leaders, some of whom, indeed, do not seem to understand the extent of their moral responsibility. A police chief in Britain serves five masters. The first, the criminal law which he is sworn to uphold and enforce impartially. The second, his police authority, be it the Home Secretary in the case of the Commissioner or a Police Committee if a chief constable. The third, the men and women he commands, whose interests may not always coincide with those of his police authority, in financial matters, for example. The fourth, the people of the police district under his command, who look to him for security and tranquillity. The fifth – and the most important – his conscience. For in Britain policemen are not merely allowed to have consciences, they are required to have them. Their authority under the law is personal, as is their accountability and in no other country in the world does their awareness of this influence police policies and operations so decisively.

A former chief constable, a product of Hendon, a University graduate and a most able thinker in the field of technical police research once argued in the *Criminal Law Review* that the role of the police should be confined to silent acquiescence in the criminal justice system. That argument might have been appropriate in the 19th century. It has no conceivable justification now. The police alone see the whole crime reported to them, most of which never reaches a court and they are no longer the semi-literate, unthinking mercenaries of long ago. No discussion of criminal justice can be complete without their participation, far too long delayed. The civil servant, only too often more intelligent, better qualified, intellectually superior and sometimes of higher integrity than his political masters, is unable to speak. The police officer is an independent officer of the Crown and fails in his duty if he does not do so. He cannot, of course, comment publicly on the acquittal of the blatantly guilty, but he alone has the resources to mount research into the failure of the bail system, the manipulation of the jury system, the obvious exploitation of legal aid and he should use those resources or direct the attention of the Press and the Universities to them. If that is thought too strong an assertion, consider the following comment by Professor J.Q. Wilson of Harvard University, one of America's most respected criminologists, in Issue No. 43 of the magazine the *Public Interest*, published quarterly by National Affairs Incorporated of the United States of America.

> Finally, there are signs of what I would call, at the obvious risk of some trans-Atlantic ill will, the 'Americanization' of English criminal justice – by which I mean that well-intentioned officials and advisers in Her Majesty's government seem to have learned little from the mistakes made by their counterparts in the United States. There is scarcely a single ill-advised recommendation of the President's Commission on Law Enforcement and Administration of Justice that the British Home Office and its various advisory councils do not seem determined to repeat.

Perhaps the politicians and the Home Office are not wholly blameworthy. As I have made it clear earlier in this book, the gap left by the silence of chief officers of police has been filled by representatives of junior and intermediate ranks elected to negotiate pay and conditions of service and without the experience, the resources or the intellectual capacity to discuss public issues for which they bear no responsibility.

The message for both police, politicians and public is therefore plain, though overdue. It is that light should now be shed on matters of which the public have long been left in the dark. Police administration, as well as the workings of the Courts and legal aid, should be exposed to extensive and impartial research. Speculation and research about the causation of crime and penology are not likely to serve any useful purpose unless related to research about the actuality of the criminal justice system. This should, as a matter of urgency, become the first priority for those entrusted with public funds for the purpose of academic research into crime and justice. Society has so far been ill served by the priority of their efforts.

# CHAPTER 20

# The Pornography Trials and Police Discipline

I was far away in Kuwait on the Arabian Gulf when the now famous porn trials of 1977 began. The arrest of twelve former or serving officers in February 1976 preceded by a number of earlier arrests had resulted in a decision to institute three separate prosecutions of which the last, involving the former head of the Flying Squad, was not completed until July 1977, by which time I had returned home. Altogether eighteen men of varying ranks from constable to commander were sentenced to over a hundred years' imprisonment, including terms of 12, 10 and 8 years in the worse cases.

The convictions of one of the commanders were quashed by the Appeal Court and his sentence set aside, but another, who had retired from the force soon after I became commissioner, got eight years. A detective chief superintendent, who, ironically enough, had been put in charge of the enquiry into *The Times* allegations of police corruption in 1969, got twelve years. Three detective inspectors got ten, seven and four years respectively. A little later, the police pensions of the worst offenders were revoked. This was an unusual step. Although the law authorizes the revocation of a pension in respect of a former policeman sentenced to not less than one year's imprisonment, the Home Office had generally not taken that action following convictions resulting in longer sentences of three or four years. Clearly the action in the porn cases was intended to allay outraged public opinion. This ended the 'firm within a firm' of which *The Times* had complained, which in its heyday had made thousands of pounds a year from pornography. Their immunity for so long was an indication of the extent of corruption within the detective branch, which was not, of course, limited to pornography. The case illustrates dramatically the need for the sweeping changes in organization and control in 1972 which made continuance or repetition of such wrongdoing not merely less likely but, once disclosed, virtually certain to bring swift retribution.

I can't say that the punishment and humiliation of the wrongdoers gave me any pleasure. It is an indication of immaturity or worse to rejoice at the downfall of another human being. But there were factors about this case which gave police and public alike reason for satisfaction. Some of those involved had persuaded or even virtually compelled juniors to the point of corruption and that danger at least was now ended. What was surprising was the failure of the Press, who after all had followed it closely, to understand the ramifications of the case.

'If the independent police complaints board, which is just opening for business, needed any further justification,' thundered a *Guardian* leader on 13 May 1977, 'all it needs to do is to point to the six complaints which sat on Commander Virgo's desk – unattended.' It would, however, have a problem. One of the most important changes in 1972 was that no one was allowed to see a complaint against him. All complaints thereafter went directly to A10. The *Guardian* had failed to appreciate that the trial related to events before the change. Moreover, even under the new arrangements, if the complaints are of crime, the new complaints board will not see them unless there is no prosecution or an acquittal.

'The whole affair [the pornography trial],' declared Brian McConnell in the *Observer* of 15 May 1977, 'makes nonsense of the claim by Sir Robert and others in the police that enquiries into police complaints should be conducted by police themselves.' Well, hardly. The long, complex and difficult enquiry *was* conducted by police themselves and ended with the conviction of all but two of the accused. More interesting still, the new Act makes not a jot of difference. The enquiry was into alleged crime, with which

264

the new complaints board is not concerned. I quote these comments because they illustrate well the instinctive prejudice and sad lack of real knowledge of most of those who have made public comments on police discipline in the last few years. It is, admittedly, a difficult and confusing subject understood by only a handful of people but that is no excuse for a pretence of knowledge. In the cases I have quoted, a false pretence.

The Judge in the final case was kind enough to make some generous remarks about both the Press and me. Even these were a little misleading, no doubt unintentionally. The legal correspondent to the *Security Gazette* had commented a decade earlier that investigatory journalism into crime though potentially valuable in arousing public interest is seldom of any real use for the purpose of prosecution and is as likely to be as obstructive as helpful. A confession or allegation in a newspaper is of little or no evidential value unless confirmed by subsequent enquiry. The Press are able to pay for information on a scale unattainable by the police and they do not suffer from the same inhibitions in printing allegations or innuendoes which if made by a policeman would wreck his career. The whole Soho scene was a godsend (if that is the right word) to the sensation-seeking Press. They could print virtually what they liked without any real fear of repercussions from pornographer or bent policemen alike. They were not in fact printing anything which the team under Gilbert Kelland did not already know. They were simply making hay while the sun shone. The only really valuable contribution by the Press was the publication of the holiday in Cyprus shared by Humphreys and Drury. That, in fact, provided the lever which enabled me to prise the lid open. It was perhaps the most spectacularly worthwhile piece of journalism I can recall, though, of course, it was not investigatory, it was merely 'information received'. The benefit which flowed from it was nevertheless almost immeasurable.

Emphasis by the Press on the Humphreys' diary was also helpful even though much of it was inaccurate. Like it or not, there is such a thing as pre-trial publicity of a prejudicial nature though not specifically unlawful. This can work both ways. A well-known figure accused of crime can benefit or suffer from Press comment which borders on contempt but never quite attains it. Trial by newspaper is in fact more likely to end with unjustified acquittal than unfair conviction. The Press comment in this case, however, was such as to give the widespread impression that 'there is no smoke without fire', and I doubt whether any of the accused benefited from it.

The characteristics which showed most clearly in pornographer and accused alike were greed and stupidity. The worst threat to the pornographers was not the law or the Courts, whose record in dealing with pornography in London before these cases makes pitiful reading, but harassment, either by police or strong-arm men. And there are cheaper ways of dealing with that, especially with the help of the Press, than by paying vast sums of money to greedy and unscrupulous policemen.

I do not wish to give the unfair impression that the Courts were wholly to blame. The law on pornography is a mess. I can't help wishing that Roy Jenkins had turned his undoubted talents to having a second go at it, rather than to initiating the Police Bill. He was just the kind of Home Secretary who might have succeeded where others had failed, especially in the light of experience. The Blackburn case, if it did nothing else, made it clear that even the Judges regarded the law as confusing, ill-defined and virtually unenforceable.

I mentioned briefly on page 136 that late in 1972 the Court of Appeal had dismissed an appeal by Raymond Blackburn against a decision by the Divisional Court for an Order of Mandamus directing me to enforce the pornography laws more energetically. I was rather surprised that neither the Home Office nor Parliament itself had seemed to regard the views of the Court of Appeal as worthy of consideration or parliamentary time. The subject was, after all, a recurring theme in those newspapers reliant primarily on sexual deviance, titillation and pious condemnation of pornography, massage parlours and so on for their circulation. After all, some of the comments of the three Judges were of general interest. For example, the Master of the Rolls said:

'The cause of the ineffectiveness lies with the system and the framework in which the police have to operate. The Obscene Publications Act 1959 does not provide a sound foundation. It fails to provide a satisfactory test of obscenity, and it allows a defence of public good which has got out of hand. There is also considerable uncertainty as to the powers and duties of the police when they seize articles. If the people of this country want pornography to be stamped out, the legislature must amend the Obscene Publications Act 1959 so as to make it strike unmistakably at pornography, and it must define the powers and duties of the police so as to enable them to take effective measures for the purpose. The police may well say to parliament "Give us the tools and we will finish the job" but without efficient tools, they cannot be expected to stamp it out.'

Lord Justice Phillimore was no less critical: 'The Commissioner may be right when he says that at present pornography causes less public unease than most other breaches of the law. In my judgement, it is high time that its gravity was appreciated by the public. It cannot fail, especially in the light of the great volume of such material which is being put into circulation, to affect the morals and the moral outlook of many people, and in particular of the young and the impressionable. It tends, of course, to encourage promiscuity and to weaken marriage.'

I could not help but reflect that in a lifetime's police experience I knew of no evidence to support the conclusions of the Lord Justice, which in the event, did not evoke any noticeable response from the legislature.

During my time as Commissioner I had consistently argued that much pornography is almost impossible to define, that definition changes continually, that contested prosecutions are no more certain of outcome than a game of chance and that the reaction of the Courts was a virtual licence for its continuance. I well remember Roy Jenkins, in a television interview, following the failure of a prosecution, stressing the importance he placed on the part played by the jury, he being unaware that the right of peremptory challenge exercised by skilful counsel had ensured a jury that was virtually certain to acquit! Moreover, even in the successful cases, the penalties which the lower Courts can impose offer no deterrence. The irony of the situation was that for tactical reasons I could not reveal to the Court that we were at last taking positive measures to end police corruption arising from the sale of pornography. Though I was not then to know how successful these were to be.

Notwithstanding the strictures and anxieties of their Lordships the situation remains unchanged so far as the law is concerned. More happily, police corruption arising from it had ended by late 1973 when transfer of responsibility to the uniform branch and the activities of the newly created anti-corruption unit had swept the deck clean.

Throughout my time as Commissioner there was occasional agitation for reform of the law on obscene publications and I therefore took the precaution of concealing an ace up my sleeve. It consisted of one or two dozen publications each of which had been both acquitted and convicted. It was my intention, had a Bill been presented to Parliament, to invite the Press to inspect these publications without first explaining their special category. The result would, I am sure, have been both amusing and instructive. A number of people were good enough to warn me that such an action might be unlawful. I was grateful but unworried. Ridicule can sometimes be more powerful than law itself.

My own inclination is that if there is to be a change in law, that the emphasis should be on control of display rather than on prohibition. I am not competent to say whether pornography depraves or corrupts. Nor are the judges or jurors who have been invited to offer that opinion. But I can say what is likely to offend and although I am not in favour of prohibition, I do no see why people should be needlessly offended by display. Control of display will not, however, be easy. Definition of that which is offensive will be difficult. And legislation will be pointless without swingeing penalties, an unpopular proposition for any Member of Parliament to contemplate.

In anticipation of this and other controversial issues likely to follow my retirement I had been interviewed by Desmond Wilcox on BBC television following my retirement. When I realized that the screening of the interview might coincide with Drury's trial, I asked that it should be deferred and the BBC kindly agreed. During the course of that interview I readily admitted that there may well be officers in the CID who had, as it were 'turned over a new leaf' as soon as virtue became fashionable. This did not imply failure to prosecute anyone against whom evidence was forthcoming. It was simply a plain statement of reality. On reflection, I am sorry that I did not make the point that the great majority of the CID must not only have been honest but anxious for reform. Were that not so, reform would clearly have been impossible. It could not have been achieved without the wide measure of support it was given by the CID generally.

CHAPTER 21

# The Police and the Media

I was extremely fortunate to be invited by the International Press Institute to a conference funded by the Ford Foundation on The News and the Law in mid-1977. It was held at Hythe and was attended by some eighty or more of the most distinguished judges, lawyers and journalists from both sides of the Atlantic. Professor Archibald Cox of Harvard and Watergate fame, Katherine Graham of the *Washington Post* and a number of distinguished judges, attorneys, editors and academics represented the United States, whilst Lords Denning and Cameron, Sir John Donaldson, Sir Gordon Slynn, Harold Evans of the *Sunday Times* and William Deedes of the *Daily Telegraph* headed a no less distinguished British gathering.

William Colby, former head of the Central Intelligence Agency, and I were there, presumably in the role of umpires or keepers of the peace, and there were observers from France and Germany.

The conference was important because it was the first joint, if long overdue, attempt to clarify the differences between the freedom and activities of the Press in the United States and Great Britain when dealing with crime and confidential information. Because we both speak the same language we assume that the same rules and conventions apply. They don't. Only a very small number of people in both countries have experience of, or access to, the reality of crime, e.g. policemen, lawyers, social workers and victims. For almost all of us, our knowledge is gained at third hand, a great deal of it from newspapers, television and radio. In both countries that can be affected by availability of space, editing and local interest. What is not generally understood is that the ground rules in both countries are totally different. American editors look upon the first amendment to the Constitution as a licence to print anything they can discover about crime or confidential information. The Supreme Court has sharply restricted the power of the judiciary to hold editors and writers in contempt for publishing material criticizing or likely to influence court decisions. Though they are by no means averse to reversal of convictions by reason of prejudicial pre-trial publicity they have always been unwilling to lay down clear rules restraining such publicity. The practical effect is that, although the accused, though technically guilty, may benefit from reversal through prejudicial publicity, the Press has not suffered any adverse consequence from its contribution to miscarriage of justice. The position in Britain is different. Once a charge is imminent, publicity may be judged prejudicial. Once preferred, the Press may not print more than brief details, the name of the accused and the particulars of the offence. If the offender is a juvenile, his name may not be published without the consent of the Court. Restrictions on publicity continue to apply throughout proceedings for committal for trial in indictable cases unless the *defence* asks for them to be lifted. During the trial itself, unless in camera, the restrictions no longer apply.

The whole purpose of these restrictions is to increase the likelihood of fair trial by the avoidance of prejudicial pre-trial publicity and the rules governing them are strictly enforced. In 1949 the editor of a national newspaper was committed to prison for three months and his employers fined £10,000 following a lead story under the heading 'Vampire will never strike again' before the trial of a man charged with several murders. In 1978 the High Court in Edinburgh fined London Weekend Television £50,000 and three of their executives a total of £11,000 for references in a television programme which prejudiced the fair trial of a nurse accused of obstructing the air supply to a patient in an intensive care unit. These are, by any standards, swingeing penalties imposed arbitrarily. In sharp contrast, whatever adverse effect the activities of the American Press have had on the administration of justice no American newspaper or editor has ever suffered any similar penalty. The practical effect of these differences in law and practice is that whereas in Great Britain trial by newspaper is unlikely, in the United States it is commonplace. Yet many people not personally involved in the professions of law and journalism remain unaware of this and draw misleading inferences or conclusions from the activities or the inexplicable silence of newspapers they mistakenly believe to be published under much the same principles.

The three days of the conference were organized by a happy Anglo-American combination of Peter Calvocoressi and his colleague, Elsie Burch Donald. There were five excellent discussion leaders from Harvard, Columbia, Cambridge and *The Times* and not for one moment was there any danger of anyone falling asleep. After some polite and tentative exchanges the arguments between the British and American points of view waxed fast and furious, though always politely – well, just. I never thought I would live to hear Harold Evans defending English libel law on the ground that it promoted good and responsible journalism. The disagreement about prejudicial pre-trial publicity raised blood pressure on both sides. One of the more amusing incidents was the spectacle of Lord Denning describing with horror the prejudicial screaming headline of an American newspaper – 'Cop slayer goes on trial tomorrow', only to be told angrily by an editor, whose accent I imagined to be Bronx, 'Waddya mean prejudicial? Da conviction was revoised on appeal. Da system woiks.' When the laughter had died down we were left with hard reality, a wide gulf between British and American practice which each finds hard to bridge. British dislike of prejudicial pre-trial publicity was countered by the part played by the Press in Watergate. Somehow, as the hours passed, both sides began to suspect that there might be something to learn from each other. The moment of conversion from disagreement to a search for understanding began when one American said, in effect, 'Look here, you British don't understand. Our Constitution was written at a time when each State distrusted authority, and federal government in particular. Freedom of the Press was enshrined in it as a specific safeguard against central authority and government institutions. Your traditions are different. You have long had a degree of trust in your institutions, not always deserved, and have tended to look on the Press with distrust.' He was so obviously right that everyone paused for thought and it was noticeable thereafter that participants began to ask rather than assert. I don't know that we came to any firm conclusions, but I thought it to be one of the most interesting and informative conferences I have ever attended and it certainly diminished my hitherto critical prejudices about the American Press.

There is, of course, great argument here about the role of the Press, the balance between privacy and freedom to investigate and contempt. During the conference no one on the British side attempted to explain the difference between the theory and practice of law, possibly because the Lord Chancellor and Attorney General were present. Section 2 of the Official Secrets Act may still be on the Statute Book, but I cannot imagine, after a government declaration of intent to repeal it, that it would ever be invoked except in the most horrendous circumstances, or that if it were invoked lightly a jury would convict. Again, it is all very well to argue that the Attorney General is impervious to political pressure, that is not a belief likely to find universal acceptance in recent years.

There is no doubt that neither a Labour nor a Conservative government is likely to find this an attractive skein to unravel. The Americans prefer definition by Constitution, Bill of Rights or statute. We prefer a grey area of discretion in which the judiciary or even public opinion will decide whether disclosure was justified in the public interest or not. For example, if Harold Evans, William Rees-Mogg, or one or two other editors I can think of, had stumbled across a Watergate, I do not think any statute would have prevented them from disclosure. Their problem would have been whether disclosure was likely to obstruct or prevent prosecution of the wrongdoer on the grounds of prejudice.

My own attitude to the Press has undergone gradual and extensive change in the last forty years. I was taught at the outset that the only things to believe in a newspaper were the date and the lighting-up time, and even then only after checking them with a diary. In fact for most of my police service the Press were generally seen as an enemy, or at least as untrustworthy. This was not entirely the fault of the police. They had to operate under a system of justice distinguished as much by complacency as ineffectiveness, and were inevitably the most vulnerable participants. Traditionally a butt for lawyers, politicians and civil libertarians, they were not in a position to air their grievances without serious adverse consequences and not surprisingly reacted with hostility. The occasional breaking of this wall clearly offered advantages for policemen and journalists alike, but it was invariably done at operational rather than command level, because police chiefs are sensitive about airing views which might offend those on whom they rely for support. For years, therefore, individual detectives and journalists enjoyed a questionable relationship of which everyone was perfectly well aware, but no one wished to expose. In fact the lack of objectivity in the reporting or revelation of the reality of the relationship between criminal justice, the police, and the Press must have constituted one of the most longlasting and successful hypocrisies ever to influence public opinion.

Now at least that is over. The police in particular have led the way in attempting to break down a tradition harmful to the public interest. Not, of course, for any altruistic reason, but because they have at long last come to realize that they suffered most from it. The adversary system in our courts, with its high profits for lawyers and criminal alike, and its disregard of truth as essential to the purpose of criminal justice depends upon the willingness of the policeman to accept a servile role. The stronger the case, the more certain it is that he, not the accused, will be on trial. Far from being the envy and admiration of the world, as is claimed by the few with vested interests in it, the British system of justice is gradually sinking in public esteem to the level of the American, than which there is none less respected in the free world including America itself. Anyone thinking that an extreme statement should take the trouble to read the issues of *Newsweek* of 8 March 1971 (Justice on Trial) and *U.S. News and World Report* of 10 May 1976 (The Revolving Door of Justice). Seldom can two reputable periodicals have so castigated one of the most important social institutions in their own country and with so much evidence and justification.

The real difficulty is that so few people know anything about it. The legal trade unions protect their vested interests with impressively iron determination, complacency and eloquence from which even the Fleet Street printing unions could learn. Politicians of all parties see no advantage in upholding the interests of the accuser or the wronged, only those of the accused. Journalists form snap judgements likely to appeal to the reader. Popular judgements may be good for newspapers' circulation. They are less likely to contribute to respect for law. Perhaps most to blame are the academics who have spent countless hours and money on speculating pointlessly about the causation of crime and hardly any time at all examining the system of justice. They and the Press could probably do more than anyone to influence the making of laws, police procedures and penal policies, but they would have to be given much greater facilities for research than hitherto. And their research should be free from the paternal but stifling supervision of the Home Office, which is never very anxious to be told of its own mistakes, or lack of vision.

The police, therefore, have everything to gain by opening their doors to the Press not because they accept the Press at its own evaluation. No one but the Press is likely to do that. However, exposure of reality is the best way to achieve reform. It is moreover likely to deter police wrongdoing, to encourage public confidence and to serve the public interest as well as that of both police and Press.

That a free Press is essential to a free society is surely a proposition beyond dispute. But whether the resources of the Press are used well or ill is always a matter of opinion. The actual conveyance of views or opinion to the public may be accurate or inaccurate, objective or misleading but this ought not to lessen belief in the need for a free Press so much as to encourage critical examination of the way in which it works.

There is unfortunately a natural basis for disagreement in that the Press regard themselves as being entitled to virtually everything that the police disclose and a great deal that they do not. The police on the other hand tend to regard the Press as being entitled to nothing but having to be given a great deal in the hope that it will further the interests of both police and public. They therefore expect the Press to give disclosures the kind of slant that the police themselves would like. The natural diversity of Press opinion and policies frequently disappoints them. Even if Press and police interpretation of particular incidents is not discordant the limited purpose of most newspapers ensures a built-in superficiality, and sometimes even distortion, which offends a service geared to factual and precise comment. That every chief inspector in some kind of difficulty becomes a police chief in the headlines is misleading and offensive to the police mind, even if the headline is created by a sub-editor less concerned with the true meaning of words than the filling of column space in a manner most likely to catch the eye. It would never occur to him that this is akin to describing a compositor as a personal aide to a Press Lord. Although I suspect a compositor is paid more than a chief inspector.

There are, too, the obvious difficulties, once disclosure is agreed, arising from the need to treat all newspapers fairly. Every journalist wants a scoop, and every journalist wants to put his own interpretation on news unavoidably shared with others. The likelihood is that the search will be for difference, of fact or interpretation; the very opposite, in fact, from the treatment the police would like. The nature and interest of the police function means inevitably that in addition to the formal arrangements for liaison there is a ceaseless search for information through informal and sometimes unorthodox channels. The result of activities of this kind is not always harmful. Indeed, it can sometimes demonstrably be in the public interest, as in the Sheffield rhino whip case. This was a case in 1963 in which two policemen were found guilty of beating two prisoners with a whip in order to obtain confessions. They appealed to the Home Secretary against their resultant dismissal from the force. A tribunal consisting of a QC and an Inspector of Constabulary found that they had been guilty of brutal and sustained assaults, that they had been under pressure to get results, that violence had been witnessed with approval by senior officers and that a senior officer had helped them to concoct a false story in mitigation before the justices. The chief constable, who was comparatively young and inexperienced, was also criticized and resigned prematurely. The real significance of the affair, however, was that it would never have come to light but for the persistent and courageous campaign of the Sheffield *Daily Telegraph* to expose what its editor rightly felt to be unacceptable police behaviour. There was ironically another no less significant aspect of this affair. The conduct of the two detectives and their chief constable was little, if at all, different from the methods by which Percy Sillitoe, chief constable of Sheffield from 1926 to 1931, tamed the razor gangs which troubled the city at that time. His strong-arm squad using 'hit first and ask questions afterwards' tactics had striking results (no pun intended), gained the approval of Press, magistrates and public alike and ensured his appointment as chief constable of Glasgow, from whence he progressed to Kent, MI5 and a knighthood. In 1963 he would have got the sack. *Autres temps autres mœurs!*

Amongst the police themselves there is an understandable lack of uniformity of approach to Press and television. Notwithstanding the justifiable pride of the police in local autonomy and in their constitutional independence operationally, there has always been a strong and understandable tendency to conformity in their dealings with the Press. The natural unpopularity of the police function has over the years ensured a service sensitive to criticism, and anxiety to avoid suspicion of unjustifiable deviation from commonly accepted standards. I happen to believe that notwithstanding the essentially commercial purpose of newspapers and the considerations that flow from that, the Press collectively are experts at assessing and meeting the needs of the public and have a moral, if not a legal entitlement to information from public services of every kind, including the police. To deny journalists access to information unreasonably is as harmful to the police as to the public interest.

One of the undoubted virtues of British journalists is a readiness to poke fun at each other and at the Press as an institution; and occasionally to prick the balloon of pomposity and self-esteem sometimes tied to editorial chairs. A classic example of the kind of thing I mean is the following quote from Roger Woddis, an occasionally brilliant satirist whose short poems or doggerel – according to your view – enhance the columns of the *New Statesman*:

> Headlines must be tall, you see,
> Whether they are true ot not,
> Time has dimmed the old decree
> Facts are sacred, comment's free.
> Who the hell was C. P. Scott?

Can you really imagine that in *Pravda*?

Happily more and more policemen are abandoning the traditional hostility which has impaired the relationship between police and Press for so long. Variety of opinion is essential to the framing of legislation if it is to command public support and only the Press can ensure its availability. Despite my ups and downs at its hands I now genuinely believe a free Press to be no less essential than laws and government for the attainment of a society not made critical or suspicious, or even divided, by unnecessary secrecy in matters about which the public ought to be informed. This is not a view I would have expressed forty or even twenty years ago. It takes time and experience to become convinced of it. The invitation to the editor of the *Sunday Times* to send a member of his staff to see the innermost workings of A10 (the anti-corruption unit) is surely the most convincing evidence of my conversion. No other profession or organization has, within my knowledge, offered such indisputable evidence of good intent.

# CHAPTER 22

# Guilty or Not Guilty

In the *Sunday Express* of 27 November 1977 Mr Fenton Bresler, QC, made the following assertion:

> Jury Trial is under attack. The fundamental right of a defendant charged with serious crime in our courts to claim the privilege of trial by jury is being eaten away at the edges and virtually by stealth. Unknown to the general public, and largely with the support of the Conservative Opposition, this Government has recently put upon the Statute Book the Criminal Law Act of 1977. This Act, when it comes into force on a date as yet not specified, will abolish entirely the right to jury trial of all persons charged with certain crucial offences.

He went on:

> The down-grading of the jury began 11 years ago when Sir Robert Mark, then Chief Constable of Leicester, was in the vanguard of a campaign based on returns from chief constables of 120 police forces alleged to prove that the acquittal rate was far higher for juries than for magistrates. Too many guilty men were getting away with it, ran the argument. That coincided with an outbreak of 'jury nobbling' at the Old Bailey, when some pretty obvious London villains were acquitted under dubious circumstances. The Home Office under that darling of the permissive trendies, Mr Roy Jenkins, both warmed to the 'intellectual' appeal of Britain's most famous post-war policeman and over-reacted to the purely local Old Bailey situation.

This comment, ten years after the change from unanimous to majority verdicts in jury trials, is revealing. It is a classic example of a barrister fulfilling one of the most difficult of the tasks which he undertakes, putting a case persuasively to the jury, on this occasion the readers, relying entirely on eloquence devoid of evidence or logic.

The statistics in the *Guardian* mentioned in chapter 5 showed that the average rate of acquittal by juries in fifteen Midland police force areas during a period of four years involving 4293 trials was 37 per cent although in two areas it was as high as 55 per cent, and 56 per cent. The further research mentioned by Mr Bresler in which every police force in England and Wales took part for one year showed an average acquittal rate in contested cases of 39 per cent, rising as high as 80 per cent and 90 per cent in some areas. The figures have never since been challenged, though the reasons for the acquittals and their significance, have been hotly debated ever since.

Far from being a 'trendy lefty' in using the evidence to achieve the change to majority verdicts, Roy Jenkins bravely ran the risk of offending the left, the Bar, the Law Society and much public opinion. Undeterred, he stuck to his guns.

It is no exaggeration to say that acquittal rates and the change to majority verdicts was the main subject of discussion and dissension amongst barristers and solicitors practising criminal law during 1966 and 1967. Mr Bresler himself was well aware of it, mentioning it at length in an article he wrote in *Queen* magazine on 9 November 1966. The argument that majority verdicts were necessary to prevent the nobbling of jurors was, it is true, put to the House of Commons by Roy Jenkins. But it was not the basis on which the plea for change was put forward by the police. Our Judges are, of course, non-elective. Their experience and impartiality are generally accepted. The real argument in favour of majority verdicts was not that of occasionally corrupt jurymen. It was that if the one person in the criminal justice process most fitted by education, training and experience to decide the issue, namely the judge, is to be denied that right, how much more illogical is it to confer it upon any one of twelve random jurymen, least fitted by deafness, stupidity, prejudice or one of a hundred other reasons to do so?

Why is it that a lawyer and journalist of unblemished reputation should, through the medium of a national newspaper, offer such misleading views? Sir Peter Rawlinson, QC, a former chairman of the Council of the Bar, of which Mr Bresler is a member, who had led the opposition to majority verdicts, had publicly disclosed in *The Times* that his view had changed in the light of experience, a generous admission indeed.

The article is noteworthy in that it highlights a very disturbing issue, the extent to which the most honourable lawyers find objectivity difficult when discussing issues affecting their professional interests. Mr Bresler is far from being alone. After I had given the 1973 Dimbleby Lecture criticizing, amongst other things, a minority of bent lawyers, 'the main theme of retaliation by individual lawyers and their trade unions was that I had produced no evidence. The common cry was, in fact, 'Put up, or shut up'. In the light of that reaction, consider the following extracts from the Memorandum submitted by the Council of the Law Society to the Royal Commission on the Police in December 1960.

'The Council believe that some deterioration in the relationship between the police and the public has occurred in recent years owing to the conduct of the police when discharging certain of their duties. Examples of such conduct are referred to in the following six paragraphs.

'The Council have considered the Judges' Rules and their interpretation by police officers in the course of questioning suspected persons. The Council think that the Rules provide sufficient safeguards if they are adhered to by police officers. While there is little evidence that they are not complied with, it has been suggested that on certain occasions the police may offer inducements to an accused person – for example, they may inform the accused that it would be to his benefit if he made a statement, and that if he did so no objection would be taken by them to a subsequent application for bail. The failure to observe the Judges' Rules, even though the statements obtained may be true, leads to the view that the police are unfair.

'Complaints regarding arrests have been made, and in isolated instances substantiated in subsequent proceedings (although other cases are also believed to exist which are not reported because it is against the interests of the accused to complain), that police officers have used undue force after arresting individual prisoners. The Council believe that although in general, police officers treat prisoners in a proper manner there are cases where this is not so, and they urge that all such allegations should be the subject of the most stringent enquiry.

'The Council have been informed that there is a tendency on the part of certain police officers to colour or exaggerate evidence. For example, words and behaviour are sometimes attributed to an accused person which, in the opinion of experienced solicitors, are inconsistent with his character and the attitude that he would be likely to adopt. Statements alleged to have been made by the accused are given in evidence by the police either containing criminal slang which, it is suggested, is introduced in order to indicate a criminal disposition or, at least, an intimate knowledge of criminals. Parts of a conversation indicative of guilt are sometimes emphasized whilst other parts consistent with innocence are omitted.

'The Council have been informed by experienced solicitors that occasions have occurred in which they have been forced to the conclusion that evidence has been fabricated by the police. Instances which have been put forward include the planting of stolen goods upon a receiver, the placing of indicative evidence on the accused's clothes, and sterotyped accounts of the conduct of the accused in importuning and drunk in charge cases.

'The Council believe that the instances set out in paragraphs above generally occur because over-zealous police officers, convinced of the guilt of the accused, introduce such evidence in order to make certain of a conviction. These instances, however infrequent they may be, must lead to a deterioration in the relationship between the police and the public.

'The Council think that there is a tendency on the part of police officers both to suggest and discuss with the accused, particularly juveniles, the question of a plea of guilty or not guilty to a charge. Whilst it is appreciated that the accused often asks a police officer what plea should be made, such a practice is to be deprecated. The Council consider that the proportion of cases, particularly large before juvenile courts, revealing pleas of guilty gives rise to disquiet amongst parents in the case of juveniles and suggests that advice to plead guilty is too readily given by police officers.'

Not a scrap of evidence was adduced in support of these public allegations, which, ironically enough, were not resented by the police because they were mostly true, but was there ever a more classic case of double standards? It was perfectly acceptable for the Law Society to make allegations against the police unsupported by evidence, but for the police to retaliate was sufficient to saturate the television screen, the radio and the 'letters to the Editor' columns, with indignant spluttering lawyers.

The law, by any standards, is an extraordinary profession. Its practitioners are always anxious to voice the highest principles of fairness and impartiality in relation to everyone but themselves. As I had made clear in the 1973 Dimbleby Lecture, it was common knowledge that a minority of criminal lawyers, both solicitors and barristers, are a cancer in society and have been so since time immemorial. Yet with very rare exceptions the only lawyers whose 'strikings off' appear in the *Law Society's Gazette* are those whose wrong-doing is self-detecting, almost always for the embezzlement of their client's funds. The smoke-screen of a lay observer on the disciplinary bodies of the profession deceives no one. The truth is, of course, that lawyers, politicans and jour-nalists do not differ from people in any other walk of life. The bulk are honourable, honest, hard-working and a credit to their professions. Some of the remainder are idle, incompetent, corrupt, or all three. The real trouble is that no really effective machinery exists to deal with them, a defect that has been remedied only in the case of the police.

It is in fact a serious weakness of our judicial system that everything stops with acquittal. Conviction opens the door to every kind of scrutiny. Appeal to the Higher Courts, to public opinion, to Parliament. Acquittal is followed by silence. The tactics of the lawyers, the competence of the judges, these are never called into question. It is beyond belief that lawyers do not indulge in gamesmanship, or worse, or that judges are not occasionally prone to error, prejudice and in some cases incompetence. The advent of the Crown Court judge has given a new dimension to the problem. Lord Devlin argued in his brilliant book *The Criminal Prosecution in England* that although the criminal justice system failed too frequently,

> an injustice on the one side is spread over the whole of society and an injustice on the other is concentrated in the suffering of one man. The English speaking peoples are so little vindictive that even those who have been most gravely injured by the criminal soon cease to resent his acquittal.

With the greatest respect to Lord Devlin, whom I much admire, though that assertion may have been permissible in 1960, when the book was written, I am certain that it does not reflect public opinion today.

The welcome change in penal policy towards treatment, rehabilitation, compensation and restitution as enjoying a higher priority than punishment justifies a demand that justice should establish the truth rather than technical guilt as a pre-requisit to punishment.

I was so concerned by the blatantly perverse acquittals at the Criminal Courts in London that I arranged for research to be done into the careers of a number of well-known criminals, some of them household names. This was reproduced in diagrammatic form. A line from the bottom left-hand corner to the top right-hand corner of the page represented the life of the subject. A horizontal line across the page represented the age of 21. A hieroglyph on one side of the line represented an acquittal, and on the other, a conviction. The results were both illuminating and hilarious, some of the subjects notching up an astonishing number of acquittals. I intended to carry this further by identifying by disguised names the solicitors and counsel instructed in each case. At this point the Home Office got the wind up. I was advised informally that an enterprising journalist would undoubtedly identify the subjects and that publication would expose me to actions for libel, defamation or professional misconduct. I therefore abandoned the project but it demonstrated only too clearly the need for a forum in which the shortcomings of the criminal justice system can be revealed without fear of the laws of libel, privilege and contempt.

My criticism of the system is sure to attract a strong reaction on the grounds of lack of evidence, although it is the law itself which denies the evidence to the public. Lord Mansfield, who practised at the Bar until 1971, bravely admitted under privilege during a debate on the Criminal Law Bill in the House of Lords on 21 July 1977, the exploitation of the system of barristers to 'get robbers off the hook' and went so far as to say 'to pack a jury so as to get a whole lot of illiterates and unemployables is not really a fair trial'. Lord Shawcross, in November 1977 speaking at the Jubilee Dinner of the Central Criminal Courts Association, criticised the acquittal of the guilty by juries and was predictably himself attacked by the usual spokesmen for the legal profession.

A notable feature of trials for anarchist activities is the availability of radical lawyers to exploit every conceivable ploy to confuse the issue, denigrate the police and achieve their client's acquittal. There are a number of members of the legal profession whose loyalty is to their radical beliefs rather than to the ethics of their profession and whose standards bring the process of justice and the legal profession into disrepute. It was said of Samuel Bentham, the father of Jeremy, by Charles W. Everett,

> He was in no doubt either as to the ends to be attained by education, nor the means to be employed to attain the ends. The end desired was either money or some equivalent form of power; the training must be both technical and social. The technical training that offered the most possibilities was law, for law was involved in almost all human relationships, and was so arranged that its practitioner could profit if the machinery of society ran well, and could profit still more if it ran ill.

If that was true in the 19th century, it is infinitely more true today.

The exploitation of legal aid has inevitably affected the justice system adversely especially against the background of 'paper committals' for trial introduced in 1967. The cost has doubled from £18m to £36m in criminal matters between 1973 and 1976. The effect has been to impose on the higher courts much of the 'sifting process' undertaken previously by magistrates courts with consequent long delays, great expense and increased acquittal rates, largely arising from cases which should never have got to a higher court. Even the Law Society, always quick to protect the vested interests of its members, has expressed disquiet at this situation, probably realizing that sooner or later it must attract public attention.

An equally unhappy development is the failure of the Courts, save in exceptional circumstances, to deal effectively with public violence. The trial of those accused of a variety of offences at Notting Hill in 1976 is a classic example of the inadequacy of the law for dealing with issues of this kind. Huge legal costs, refusal of juries to convict, lengthy delay, virtually unlimited falsehood and misrepresentation, all these, though seemingly successful from the point of view of the offender and the defence lawyer, bring the criminal justice system and the legal profession into mounting disrepute.

The suggestion that the whole judicial process should be handed over to the lawyers as in America and Scotland has the most alarming implications. A cursory look at the American system of District Attorneys is sufficient to induce a sense of both pity and despair. Indeed, after eight visits to the United States, I have yet to meet a single person who does not feel that their system of justice is the most unsatisfactory aspect of a society that is in so many ways admirable and an example to the world.

The arguments for and against depriving the police in England and Wales of the right to decide whether to prosecute or not in the majority of cases should be examined with great care, because the present situation is unique and has served the country well. Every citizen still retains the right to prosecute should he wish to do so. In practice the police undertake that task for him. Contumacious prosecutions by private citizens can easily be prevented by the right of the Director of Public Prosecutions to take over any prosecution if he thinks that step necessary to the public interest. There is, too, the safeguard that a private citizen may be faced with the costs of the prosecution if it is clearly unjustified.

The lawyers argue that they are better fitted by training and impartiality to evaluate the evidence and to decide whether to prosecute or not. But in practice most prosecutions before the lower courts and all prosecutions in the higher courts are already handled by lawyers instructed by the police. Although the relationship is that of lawyer and client, I have never in forty years known a police chief to disregard, or not to follow the advice of the lawyer in charge of a particular case. In other words, in every case of moment the real responsibility for its prosecution already is borne in fact by lawyers. There is no conceivable justification for adding to their discretion in the pursuance or conduct of prosecutions the right to decide whether to prosecute or not. That right is presently exercised by the police on behalf of the people, not of the government, central or local, and their compulsory divorce from politics, trade unionism and financial consideration for their services, equips them uniquely to fulfil it. Even the smallest police force is now sufficiently large to employ properly qualified legal staff so the argument for change virtually disappears altogether.

More to the point, I think is the increasingly urgent need to remove all but a handful of motoring offences from the criminal to the civil law. The trial procedure is now appropriate for serious offences such as causing death, dangerous, reckless or careless driving, driving whilst uninsured or under the influence of drink or drugs, but it is surely excessively ponderous, costly and to some extent offensive, as a means of dealing with the vast majority of motoring offences. All 'absolute' offences, parking, lighting, those relating to the condition and ownership of vehicles, should be dealt with as civil matters by ordinary magistrates sitting in a civil capacity as when dealing with family affairs. The burden of proof in all such cases should be reversed since there would be no question of deprivation of liberty or conviction of crime. Any penalty could be described by an inoffensive term such as 'levy' and the stigma of conviction would be avoided. It would be necessary to abolish 'totting up' but that would, I think, be a very small price to pay for a change that would be universally popular. 'Totting up', by the way, for anyone happily unaware of its meaning, is the arrangement under the 1972 Road Traffic Act authorizing the endorsement of a driving licence after conviction for any one of a number of offences. The endorsement lasts three years and two further endorsements during that period mean mandatory disqualification from driving for a minimum of six months. It is intended as a kind of surety for good driving behaviour.

The lawyers might, of course, see the change as involving loss of earnings and be inclined to oppose it on other grounds such as diminution of liberty. But I doubt whether those arguments would carry much weight. Their services would still be available to the motorist in the civil court and the process would not apply to any offence likely to involve a custodial sentence.

The greatest obstacle to be overcome by those seeking rational public discussion of police powers, criminal trial and penology is that it arouses in every section of society emotion for which there is rarely any evidential or logical reason. The worldwide myth of the omniscient and incorruptible Metropolitan CID, under the misleading label of 'Scotland Yard' was as mistaken as the unthinking belief in the virtues of trial by jury, the impeccable standards of British lawyers and the efficiency of the British system of justice. The first has, after a century, been thoroughly exposed. The other two have never undergone impartial scrutiny.

Almost a century ago, Jeremy Bentham wrote:

If all criminals of every class had assembled and framed a system after their own wishes, is not this rule (that suspects cannot be judicially interrogated) the very first which they would have established for their security? Innocence never takes advantage of it. Innocence claims a right of speaking as guilt invokes the privilege of silence.

The *Justice of the Peace Review*, hardly the most revolutionary of periodicals, said on 18 November 1972 of the Criminal Law Revision Committee's reaction to this situation:

It has been objected, for example, that an innocent person accused in vague terms, or of an incident which took place long ago, or of an involved and complex matter, may not reasonably be expected to respond immediately by offering the investigating officer a complete statement of his side of the case. But no one would expect him to in these circumstances, any more than if the interview had taken place while the accused was ill or recently awoken or in the existence of any other factors which would account for the accused's failure to give a full or, indeed, any explanation of his conduct. Under the committee's proposal everything would turn (as with any other piece of evidence) upon what it is reasonable to expect from that particular person faced with that particular inquiry in those particular circumstances. To expect more would be oppressive to the accused: to expect less (as we now do) is to fetter justice to no good effect. We cannot think of a single improvement in criminal procedure which would go so far towards rectifying the unjust acquittal of guilty men, which is the foremost defect of our criminal procedure today, without increasing even in the minutest respect the possibility of innocent persons being wrongly convicted. By expecting of the accused that which any honest citizen is not only willing but morally obliged to render, namely co-operation with the police in the investigation of crime, the draft Criminal Evidence Bill proposed by the committee will go a long way towards adapting our criminal trial procedure to the demands of the mid-20th century. We would all do well to remember the words of Mr Robert Mark, the new Metropolitan Police Commissioner, in his address to the Royal Society of Medicine when he said: 'Most people have been brought up to think of the English judicial system as reasonably effective: a belief arising from an astonishing general unawareness of the truth. It is, in reality, effective only for dealing with the compliant, the weak, the stupid, the illiterate and the spontaneous wrong-doers who comprise the vast majority of cases. It is ineffective to an alarming and harmful extent in dealing with the non-compliant – those who set out to break the law and who are able, by experience or through advice, to exploit its weaknesses.' Although recent research has indicated that Mr Mark may perhaps have painted a gloomier picture of the trial scene than is wholly justified by the facts; nevertheless they remain words to be heeded.

It is perhaps an apt footnote that the same eminently

conservative periodical had said a little earlier on 19 August 1972:

> The most extraordinary thing about the jury system is that it has lasted so long.

But, of course, when that comment was made there had not been any significant public declaration that lawyers, as well as criminals, do very well from the proceeds of crime.

If certainty is the objective of the law, the jury can hardly be said to have contributed to it. Oddly enough, perhaps that is why it has lasted so long, and could, with advantage, survive. It is not the principle of the jury system which has cast increasing doubt upon its value. Rather is it the complacent and unquestioning acceptance of its exploitation and its fallibilty, encouraged by those with a vested interest in its continuance free from impartial and objective research.

# CHAPTER 23

# The One Who Got Away

Few things could have given me greater pleasure than to read in the *Daily Telegraph* of 25 November 1977 part of a speech by Roy Jenkins, President of the European Economic Community, to the Royal Institution in London in which he is reported to have said:

> A party that wins a bare majority of seats in the House of Commons enjoys the full fruits of sovereignty, even if it has won the votes of well under half of the electorate. So long as its members obey the whip such a party can force through whatever legislation it wishes, even in matters which in most democracies would require an amendment to the constitution.

He went on:

> The net result is that British Governments find it all too easy to carry through harmful changes and extraordinarily difficult to carry through beneficial ones.

There is was, in his own words, a description of the enactment of both the Police Bill and the Bail Bill and the blithe disregard of the need, unlikely to be acceptable to the trade unions, to treat the maldistribution of police manpower with special urgency.

About a year earlier, on 10 May 1976, the *US News and World Report* had said – 'Americans for years, have been frightened by the constant rise in crime. Now along with that is growing anger. The anger is about the way the nation's system deals with criminals.' It then went on to describe the case of a man arrested seven times, three of them for armed robbery, finally pleading guilty to an attempted petty larceny charge and being released on bond pending sentence. The whole article was a carefully researched, well-balanced critique of the American justice system, with particular reference to the abuse of bail, which in the larger cities is encouraging a sense of near despair in all but the guilty and the lawyers. I sent a copy to the Home Office but received no acknowledgement.

The Home Secretary having expressed his concern about the bail system undertook to introduce a Bill to liberalize it. The impression given by those urging reform was that the bail system was being administered with excessive severity. In fact this was the reverse of the truth. Of 112,000 persons charged in England and Wales in 1967 with indictable, or the more serious non-indictable offences, 38,000 were remanded in custody and 74,000 released on bail. By 1975 of 268,300 persons arrested for the same categories, fewer (35,300) were remanded in custody. The number released on bail had increased threefold to 233,000. Worried by the disregard of reality and the influence of the reformers I ordered a pilot study on bail and the results showed that between 1 September and 4 December 1976 there were 928 occasions on which an adult accused of an indictable offence 'jumped' bail. 150 of these had been granted bail despite a previous record of absconding. A projection of the results suggested that something in the order of 4000 adults live off crime in London, having 'jumped' bail and therefore being unable to follow employment or to apply for social security. The research suggests also an annual total of roughly 3000 arrests for crime committed whilst on bail.

One particularly tragic case in this category was highlighted in the *Sunday Times*, the brutal murder of a young girl bank clerk in South London by a man already on bail.

A search of Hansard during the debate on the Bail Bill will not reveal any embarrassing details of this kind. The theme was predictably that prisons were overcrowded, that prisoners remanded in custody were sometimes acquitted or not given a custodial sentence. Governments of all complexions have understandably not been willing to spend any more than is necessary on police, prisons, probation services or ancillary measures affording more options to Courts. This is understandable, but there should surely be more research, greater disclosure and more public discussion of the issues involved before reforming zeal, no matter how praiseworthy and well intentioned, is allowed to outrun commonsense.

No one who has seen them would deny that some of our prisons – Dartmoor, the Scrubs, Wandsworth, Leicester, Durham, to name but a few – are a thorough disgrace to a supposedly civilized society, and a cause for shame for every post-war government. That doesn't mean that their occupants should necessarily be let out. It means that more money should be spent on building modern prisons and that there should be a meticulous review of sentencing policies and procedures so as to make imprisonment a measure of last resort. The Bail Act, like the Police Act, is a classic example of doctrinaire reaction to vocal minority pressure pushed through without adequate research, logic or mandate and after a Parliamentary debate remarkable for its irrelevance. It is at least a little encouraging now to see a former Home Secretary, surveying the scene from a more objective vantage point, publicly recognizing this unfortunate parliamentary tendency.

I do not want to see increased severity or harshness in our trial or penal systems. Neither do I wish to see woolliness or groping in the dark. I would like to see police, probation officers, lawyers, academics and civil servants concentrating on the definition and production of statistics and research, which for the first time, could serve a useful purpose as a tool of management and planning. It ought not to be impossible, but it is a pity that the responsibility is so widely dispersed. It clearly makes co-ordination and collaboration difficult.

Of course, avoidance of the need to keep criminals in prison for long periods after conviction, an expensive and sometimes contentious business, could be avoided with a

IN THE OFFICE OF CONSTABLE

little more imagination and willingness to learn from experience. The case of one of the Great Train Robbers, one Ronald Biggs, is an indication of this. Quite apart from its usefulness in suggesting a new approach to the problem of what to do with criminals sentenced to long terms of imprisonment it adds a rare and welcome touch of humour to the history of crime.

The Great Train Robbery is much too well known a part of our social history to recount at length. Suffice it to say that in August 1963 a gang of criminals, of whom Biggs was one, held up the Glasgow to London train in Buckinghamshire and relieved it of £2¼m in used untraceable banknotes. The perfect crime, in fact. The wonder is that it had not been done long before. Vast sums of new and used banknotes had been moved between London and the principal provincial cities without any adequate protection for decades. The booty was so enormous and unexpected that it immediately posed grave problems. It attracted the attention of the world and ensured exorbitant demands from anyone to whom the robbers turned for help. One by one they were arrested, though very little of the money was ever recovered. Society was so outraged by the amount of money stolen, rather than by the injury inflicted on the train driver, that the ringleaders received sentences of thirty years' imprisonment. This tended to have the belated and unforeseen effect of turning them into folk heroes. One, Bruce Reynolds, stayed on the run for several years. Two of the others, Charles Wilson and Ronald Biggs, later escaped from prison, though the former was later recaptured. Most of them, incidentally, have now been paroled.

It was, however, left to Biggs to revive memories of the rather convenient and useful punishment of banishment, probably the most memorable figure to undergo that fate since Henry IV in 1398, before his accession. He was doing his time in HM Prison Wandsworth, when on the afternoon of 8 July 1965, a furniture van with a hole in its roof and carrying mattresses to soften a fall drew up outside the prison wall, behind which Biggs was taking exercise with three other prisoners. Two rope ladders were thrown over the prison wall. The other prisoners impeded the attendant prison officers and the intrepid Ronnie was up the ladder, over the wall and into the van in a trice. The escape took one or two minutes and no doubt cost a lot of money.

Nothing was heard of our hero for some years when he was traced to Australia. The Yard then took the appropriate measures to effect his arrest by means acceptable both to the Australian and British governments. Unfortunately that was all that was necessary to forewarn him and the bird had flown even before detectives had set off from London airport. In fact, he managed to get to Brazil where, after some years, he established contact with the *Daily Express*. No doubt by this time the money had run out, he could not run the risk of committing crime for fear of discovery and the benefits of social security were denied to him. The length of time since the robbery, the parole of some of the participants, the possibility of a lucrative deal with the *Daily Express*, these and many other factors must have given the prospect of home an attraction it had hitherto lacked. By this time the Policy Committee and the CID were both doing well, and I was continually extolling the virtues of delegation. They took me at my word for which I cannot complain since I enjoyed much the reflected glory for some of their more successful exploits. Having gone through the usual channels on discovering Biggs in Australia, the CID were a little put out to find that the bird had flown before they could even leave Heathrow. This time they did not tell anyone, not even me. The resultant comic opera did no real harm, though I suspect it wounded the pride of Jack Slipper of the Flying Squad, who was sent to bring in the wanted man. No one seemed to have given much thought to the difficulties of doing the 'I want you, Ronnie' bit in a faraway land that shows more interest in football than criminal justice. It never occurred to anyone that all that needed to be done was to fly his wife out there and await results. I suspect that Ronnie would have emerged like a rat from a drainpipe. However, the result was not all that bad. The infallible CID were seen to be capable of error, and therefore more likely human, the British taxpayer is spared the cost of keeping Biggs and he isn't even in a position to make a fortune out of his memoirs when eventually paroled. On reflection it might have been even funnier had we simply issued a statement from the Yard saying,

To whom it may concern –

Mr Ronald Biggs, formerly of HM Prison Wandsworth, is alive and well and now living at such and such an address in Brazil.

Ah, well! There's always a next time.

The case does, however, raise the intriguing possibility of offering some of our 'lifers' or long sentence prisoners the choice of voluntary banishment. This would save the cost of keeping them, of prison staff and ensure that the country would be rid of them. They would be denied the possible profits from recounting their real and fictional exploits in the Press and on television, the exploitation of social security or the opportunities for further crimes in Britain. It would, of course, have to be clearly understood that if they returned their sentences would start from scratch, that there would be no parole and that they would be criminally bankrupt. The strain on prison accommodation would be lessened and we would be spared the continual boredom of listening to penal reformers hawking their consciences around for sale to Press and television. Bear in mind this would not be transportation. It would be voluntary. Were this to come about I think the intrepid Ronnie, despite his domestic problems, would have earned himself an honourable place in British penal history.

# CHAPTER 24

# The Police and a Changing Society

What is the future role of the police and what lessons can we learn from the past? So long as we remain free from external interference, it is unlikely that the move towards a socialist society so marked in the second half of my lifetime will reach the authoritarian extremism of Eastern Europe. If, however, that were to happen there would be no point in philosophizing about policing. I doubt whether there is any difference between the cells of the Gestapo and those of the KGB. The dead of Auschwitz and Treblinka are indistinguishable from those of Katyn though the nationalities of their murderers differed. Though the extremists of the National Front, the Socialist Workers Party, the International Marxist Group and the like may cause apprehension to the vast majority of moderates, Labour, Liberal and Conservative alike, I do not think they present a serious threat to this country other than in the event of a catastrophe such as a third world war. In fact, in a curious way, their very existence offers a reasonable assurance of continued moderation because each offers a frightening glimpse of the possible.

The police of the future will inevitably reflect social change probably more rapidly than in the past, because of the acceleration to centralized control of the last decade. When socialists in the Commons and the Lords speak of a police force accountable to Parliament, or a national police force, they are not thinking of justice. They are thinking of police as a tool of government. This would not, of course, be the end of the world. That description can already be applied to the police of almost all countries, including those we regard as democratic. But it would mean an end to the conception of policing initiated by Rowan and Mayne under the sponsorship of Robert Peel in 1829, a different role for the police, a different relationship with the public, and a different kind of policeman. Whatever the views of politicians, civil servants and journalists, the more senior and experienced policemen today have a real sense of pride in their impartiality operational independence. It is probably true that only in the post-war years has that pride had any basis in reality.

Until the celebrated case of Fisher v Oldham Corporation/1930. 2 K.B. 364/ the extent to which public authorities, whether the Home Secretary in the Metropolis or the Watch Committees and Standing Joint Committees of the provinces, could properly exercise influence in operational, as distinct from administrative, matters, had always been doubtful. Chief officers had not shown a noticeable willingness to resist encroachment upon their operational sphere by authorities exercising a discretion in respect of their salaries and allowances. 'Fisher' had, however, made it plain that the powers of a police officer, whether conferred by common law or statute law, are exercised by him by virtue of his office and cannot be exercised on the responsibility of any person but himself. This was understandably not a judgement likely to commend itself to local authorities or the central government and it is unlikely that it had any immediate impact on their relationship with chief constables. It was, in fact, continually challenged by the Association of Municipal Corporations and its scope was questioned by Dr Geoffrey Marshall in *Police and Government* published by Methuen in 1965. However, the Court of Appeal restated the position with even greater emphasis in the case of Regina v Commissioner of Police of the Metropolis *ex parte* Blackburn in 1968 when it asserted 'every constable in the land should be and is independent of the Executive . No minister of the Crown can tell him he must or must not keep observation on this place or that, or that he must, or must not, prosecute this person or that, nor can any police authority tell him to do so.' No less significantly however, police forces in the meantime had been reduced in number and the influence of local authorities in their administrative affairs had been severely limited by the 1964 Police Act. In other words, chief officers were for the first time able to put theory into practice without fear of adverse personal consequences. I think it a not unfair assumption that prior to 1964 police freedom from political or executive influence in operational matters was less likely than today. The change has, without any doubt, sustained the morale, and to some extent the quality, of the service during a period of intense difficulty. Manpower shortage, rising crime, industrial unrest, terrorism, and, in the most vulnerable areas, racial problems have lessened the attraction of a police career. The resilience and achievements of the service, throughout that period, owe more to a sense of vocation, group solidarity and pride than to material factors. If ever the police in Great Britain cease to represent government by consent and become the servants of those who rule, their relationship with the public will inevitably change. Improvement in their material conditions would be compelled, since the vocational appeal would be gone, except perhaps to the kind of man at present not acceptable to the police. The damage would not be much less if the police were ever formally associated with trade unionism whilst retaining their present organization. There is no impartiality about trade unionism in politics and impartiality is essential to the present police ethos.

The greatest challenge for the police of tomorrow, therefore, is the threat of change in their constitutional position, particularly a threat concealed in the seemingly attractive disguise of a better deal in terms of pay, working hours, pensions, etc. A number of police officers at every level are no doubt aware of this. If so, they have not been sufficiently vocal about it. The Joint Central Committee of the Police Federation should not be encouraged by the silence of a majority of dissenters to play the role of Faust to the Mephistopheles of the left or right. I do not see any present real danger of this. The Police Act of 1976 might have been the first step along this dangerous road but in its present form is likely to prove no more than a fatuous if costly irrelevancy to be discarded or varied at a convenient moment. There is no doubt however that as political, industrial and racial tensions rise the police will increasingly become the focus of political controversy centred upon their control and accountability. The history of race relations in recent years is an indication of this. Government policy opened the doors to thousands of Commonwealth immigrants to serve an expanding economy. Natural justice demanded that on arrival they should enjoy the same conditions as every other citizen. The scale was so overwhelming that planning and deployment were left to settle themselves. The idealists – and every politician is in theory an idealist – saw no difficulties arising from differences in ethnic origin, culture and so on. In fact the conception that in Britain everyone is fair-minded, tolerant and free from colour prejudice is such obvious nonsense that the most remarkable feature of this change in our way of life is that it has not fulfilled the blood-curdling predictions of Enoch Powell. That in itself is a tribute to the innate decency of the British people rather than to the wisdom of their rulers. The trouble is that things are likely to get worse rather than better though the problem is not necessarily insuperable in the long run. The great majority of immigrants came with the laudable intention of finding work and leading normal useful lives. But the very nature of the operation ensured that they got the most menial jobs and the tangible, though unmentionable, reality of colour prejudice ensured that they would generally live together in ghetto areas. The end of a booming economy was sure to hit the immigrant hard. He then suffered a second blow in that his children, born here, were unlikely to get jobs and thus more likely to get into trouble.

Government reaction to all this, both Conservative and Labour, has hardly been dynamic. Broadly speaking it has consisted of saying first, the problem doesn't exist, second, if it does exist we mustn't reveal and discuss it for fear of making it worse and third, if it does exist, it isn't our fault! For example, for many years, no attempt was made to identify the racial origins of those accused of crime. Eventually, it was thought necessary to do so if only to illustrate the need for positive remedial rather than punitive action. But by common consent the figures were not published because it was argued reasonably that their sudden appearance might open the door for the instant wiseacres, cause misunderstanding, inflame prejudice, and make matters worse. The situation steadily deteriorated, however, without there being any publication of information against which the public could assess it. Moreover, in the absence of factual information political pressure groups, politicians and others with vested interests were able to indulge in generalizations and accusations which no one could disprove.

The Select Committee on Race Relations was of particular interest in that its establishment was compelled by rising public unease and the anxiety of politicians and the Community Relations Commission to demonstrate awareness of it.

The record of the Metropolitan Police in the field of race relations compares well with that of the Community Relations Commission or of the government itself. And it was achieved at a much greater cost. Policing the ghettoes of London, created by the idealist and the inept, requires not only as much physical courage and dedication as policing parts of Victorian London but a great deal more moral courage than has been required by the police at any time since Peel.

Police have suffered many casualties in trying to cope with crime and vandalism by black youngsters, themselves to some extent victims of a situation which must offer them little hope. Black activists, white leftwing opportunists, people employed in the race relations industry see the police as the most obvious and vulnerable target on which to vent their resentment. As in Northern Ireland, no one has a constructive answer so allegations and blame are dispensed with equal lack of scruple.

The police have no influence on employment, housing and education. The problem of alienated black youth is dumped on their lap without any means to resolve it. Their efforts to do so constitute one of the most admirable chapters in their history so far. Beset with every kind of difficulty, hostility, violence, reverse prejudice from politicans, Press and courts, exploitation by political pressure groups and lawyers, they have never ceased to try to persuade black youths that there is a place for them in our society and in the police in particular. Joe Simpson deserves to be remembered for establishing early an elaborate Community Relations scheme on quite a large scale when the police themselves were scarcely ready to accept it. Since then the force has gradually come to accept, despite continual provocation and misrepresentation, that if they are to represent the whole community, of which, in London, the immigrant is an important part, coloured recruits must be attracted into the force. There are obvious difficulties and few helpers. But it is basic to the philosophy of policing that we should recognize only one colour, blue, and nothing must be allowed to deter us from persuading adequate numbers from minority groups to join the service.

I was told by the authors of Penguin's *The Fall of Scotland Yard* that I had failed badly in this. I doubt whether history will ratify that judgement. The number of coloured officers rose in my time from 1 to 80, with a further 100+ in the Special Constabulary, a small beginning but by no means an insignificant one. And losses have been small, smaller than of white recruits.

A typical instance of the many difficulties with which we had to contend was a defamatory press campaign, long and sustained against a Constable Pulley, who, when stationed at Notting Hill thought it proper to enforce the law impartially against black and white alike. The outcome was a civil action in which the allegations were exposed in court as baseless and wicked propaganda, Pulley being awarded £5000 damages and costs. I was anxious that he should pursue similar action against everyone involved in this unscrupulous campaign but he felt that honour was satisfied. The incident was followed soon afterwards by an exchange of letters with the legal officer of the so-called National Council for Civil Liberties:

Dear Sir Robert,
We have recently been informed that PC Pulley has been transferred back to the Notting Hill Gate area. I am sure that you are fully informed as to the previous allegations concerning this officer. It is not my purpose in this letter to argue whether or not the allegations were justified beyond saying that they were sincerely believed to be true by the black community and indeed by many other persons. Because of this, no matter what his conduct, his presence is potentially explosive and I feel that it is in the interests of the officer and the community generally if he were to be transferred from this area in which there is such a history of allegations. This is not pandering to popular dictates but is solely in the interests of community relations.

Sincerely, Lawrence Grant
Legal Officer

and my reply:

Dear Mr Grant,
I have received your letter of 30 April. Constable Pulley was originally transferred from duty at Notting Hill at his own request and I shall be interested to see on what evidence your assumption of his return is based. He has not in fact been transferred back to the Notting Hill Gate area though his present duties may take him there, as to many other parts of London, from time to time.

I note all that you say about him. He was in fact awarded £5000 damages in a recent court action against a national newspaper for the defamation on which your remarks seem to rely. He generously, and perhaps mistakenly, decided not to pursue similar actions in respect of other newspapers and organizations which had publicized similar statements.

I shall be obliged if in future you think it necessary to make statements about one of my officers which suggest grounds for criticism that firstly you verify your facts and secondly that you support your allegations with the evidence, if any, on which you rely.

Yours sincerely, Robert Mark

Needless to say, that was the end of that. I still regret Pulley's magnanimity. The money was not important but he could have given a number of journalists and political agitators a much needed reminder of Bertrand Russell's assertion:

A habit of basing convictions upon evidence, and of giving to them only that degree of certainty which the evidence warrants, would, if it became general, cure most of the ills from which the world is suffering.

The Notting Hill Carnival of 1977, despite a limited degree of tolerated crime, did at least reveal more clearly the nature of the problem. It may well prove, however, an ominous harbinger of things to come. Somehow or other, polarization must be avoided. Coincidentally, other social elements than the police, magistrates, journalists, politicians, judges and even the law officers of the Crown should be persuaded or shamed into exposing themselves to this kind of experience in person, and without such weighty protection as to make it unreal. The more people who undergo it the more likely its gravity will be appreciated. Ironically enough Scotland Yard and the Metropolitan Police and civil staff are possibly an outstanding example of a happily integrated and harmonious multi-racial organization. No one know just how many coloured staff there are in a wide variety of jobs but there are many and there has never been the slightest difficulty or tension arising from this by now well-established development.

I do not want to give the impression that the problem is insoluble. Having visited more than thirty American campuses in 1977 I feel hopeful for the first time that a reasonably happy multi-racial society is capable of achievement. But so much depends on the years of endeavour which will be long, and compulsion by statute is likely to extend rather than shorten them. My feelings on this matter are aptly summarized by the preface to the book *Target Blue* by Robert Daley which deals with one year in the tenure of office of Commissioner of Police for New York, Patrick V. Murphy, an exceptional policeman of outstanding integrity and moral courage. The words of the preface were spoken by Sergeant William Moriarty of the New York Police Department over the bodies of two patrolmen, Foster and Laurie, one coloured, one white, who had been assassinated on a New York street in January 1972. He said:

> They were killed because of their colour, which was neither black nor white, but blue.

These words should be taught to every police recruit. They say so much more in one sentence than seems possible. The nearest example of this police reaction in London was in 1973, following the stabbing of a sergeant in Notting Hill by a coloured woman. He was a popular man, a former rugby player and his life was in serious danger. After visiting him I went to Notting Hill police station where men were being concentrated to go out and make the arrest in expectation of a minor riot. Tension and apprehension were running high, until one young inspector, whose name I do not know, remarked audibly to a colleague, 'It's just as well to remember that some of the medical and nursing staff fighting for his life are black.' He could not have devised a better way to lower the temperature. Even had it not been true, I would nevertheless have blessed him. It was this incident and the words of Sergeant Moriarty which led me during the remainder of my term of office continually to hammer home the message – 'The Metropolitan Police recognize only one colour – blue'.

No one will gain more than the police from established

racial equality. No one will pay a higher price, or suffer more unjustly, in its achievement. The police in the ghettoes of London and other large cities demonstrate the Christian ethic in more practical terms today than any other institution or organization including the Church. The wider the awareness of this, the sooner will tension lessen and reason prevail. Police, Press, television and radio, can together do much to achieve this desirable end. It is essential that there should be an open relationship between them and that the prejudiced and the propagandist should be made aware of the likelihood of exposure.

These, then, are the two great problems for the next generation of policemen. Resistance to political encroachment on their operational freedom, and exposure to the brunt of social change. By comparison with those two, crime is never likely to be more than the conventional costly nuisance it is today and terrorism, as today, in reality a comparatively insignificant issue. Freedom and public order, in the widest sense, must be the priorities for the police of tomorrow – and I mean freedom from domestic, not foreign, masters.

# CHAPTER 25

# Security and Crime Prevention

There is one aspect of police activity which has understandably always exposed us to speculative criticism from extremists, civil libertarians and sometimes from moderates, uneasy at the lack of information about this hazy area and the unwillingness of government and police to discuss it. I am referring to the activities of Special Branch, criminal intelligence gathering, target criminals (this term is explained later on in this chapter), telephone tapping, closed circuit television, computers and so on. I have often thought it a pity that more light could not be shed on these activities because excessive reticence encourages the political extremist and even the curious to voice speculation and criticism, which, for lack of rebuttal, gains more credence than it really deserves. This is heightened by the emergence of a new genre in literary and cinema fiction, the spy thriller. The interests of the state naturally require some reticence in these matters, but that does not mean that there is not an advantage in revealing as much about them as possible if only to offset fictional or political misrepresentation.

The first point on which there is no need for equivocation is that every state in the world requires security services. Those of authoritarian societies operate without any of the restrictions imposed upon their counterparts in Great Britain. There are no facilities enabling citizens of the 'new democracies' to question the activities of their security services. There is a special irony in that those who are most active in questioning the activities of the police and security service in Great Britain are either silent about, or positively approve, social systems in which questioning of either is forbidden. Semantics can confuse people when discussing this kind of thing. 'Fascism' or 'Nazism' conjures up visions of blackshirts, brownshirts, genocide and governments immune from the process of law as we understand it. Nazism has particularly horrible significance for the elderly because of the massacre of 6,000,000 Jews. In reality, however, both are simply forms of authoritarianism. Any society whose judicature is a tool of government is authoritarian.

To the ordinary simple individual the differences between the Greater German Reich of 1933–45 and the Soviet Empire of today are difficult to discern, especially against vivid memories of Soviet tanks and infantry crushing the people of Hungary in 1956 and the 'disinterested help' from the Soviet Union which was required to overthrow Dubček, the Prime Minister of Czechoslovakia, in 1968. There is no possible reconciliation between some of the different forms of government in a competitive world divided by different ideologies. Every country therefore protects its own interest as best it can, both at home and abroad. Each has its counter espionage or security service and its intelligence gathering or spying network. To some extent, both enjoy, though on a rather higher plane, the same cloak of diplomatic immunity as parking and drunken driving. The essential difference between our security service and those of authoritarian countries is that ours has no executive authority. Its members are ordinary citizens without any police powers. They collate, they evaluate, they advise. They work in close collaboration with the Special Branches of the police, who are part of the Criminal Investigation Department and whose members are perfectly ordinary police officers without any special powers or immunity. The members of the security service are well trained, efficient and, believe it or not, dedicated to the maintenance of democracy. In comparison with their counterparts of the KGB or the Gestapo they are about as frightening as a powder puff. They are nevertheless necessary because they specialize in sensitive problems and they provide a convenient scapegoat if things go wrong, convenient because they are anonymous and are not overtly associated in the public mind with the police or government. With the help of the Special Branches they take a close interest in organizations exploiting the freedom of democracy in order to subvert it. Much that is written about them in the Press and elsewhere is inaccurate or speculative. The Ian Fleming school of fiction is responsible for a good deal of spurious folklore.

Most Special Branch work is boring, unromantic and certainly not dangerous. I know. I did it for several years and was glad to escape from it. Keeping watch on ports and airports for terrorists and extremists of the left and right sounds exciting. It isn't. It is dull, unrewarding and not to be endured for any longer than necessary. I was the proud possessor, if that is the right word, of the only scrambler telephone in Manchester for two or three years. It was even made available to the Prime Minister during his occasional visits. No message of any special significance was passed over it in my time even though Manchester was far from being free from subversive activity. The simple truth is that fascists, communists, Trotskyites, anarchists *et al* are committed to the overthrow of democracy and to the principle that the end justifies the means. Democracy must therefore protect itself by keeping a careful eye upon them. It is not difficult because they have never represented a serious threat. Paradoxically, they are less likely to do so if the state continues to treat them, as at present, as a bad joke. In my time in Manchester the Special Branch numbered three rising eventually to twelve, many of whom were almost wholly concerned with processing a flood of applications for certificates of naturalization. Hardly a threat to democracy in that great city!

Criminal intelligence gathering and target criminals were both born from the refusal of successive governments, Conservative and Labour, to allow the police adequate resources to fulfil their primary function of prevention. We were therefore driven, as in wartime, to selective fire-watching. We have long had a shrewd idea of the patterns of major crime and of those involved, but have always been hampered by the reality that our system of criminal justice encourages rather than deters it. Moreover, the public and Press are more concerned with the incidence of daily crime affecting individuals and therefore newsworthy, burglaries, muggings and assaults, rather than with sophisticated crime on a larger scale against commercial enterprises commanding less public sympathy. Whilst trying to cope with the former it became increasingly important to concentrate comparatively small numbers of hand-picked men and women to specialize in intelligence gathering and surveillance directed against the latter. This consisted, in practice, of directing our attention continuously, for the first time, to individuals rather than on crimes which had been committed or which we thought were likely to be committed. There has always been a small nucleus in London of people living off crime. Knowledge of them had always been useful in investigating serious crimes. We decided, however, that it would be worthwhile to discover everything we could about their movements, their associates, and their weaknesses simply as an insurance against the probability that they would commit further crimes. Thus the description 'target criminals'. These precautionary tactics achieved great success in dealing with fraud, high value robberies and so on. We had extended our research to cover kidnapping and extortion but happily this never reached European proportions.

Of all the methods we use to combat criminal and subversive activities the one causing most public unease is telephone tapping. People tend to forget that the Post Office is an independent government department not subject to police influence. The Birkett Committee of 1956 laid down stringent rules governing telephone tapping and these were approved by Parliament. In my time as Commissioner I know of no case in which those rules were broken. So far as I am concerned any attempt to break them would have led to immediate suspension and the sack. However, I am certain that the Post Office would flatly refuse to break them, and the trade unions who are powerfully represented in the GPO would have something to say if it did. There is nevertheless an endless succession of publicity-seeking trade unionists, politicians, journalists and oddballs of every kind who claim to have undergone this experience. It seems to be regarded as a kind of status symbol. I can only say that in the last five years I have never heard a justified claim of telephone tapping apart from those admitted during the course of judicial proceedings which had been properly authorized by the Secretary of State.

Closed circuit television for the purpose of crowd and traffic control used to be a frequent target for the political activist. Their objections always seemed to me to be emotional rather than logical. There was considerable public objection some years ago to the use of television cameras as fixed on public buildings by the Liverpool police as a deterrent to crime. In the event the experiment was not successful enough to justify its expensive continuance.

Participants in industrial disputes and political demonstrations have frequently objected to being photographed or televised and politicians have in the past tended to receive their complaints sympathetically. Chief officers have occasionally been asked to destroy such photographs and the weaker have on occasion agreed. This kind of objection does not, as I said, rely on logic. When Commissioner I was asked by the Home Office to order constables on embassy protection duty not to enquire the names and addresses of people. handing in petitions. I flatly refused, but offered to withdraw the constables instead. I pointed out that a constable had a perfect right to put the question as the recipient had the right to refuse to answer it. But at least that would alert the constable. The request was put to me a second time but I declined to interfere with the civil liberty of a constable in that way.

Against such a background it is perhaps easier to see why the large number of closed circuit television cameras necessary to control London's traffic, and the smaller number used at the places where political demonstrations are traditionally held, used to give rise to objection and mutterings about 'Big brother is watching you'. These have tended to lessen because even the most sensitive libertarians now appreciate that the cameras cannot see anything not visible to the ordinary observer on the street. They merely overlook streets and public places and more than anything else allow limitation of employment of police. Political demonstrators and road users alike benefit greatly. The cameras are evidentially virtually worthless. They offer no threat of any kind to anyone and in fact are of great benefit to police and public alike. In particular, they help the police to avoid excessive and possibly provocative display of manpower.

The size of Special Branch has also been the subject of much ill-informed public guesswork. In London it has only varied slightly since the war. What has happened is that the reduction from 123 to 43 in the number of police forces has allowed greatly improved co-ordination in Special Branch work generally. The 43 Special Branches remain just as autonomous in their own areas but they work more closely together and are more standardized and very much more efficient.

The Police National Computer at Hendon is not in fact controlled by the Metropolitan or any other force. It is sited at Hendon for security reasons and is controlled by a committee accountable to the Home Secretary. The computer offers immediate access to all forces in Britain. It will eventually allow the centralizing of criminal records, of wanted and missing persons, of fingerprint indices and, in conjunction with the Department of the Environment computer at Swansea, which centralizes records of vehicle owners, licensed and disqualified drivers, will represent the most important advance in police technology in this century. Retrieval of information by any one of the visual display units at police stations throughout the country can be unbelievably fast. It is possible now for a police officer to enquire by personal radio (or batphone, in police jargon) from his sub-divisional station about a motor vehicle and for the station officer, using the VDU (visual display unit) link with the computer, to give him details of ownership within one or two minutes. I can give a simple example of this from personal experience. During the height of the IRA bombing campaign I arrived home late one night with my wife from a police social function to find my neighbours out of their homes looking with anxiety at a car parked against my garden hedge. They thought it might be a car bomb. The home beat constable from the local station arrived and was able to tell them within two minutes that it belonged to someone who lived a few hundred yards away who, for one reason or another, had decided to walk home. Before the advent of the computer and personal radio we would have cleared the area, called the Bomb Squad and it would have taken three or four hours, not two minutes, to resolve the matter.

Nevertheless people are uneasy about the storage of information on computers about literally millions of vehicles and persons. The civil libertarians in particular view the development with apprehension and I do think they have a point in insisting that great care should be taken to ensure that the computers are only available to properly authorized sources. Nevertheless, against that risk, the benefit to police efficiency is immeasurable. It is also important to emphasize that this facility, with all the other specialized activities I have mentioned, is within the knowledge of the Home Secretary and his senior advisers. Both Labour and Conservative ministers have found them unexceptionable and have never questioned the strict adherence of the police to the principles which they have from time to time explained to Parliament. These activities are all open to error or to misrepresentation, but suggestions that in some curious way they have sinister connotations are in the circumstances neither reasonable nor supportable by evidence or logic. The system, necessary as it is, will bear comparison with that in any other society, eastern or western.

# CHAPTER 26

# A Look at the Future

What about future problems outside the immediate scope of the police but likely to affect them in one way or another? It is possible to foresee some in which they will be mere spectators although the results will affect them greatly. Inflation, unemployment, improvement of deprived areas, dispersal of minorities, all these will bear upon the police, directly or indirectly, because they will change the social tensions in which they have to work. The openly proclaimed drive by the government and the TUC to egalitarianism is not, and cannot be, an isolated social trend. It involves changes in the standards which hold society together. Paradoxically it allows greater social freedom by the relaxation of customs affecting behaviour and morals whilst coincidentally eroding freedom of activity through economic and restrictive measures designed for the benefit of the majority. The once poor rightly feel a sense of social progress. The once prosperous feel only enforced deprivation. There is a subtle change from the courts to the tax collector for the purpose of controlling society, and since the poor have always outnumbered the middle class and the wealthy, there is no hope of reversal of this process by conventionally democratic means. The management of the economy will gradually ensure that the members of the most powerful trade unions are the equals of judges, surgeons, businessmen and academics. This is far from being a look into the distant future. Judges, generals and top civil servants appear to be well paid today, but taxation reduces their actual remuneration close to that of less skilled occupations. A judicial ruling against a trade union is now all that is necessary to provoke the suggestion from the leader of the House of

Commons that the law will be changed. Indeed, the extent of trade union immunity from the law is likely to be one of the liveliest political issues of the next decade. There does not seem to be any prospect of radical change, for public or law enforcement officer alike. The spectacle of a shadow employment minister tipping a respectful forelock to the unions on television before he has even assumed office is not likely to attract the several million floating voters, who might prefer to see the unions compelled into reasonable, rather than dominating, partnership. The professional classes are fragmented, disorientated and obsessed with self-interest. Once qualified, new entrants are increasingly likely to see advantage abroad rather than accept egalitarianism at home. Moreover, the government enjoys a built-in advantage in that any move to reverse present policies can be condemned as backlash, a move to the extreme right for which even the most aggrieved feel a historical distaste. Superficially, the situation seems unlikely to change. Doctrinaire determination, self-interest, obsession with power, all are only too evident in those who make the rules today. There is, however, some cause for hope. The traditions of decades are not insignificant or to be lightly brushed aside. The former upper classes accepted, grudgingly and belatedly, the right of the majority to a better life and to a better opportunities. Their children accepted it more readily as socially just. There is no reason to suppose that the same trend will not emerge just as significantly in the workers themselves and even in their rulers. The extremists of the left no more represent the working class of this country than those of the right represent the former upper class. Perhaps more than any other nation we are subject to the pendulum principle of aversion to extremism in any form. Already workers have rejected the extreme policies of trade union leaders and an Anglo-Indian running a small business has courageously and successfully stood firm against politically motivated violence on the streets at Grunwick. Under the present government individual freedom is increasingly in peril but it is far from dead. If it is to be kept alive, it is necessary, to turn a phrase, that good men should do something. And that which they can usefully do need not necessarily involve direct or indirect confrontation with either left or right.

There should, as a first priority, be ever widening insistence on evidence of need for any change, legal, fiscal, political and on its clear explanation to the general public. This should be followed by insistence on impartial monitoring of the effect of any authorized change, the results being widely publicized. I believe the characteristics of the British people are such that adequacy of information on any issue, coupled with a belief in the integrity of its authors, would facilitate and probably achieve generally acceptable solutions to most of our problems. At present, sad to say, both these essentials are lacking. We do not have a Freedom of Information Act and are unlikely to achieve one. Easily understandable information about abuse of social security, the Polish shipbuilding deal, the apportionment of expenditure throughout the National Health Service, the problems of education in inner cities, the overmanning of industry in subservience to the unions – this is unlikely to be forthcoming. Not even Parliamentary Questions can do much to fill the gap. The whole art of answering Parliamentary Questions is to avoid giving away any information that might embarrass the government without actually telling a lie. Thus, a Home Office spokesman of the left or right will comfortingly assure the House that police strength has risen by 3000 without disclosing that it had fallen in the six largest cities, where it is most needed. This kind of thing has been going on for years, has been accepted by all parties and is the window dressing which obscures the less successful activities of government.

I suspect that those who urged the abolition of section 2 of the Official Secrets Act, which restricts the disclosure of information acquired in the public service, do not even now understand the advantages to be gained. It is not that someone might be able without fear to disclose the truth about a major scandal. The real advantage would be that employees would be able to speak as freely about the maladministration and failure of government policies as about those of private corporations and other undertakings and thus not so much expose scapegoats as ensure greater efficiency by more open administration. If, as I believe, it is right that the police, one of the most vulnerable and sensitive of all public services, should be administered as openly as possible, how much more important is it that the same openness should be required of the government, of trade unions, of private and public utilities? And should not those purporting to seek political change by pressure of public opinion themselves be required to expose their administration to impartial scrutiny?

It does not surprise me that the government has not implemented its declared intention of repealing section 2. Proclaiming the virtues of freedom and putting freedom into practice are two entirely different philosophies when viewed from the seat of power. I would like to see the repeal of section 2, but in the event of that not being forthcoming, I would hope for its increasing disregard by civil servants in particular and anyone feeling that secrecy on any issue was harmful to the public interest. I do not mean to imply that individual privacy should be subject to intrusion or exposure without very good cause, or that matters affecting the security of the state subject to government control should be revealed. Still less do I imply a disregard to judicial dicta. Indeed, so strong is my confidence in the commonsense reaction of the ordinary public in any situation in which they are told the truth that I believe convictions under section 2 would nowadays be difficult to obtain except in cases clearly motivated only by self-interest, e.g. disclosure of information for payment or other kind of profit. Those who have criticized my comments about the jury system have usually assumed that I seek its abolition. I have never suggested or even hinted at such a move. I have opposed unanimous verdicts, for which the Scots, with their ancient tradition of verdicts by a straight majority, will no doubt forgive me. I have ridiculed the right of peremptory challenge and the pretence by the legal trade unions that, because it is in law vested in the accused, it is not in practice frequently exercised by counsel, in the hope of ensuring a favourable jury. But I have always insisted that cases in which the state is directly, or by implication a party, should be tried by a jury. The unauthorized revelation of maladministration in government or any public undertaking would almost certainly not involve any real risk these days, for three reasons. First, because the Attorney General would not risk a prosecution. Second, because a jury would be unlikely to convict. Third, because in the unlikely event of conviction, the judiciary, if satisfied of the disinterested motives of the accused, would be unlikely to impose any penalty. The situation illustrates the difference between American and British criminal law. The Americans prefer certainty and definition. We prefer an area of discretion in which the accused, the jury and the judge are entitled to apply their own interpretation of a moral issue. The trouble is, we do not exercise that discretion sufficiently.

I would welcome, too, the televising of Parliament because it would expose its unsatisfactory standard of knowledge and discussion of important issues. It would be a painful process and through provision of a special channel ought not to lessen the availability of more attractive television. But it would emphasize the need for accuracy, information and logic. Though its intended entertainment value would be nil, as a corrective and an inspiration to improved performance it could be of great value.

If, as seems likely, the legal trade unions, through their representatives in Parliament, press more actively for the discretion to prosecute to be vested in lawyers appointed by the Crown I would hope, as I have said, that police and public would resist. But if, as is usually the case, the self-interest of the legal establishment were to prevail, it would, I think, be the right moment to consider more fundamental change, the abolition of the adversary system and the nationalization of that part of the legal profession practising criminal law, whether for prosecution or defence. I do not

27

mean that criminal lawyers should be administered by a Minister of Justice. A governing body drawn from the legal trade unions and a ministry could no doubt administer an inquisitorial system approved by the judges and Parliament whilst retaining most of the essential rights of wrongdoers under the adversary system. Attacks on the police as an automatic defence would be lessened. The profit motive for the lawyer which ought to have no place at all in the examination of criminal issues would be eliminated. Such a system need not prevent a lawyer from relinquishing salaried and pensionable employment in criminal practice in order to change to civil law on a self-employed basis. He should be able to withdraw at will, taking his pension contributions with him, but receipt of a fee or other remuneration from a defendant, directly or indirectly, should then be made a serious offence not only followed by permanent disbarment, but by exclusion from employment by anyone engaged in the practice of criminal law. The proposal is not so revolutionary as it sounds. Justice ought not to be geared to profit either for prosecution or defence and there is a strong case for arguing that everyone charged with crime should be entitled to legal aid without regard for his financial background. But not under the system which presently administers the grant of legal aid in criminal cases. It would be essential to ensure that those who practised criminal law would be so generously rewarded as to ensure a sufficiency of practitioners of very high standard, not always the case at present, at least in London.

There are always those who regard our present system as sacrosanct. But is it? Apart from those countries on whom we imposed it, not all of whom have retained it, no one else seems to want it. And, as I have said, it has played a formidable part in undermining the security and stability of urban social life in the United States. Already, in this country, we see creeping similarities of great potential danger, in particular, the unjustified release on bail of people charged with violence, even murder, without any attempt by the government to discover and publish any statistical evidence of the need for, or consequences of, such change. I do not pretend to like nationalization, at least in the field of commerce. I doubt if there is a single commercial activity of which it would be said that nationalization has not resulted in bad administration, increased cost, reduced efficiency, lower productivity and a hitherto unimagined ingenuity in misrepresentation for doctrinaire political purposes. Criminal justice, however, like the armed forces and the police, should be free from suspicion of any motivation other than dedication to the public interest. That is not a claim which criminal lawyers could make today. An enquiry by the *Daily Mail* as long ago as 1973 showed that:

Many solicitors are taking on more ciminal legal aid cases than they can properly handle.

The scheme is encouraging defendants to by-pass magistrates' courts and elect for trial by jury instead – in most cases entirely free.

The work of Crown courts is being choked with triviality. (It recently took a day and a half at the Old Bailey to try a man for attempting to steal a milk bottle.)

At most courts there is little, if any proper examination of defendants' financial means. No checking machinery exists. In 1970–71 – when criminal legal aid cost more than £8 million – only £165,000 was finally recovered from defendants.

Criminal legal aid is now costing more than £11 million a year compared with £1,300,000 ten years ago. But the hidden costs involved – such as extra courts, judges and staff, witnesses and jurors' expenses, and police man hours – are enormous and incalculable.

Some solicitors, inundated with remunerative legal aid work, are suspected of advising almost all their clients to elect for jury trial. In this way the solicitor can pass the case straight on to counsel, without bothering to study the papers.

According to *The Times* on 24 November 1976, Mr David Edwards, secretary of the Law Society's legal aid committee said:

> The maladministration of criminal legal aid is a scandal. Civil legal aid is tightly controlled, whereas criminal legal aid is not subject to any control; once it has been granted it is allowed to rip.

It continued:

> It is of interest that Mr Edwards, an official of the organization that, among other things, is supposed to be looking after the interests of lawyers, should have joined the growing list of critics of apparent abuses of the criminal legal aid scheme.
>
> He points to the high proportion of legal aid costs that go to cover lawyers' waiting time in congested courts. In London magistrates' courts they account for about a quarter of the total legal aid bill for a case.
>
> He also believes that there should be much tighter control of the number of times that a lawyer needs to be present in court for straightforward remands of his legally-aided client.

Under the present system legal aid in criminal cases has turned out to be the biggest bonanza since the Klondike! Much more regrettable, however, is that the admirable purpose for which it was conceived is not being fulfilled and that its flagrant abuse does not enhance the image of a profession, most of whose members are not involved in it and do not deserve the stigma rightly attached to those who exploit it. It is a welcome, if surprising, development to see the Law Society roundly denouncing its own black sheep. That, at least, is new in my experience.

The truth is that few people are satisfied with the present system, apart from wrongdoers and a minority of criminal lawyers. It is high time that the cpmplacency and emotive eloquence extolling its virtues were examined critically by a selection of people without any professional, political or financial interest in the eventual findings and recommendations.

There is, too, the role of the police, long overdue for examination. Norval Morris and Gordon Hawkins, the authors of *The Honest Politician's Guide to Crime Control*, published by the Chicago University Press in 1970, argued *inter alia* that a man should have the right to go to Hell in his own way, provided that he harmed no one else and that, in any case, the criminal law is not a satisfactory instrument for compelling people to the good life. The first proposition is oversimplified. What about those who are not fit to decide for themselves? The young, the mentally subnormal and so on? But taken together the two propositions do not represent a bad approach from which to assess how far policing should encroach upon people's lives. We have, as a service, for too long been the peg on which every problem not wanted by someone else has been hung. Sin, for example, which in canon law was regarded as crime, ought no longer to be of interest to the police as current opinion takes it off the statute book. Suicide is no longer a crime. Homosexuality between consenting adults in private is no longer a crime. Adultery was a crime in many states of the Union – still may be, as far as I know – but fortunately for police and public alike is not so regarded here. Sin which is not criminal is a matter for the Church, not the police, and in these days of unnecessary demarcation disputes is an issue which police should leave severely alone. They should firmly resist requirement to regulate or control any activity not regarded by the public generally as being rightly within the ambit of the criminal law. Police leaders in particular should be especially careful in a multiracial society not to confuse their role with that of the cleric. They may at times be mutually supporting, but confusion of one with the other is sure to detract from both.

If trade unions are to continue to play an ever increasing role in government, ought not their elections and their more important decisions to be by secret ballot under impartial supervision, in the manner of a general election? It is inconceivable that their power will lessen. Surely, therefore, it is in the real interests of all their members as in that of the public that they should be subject to the same scrutiny, the same checks and balances as those who aspire to govern by universal suffrage? I am not anti-trade union. I have no doubt that my forebears, if I knew them, would a hundred years ago have been fighting for the right to establish trade unions and for collective bargaining. I certainly would. But today, a product of the working class, I desire no less ardently the subjection of the unions to democracy, a description to which some of them today cannot pretend.

Political parties, trade unions, the legal profession, the Press all claim today that they serve the public and are therefore entitled to certain rights and privileges. But what about accountability? Should that not go hand in hand with rights and privileges? The police service, the handmaiden and, to some extent, the victim of them all, has accepted the need for accountability – though, in my case, admittedly not to political nominees. Has not the time arrived to increase the accountability of all those who claim to be public servants? And if they are not willing to be accountable should we not dismiss their claim? I believe that the overwhelming majority of politicians, journalists, lawyers and trade unionists want the public interest to prevail. Given the disagreements resulting from personal ambition, professional loyalties and genuine dissent, I am nevertheless convinced that there is so wide a measure of common interest as to encourage support for a more open, more factual and more honest appraisal of the working of our society, which would allow a more harmonious and constructive relationship between some of those who have traditionally regarded each other with distrust if not actual hostility. If, as I believe, the worst of all crimes is the furtherance of political or industrial aims by violence, perhaps the natural conclusion is that the greatest of all our needs today is openness of administration, greatly increased dissemination of factually correct information and exposure of attempts to mislead. For those reasons I believe the means and process of communication between all sections of society and particularly between government and people to be now amongst the most important of all our activities, affecting more widely than ever before the freedom and stability of society. The validity of this belief depends on the sufficiency and diversity of the means to communicate and the ability of people to understand what is put before them. The means are now all embracing. There can scarcely be a home which does not have a newspaper, radio, television or all three. The standard of literacy, too, has greatly improved in this century. We thus have, to a greater extent than ever before, the means to inform the public about facts or opinions relating to any matter affecting them. In theory, this should have a profound influence for good, but it has its dangers and disadvantages.

If, for example, newspapers, television and radio are controlled by the government as the Press and radio were in Germany between 1933 and 1945 they can be used to influence or condition people rather than to present them with information from which they can draw their own conclusions. If those who produce or print newspapers or transmit broadcasts exercise censorship by withdrawal of their resources or technical skills their value may not be merely reduced but undermined. If the means to communicate become so extensive as to make it impossible to satisfy their capacity, their attraction and usefulness will diminish. There can be no doubt of their importance, particularly that of television. An unattractive appearance, lack of histrionic ability, a momentary loss of self-control under pressure, any or all of these can demolish the usefulness of a public figure who in reality may have much to offer. By contrast, a smooth performer before the television camera without any other real merit can achieve public support.

The competitive nature of the communications industry inevitably heightens the commercial value of disclosure, which is the prime function of a free Press. Unfortunately, competition makes co-ordination impossible, and many would argue, undesirable, with the result that the public are fed with a continuous diet of dissent for commercial or political purposes. This is an inevitable but not always recognized aspect of a free Press. Its viability, or circulation, depends on dissent, a reality both bad and good, in that it makes agreement less likely where it is both possible and in the public interest but has the compensatory effect of protecting the public from what is sometimes called 'guided democracy', a euphemism is less free societies for authoritarian or semi-authoritarian control.

Dissent is the very essence of democracy. The role of the police is not to suppress it but to ensure that it does not express itself unlawfully, and if it does, to contain it by lawful means. This is a lesson that policemen often take years to learn. It can be a bitter lesson because the more dissatisfied or frustrated the dissenter, the more he will sometimes vent his displeasure on the police. This is as true, incidentally, of domestic disputes as of industrial and political demonstrations. That is why the lot of the policeman is so frequently unhappy. Apart from containment, his only permissible reaction is to expose untruthfulness or inaccuracy in dissension, if he is aware of it. The latter responsibility is not, of course, his alone. It should be shared by everyone and the Press in particular. No one would expect leaders in the *Morning Star* to express the same kind of views as those in the *Daily Telegraph* but the facts to which they relate should be correct and open to examination. Violence and extremism in controversial issues of widespread interest can never be eradicated by suppression, except in authoritarian societies. In a free country there is no other course but to contain them and demand their justification by evidence and logic. It is important that this should be ever more widely understood, especially by those who think it the task of the police to take action against those with whom they disagree. That which is not unlawful is by implication lawful, however distasteful or objectionable, and it is not for the police to react to the varying pressures and prejudices of public opinion, even though expressed in Parliament, local councils or churches. The German police in 1933 abandoned their duty to protect minorities who, until then, had enjoyed freedom under the law. It was not long before the National Socialist German Workers Party became immune from the law. One of the tests of a free society, of which people should occasionally be reminded, is the right of a minority, however odious to its opponents or even to the public generally, to express its views or pursue any other activity which does not contravene the law.

Keeping the peace and maintaining impartiality in political demonstrations, industrial disputes and racial incidents is not an activity likely to commend the police to those with whom they come into contact. Though they have a right, indeed, a duty, to comment on proposed or existing legislation, they must apply the law as it stands, suppressing any personal feeling, observing strict neutrality, sticking strictly to the truth in the midst of criticism and controversy. Truth and impartiality should be so inherent to the police function as to make the service the embodiment of both in the public mind. If that sounds pompous, I am sorry. I do not know how else to put it. Certainly they need courage, both moral and physical, self-control, compassion, and tolerance to a greater extent than most people, but without truth and impartiality they cannot possibly discharge their unique and supremely important task. Let me not now pretend that they have not been wanting in both. I have written with more frankness about police wrongdoing than is customary in a policeman's autobiography because the need for public knowledge of it is essential to attract attention to the conditions which govern an urban policeman's life, to which some of the blame for that wrongdoing is attributable.

The history of our people is not one of an excess of brilliant individuals but of innately decent mediocrity in all walks of life. Churchills, Pitts, Wellingtons and Nelsons loom all the larger because of their comparative rarity. We have shown an extraordinary capacity for survival despite, not because of, our political masters, largely because of the longlasting confidence of most people in the resilience, the moderation and the sense of fair play which they think is likely to be shown by the overwhelming majority even in times of crisis. The key to survival is not to be found in the genius of a few individuals but in general confidence, misplaced or not, in the system in which they flower. It is in that context that the police of Britain should be judged. The more rational and open the system of justice they serve, the less likely they are to fall short of the standards required of them. Do not, therefore, let them ever be considered in isolation. Let them always be considered as one part of a process of which the ideal, not unattainable, should be acceptable and humane laws, a trial system designed to establish the truth, a penal philosophy which puts the protection of society, the compensation of the victim, restitution and the rehabilitation of the offender before such punishment as may rightly be necessary to mark society's disapproval of anti-social conduct and let the accountability of all those involved be such as to satisfy the people rather than the practitioners. Juvenal stopped a little short. It is not in this instance just the guards who need guarding. Virtually everyone involved in the administration of justice other than the police has enjoyed for far too long an undeserved immunity from critical examination of their standards and conduct.

It is a matter for satisfaction that the police themselves have recognized the need for change and that they can at last with advantage expose themselves to critical examination. They have no need to spend large sums of money promoting their image on television, to pretend hypocritically that they are without fault or that they have qualities they do not possess. They demonstrate collectively the qualities which make Britain, with all its anxieties and problems, still one of the most agreeable countries in the world and are readily seen, with their faults and virtues, as being among the best exemplars of it.

# POSTSCRIPT

The year since publication in hardback of this book has not
been without incidents; and one in particular I should like
to mention here: on 21 February 1978 I received a telephone
call from Canberra asking me to assume the role of Con-
sultant to the Australian Government as soon as possible.
The invitation followed the bomb explosion at the Sydney
Hilton on 13 February during a meeting there of heads of
State and the subsequent employment of troops in aid of
the civil power.

The Prime Minister, the Right Honourable Malcolm
Fraser, agreed to the suggestion that I should be accompanied by Sir James Haughton, CBE, QPM, formerly Her
Majesty's Chief Inspector of Constabulary. We arrived in
Canberra on 1 March and remained in Australia until 5
April. During a hectic six weeks I visited the six State
capitals, listened carefully to a wide variety of opinion, was
careful to keep in close touch with the news media as
representing informed public opinion, and then produced
my report which contained a number of recommendations
covering many aspects of the policing of the Commonwealth.
One of the most important was the amalgamation of the
Commonwealth police with the Australian Capital Territory
Force to form an Australian Federal Police Force. Another
was the creation of a Common Police Services Committee
to improve the co-ordination of policing throughout the
Commonwealth.

The Federal Government agreed to my request that the
report should be published so that it should be widely
discussed. It received an excellent press and gained the
approval of the legislative assemblies and the Federal Government. A police task force of serving officers and civil
servants was set up by the Minister for Administrative
Services in Canberra to consider implementation of the

report and its work is now well advanced. The main recommendations are expected to take effect later this year. They
will inevitably have a far-reaching effect on the development
of policing throughout Australia.

27.2.79

# Index

## Compiled by Douglas Matthews

Mark, Sir Robert [*contd.*]
army, 38; military training,
39–40; service with Phantom,
45–9; in Control Commission,
50; demobilization and return to
police, 50–1; on police
procedure, 54–5; pay, 59, 67;
promotion, 59–60; lacrosse
playing, 59, 62; Police College
course, 63; applies for jobs, 64;
appointed Chief Constable of
Leicester, 64–5; on parking and
motoring offences, 69–70, 97,
289; relations with Press, 71–2,
141–3, 178, 188–91, 194,
200–1, 273–9; lectures, 72, 115,
120–1, 175, 233 (*see also*
Dimbleby Memorial Lecture);
book reviews, 72; on criminal
justice and lawyers, 72–4, 129,
138, 155–6, 161–70, 274–5,
282–92, 319–20, 329; and
Leicester amalgamation, 78;
appointed Metropolitan
Assistant Commissioner, 79, 83,
88, 92; on Standing Advisory
Council on Penal System, 79;
honorary degrees, 79, 246–7;
receives Queen's Police Medal,
92; reforms in Metropolitan
Police, 92–5, 133–45; appointed
Deputy Commissioner, 99–100,
109; on police discipline and
wrongdoing, 103–4, 109, 112,
117–20, 128–31 learns to ride,
108; and Northern Ireland,
109–10; Visiting Fellow of
Nuffield College, 116; in army
review working party, 116; tours
of North America, 122–4,
189–90, 233, 253; appointed
Metropolitan Police
Commissioner, 124, 128; and
pornography laws, 144, 173–4,
267–9; on paroling Great Train
Robbers, 189; at Balcombe

Street, 192–5; at Spaghetti
House siege, 199; opposes
Jenkins's Complaints Board
procedure, 214–28, 238–43;
retirement, 225, 238, 241–4,
245, 248, 252–3; politics, 234;
salary and pension as
Commissioner, 242–3; joins
Phoenix board, 246; honours,
246; takes last Cadets Passing
Out Parade, 248–52; on bail
system, 294; and coloured
policemen, 304
Marshall, Geoffrey, 300
Mason, Ronald, 173
Mathew, Sir Theobald (Director
of Public Prosecutions), 35, 141
Matthews, Mr & Mrs (of
Balcombe Street), 193, 194
Maudling, Reginald (Home
Secretary), 120, 124, 141, 211
Medico-Legal Society, 115
Merricks, Ray, 106
Metropolitan Police, organization,
85–7, 96–7; and Heathrow, 86,
175–6; moves to Victoria Street,
92; 'assessment' system, 92–3;
relations with Home Office, 92,
96–7, 100; married quarters,
93–4; police women in, 95,
231–2; resentment of RM,
100–1; 109; and race, 105–7,
141–2; wrongdoing and
discipline in, 101–5, 109,
117–19, 122–3, 128–31, 185;
CID, 101–2, 104–5, 109, 112,
115–32, 134–5, 143–4, 170–3,
196–7, 210–11, 269; and BBC's
'Cause for Concern', 105; and
emergency control, 107–8;
*Times* and, 112–13, 120–1;
Special Branch, 129, 178–9; and
Press, 129–30, 134, 137–8,
141–3, 149–50, 188–91, 201,
204–6; reforms, 133–45, 155–6,
269; staff associations, 134, 136;

INDEX

Wilson, John (Assistant
  Commissioner, Met Police),
  204–5
Windsor Pop Festival, 227
Woddis, Roger, 278
Wodehouse, P. G., 78
women police, 95, 231–2

Woodfield, Philip, 79–80
Woods, Sir Colin (Deputy
  Commissioner, Met Police),
  102, 131, 136–7, 143, 175
Workers' Revolutionary
  Broadsheet, 205

**Russell**

A. J. Ayer

Bertrand Russell was the most famous philosopher of his time. He did pioneering work in mathematical logic and his contributions to this and other branches of philosophy had an enormous influence on his contemporaries. He was one of the originators of the analytical movement which has dominated philosophy in the English-speaking world throughout the greater part of this century.

'Undoubtedly Professor Ayer's book is the best available short exposition of Russell's philosophy, and, not coincidentally, of his own views as well.' *Times Literary Supplement*

'This must be one of the best expositions of the work of one philosopher by another that has ever been written.'
Mary Warnock, *New Society*

'. . . here is a brilliant and very useful book.'
Bernard Crick, *New Statesman*

'. . . this could prove to be the clearest, simple exposition that exists of Russell's thinking and a proper memorial to a no mean performer in the field of popular presentation.'
*Daily Telegraph*

# Keywords

Raymond Williams

*Alienation, creative, family, media, radical, structural, taste*: these are seven of the hundred or so words whose derivation, development and contemporary meaning Raymond Williams explores in this unique study of the language in which we discuss 'culture' and 'Society'.

A series of connecting essays investigate how these 'keywords' have been formed, redefined, confused and reinforced as the historical contexts in which they were applied changed to give us their current meaning and significance.

'This is a book which everyone who is still capable of being educated should read.'          Christopher Hill, *New Society*

'. . . for the first time we have some of the materials for constructing a genuinely historical and a genuinely social semantics . . . Williams's book is unique in its kind so far and it provides a model as well as a resource for us all.'

Alasdair MacIntyre, *New Statesman*

# The Fontana Economic History of Europe

General Editor: Carlo M. Cipolla, Professor of Economic History at the Universities of Pavia and California, Berkeley.

'There can be no doubt that these volumes make an extremely significant addition to the literature of European economic history, where the need for new large comparative works has long been felt . . . It is overall a project of vision and enormous value.'

*Times Literary Supplement*

## 1. The Middle Ages

Contributors: Cipolla: J. C. Russell: Jacques Le Goff: Richard Roehl: Lynn White Jr.: Georges Duby: Sylvia Thrupp: Jacques Bernard: Edward Miller.

## 2. The Sixteenth and Seventeenth Centuries

Contributors: Cipolla: Roger Mols: Walter Minchinton: Hermann Kellenbenz: Aldo de Maddalena: Domenico Sella: Kristof Glamann: Geoffrey Parker.

## 3. The Industrial Revolution

Contributors: André Armengaud: Walter Minchinton: Samuel Lilley: Gertrand Gille: Barry Supple: R. M. Hartwell: J. F. Bergier: Paul Bairoch: Donald Winch: M. J. T. Lewis.

## 4. The Emergence of Industrial Societies

*Part 1:* Contributors: Claude Fohlen: Knut Borchardt: Phyllis Deane: N. T. Gross: Luciano Cafagna: Jan Dhondt & Marinette Bruwier.
*Part 2:* Contributors: Lennart Jörberg: Gregory Crossman: Jordi Nadal: B. M. Biucchi: William Woodruff: B. R. Mitchell.

## 5. The Twentieth Century

*Part 1:* Contributors: Milos Macura: A. S. Deaton: Walter Galenson: Giorgio Pellicelli: Roy and Kay MacLeod: Georges Brondel: Robert Campbell.
*Part 2:* Contributors: Hermann Priebe: Angus Maddison: Carlo Zacchia: Fred Hirsch and Peter Oppenheimer: Benjamin Ward: Max Nicholson.

## 6. Contemporary Economics

*Part 1:* Contributors: Johan de Vries: Claude Fohlen: A. J. Youngson: Karl Hardach: Sergio Ricossa: John Pinder.
*Part 2:* Contributors: Lennart Jörberg: and Olle Krantz: Josep Fontana and Jordi Nadal: Hansjörg Siegenthaler: Alfred Zauberman: B. R. Mitchell.

# Unended Quest: An Intellectual Autobiography

Karl Popper

Internationally hailed as one of the most outstanding philosophers writing at present – on politics, on science, on human knowledge, on society – this unique book is Sir Karl Popper's own account of his life and of the development of his ideas. In fascinating detail he traces the genesis and formulation of his major works: *The Open Society and Its Enemies*, *The Logic of Scientific Discovery*, *The Poverty of Historicism*, *Objective Knowledge*, and *Conjectures and Refutations: The Growth of Scientific Knowledge*.

'. . . a splendid introduction to the man and his ideas.'
Martin Gardner, *The New Leader*

'. . . a remarkable document of intellectual history.'      Lewis S. Feuer

'This autobiography is part discussion on method; part intellectual history of Popper's major ideas; and part a continuing discussion of his ruling preoccupations.'      Tyrrell Burgess, *New Society*

'. . . few broad areas of human thought remain unillumined by Popper's work.'      Bryan Magee

# Hitler: The Führer and the People
## J. P. Stern

His life, his times, his policies, his strategies, his influence have often been analysed. But rarely is the most elementary question of all raised – how could it happen?

How could a predominantly sober, hard-working, and well-educated population have been persuaded to follow Hitler to the awful abyss of destruction? What was the source of his immense popularity? What was the image projected in his speeches, his writings, and his conversation?

*Hitler: The Führer and the People* is a compelling attempt to reconstruct the nature of Hitler's political ideology, its roots, logic, and function.

'Who really wants or needs another book on Hitler? The short answer is, when the book is as good and original and brief as Professor Stern's, that we all do.'
Donald G. MacRae, *New Statesman*

'Stern's book is, on all counts, a significant achievement.'
Geoffrey Barraclough, *New York Review of Books*

'. . . an excellent book, all the more so because it concerns itself, via Hitler, with the more general problems of the relationship between society and the individual leader, between ideas and action, between myth and reality.'
Douglas Johnson, *New Society*

'His short book is one of the most remarkable studies of Hitler and Nazism to have appeared.'    Christopher Sykes, *Observer*

# INTO UNKNOWN ENGLAND 1866-1913

## SELECTIONS FROM THE SOCIAL EXPLORERS

### *Edited by Peter Keating*

How did the poor live in late Victorian and Edwardian England?
In the slums of London and Birmingham? In the iron-town of
Middlesbrough? In a Devon fishing village? In rural Essex?

This is a fascinating sequence of extracts from the writings of
those individuals, journalists and wealthy businessmen, a
minister's wife, and a popular novelist, who temporarily left the
comfort of their middle-class homes to find out how the other
half lived. Peter Keating includes material from Charles Booth,
Jack London, B. S. Rowntree and C. F. G. Masterman as well as
by such lesser-known figures as George Sims, Andrew Mearns
and Stephen Reynolds.

'. . . a brilliant and compelling anthology . . . *Into Unknown
England* is not only an education in itself, throwing into three-
dimensional chiaroscuro the flat statistics of "scientific" history,
but a splendid example of prose which is always immediate and
alive.'
Alan Brien, *Spectator*

'The writers collected here used all the techniques they could to
solicit sympathy. Their descendants are a thousand television
documentaries.'
Paul Barker, *The Times*

'. . . a rich collection of passages, intelligently presented.'
*The Guardian*

# Edmund Burke
# On Government, Politics and Society

*Selected and Edited by B. W. Hill*

Quoted more frequently than almost any other political writer, Edmund Burke has been cast in many roles – as arch-defender of established authority, radical critic of traditional orthodoxies, exponent of liberal values. Yet the historical Burke is a much more complex and fascinating thinker than any of these views allows.

The aim of this new selection is to reveal the range of Burke's outlook as politician, imaginative writer, and philosopher by drawing upon the extensive speeches and pamphlets on the American Colonies, the Monarchy and the Party system, and the Government of India, as well as the more widely known *Reflections on the Revolution in France*.

In his long introduction and editorial comments, Dr Hill presents Burke as an eclectic thinker, but a consistent advocate of social morality, a friend of good caring government, and an opponent of extremist politics whether of the Right or the Left.

'Almost alone in England, he brings thought to bear upon politics, he saturates politics with thought.'                        *Matthew Arnold*

'Burke *is* an extraordinary man. His stream of mind is perpetual.'
*Samuel Johnson*

'No English writer has received, or has deserved, more splendid panegyrics than Burke.'                        *Leslie Stephen*

'There is no wise man in politics, with an important decision to make, who would not do well to refresh his mind by discussion with Burke's mind.'                        *Harold Laski*

# Fontana Paperbacks

Fontana is a leading paperback publisher of fiction and non-fiction, with authors ranging from Alistair MacLean, Agatha Christie and Desmond Bagley to Solzhenitsyn and Pasternak, from Gerald Durrell and Joy Adamson to the famous Modern Masters series.

In addition to a wide-ranging collection of internationally popular writers of fiction, Fontana also has an outstanding reputation for history, natural history, military history, psychology, psychiatry, politics, economics, religion and the social sciences.

All Fontana books are available at your bookshop or newsagent; or can be ordered direct. Just fill in the form and list the titles you want.

FONTANA BOOKS, Cash Sales Department, G.P.O. Box 29, Douglas, Isle of Man, British Isles. Please send purchase price, plus 8p per book. Customers outside the U.K. send purchase price, plus 10p per book. Cheque, postal or money order. No currency.

NAME (Block letters) _____

ADDRESS _____

_____

_____

While every effort is made to keep prices low, it is sometimes necessary to increase prices on short notice. Fontana Books reserve the right to show new retail prices on covers which may differ from those previously advertised in the text or elsewhere.